VIOLENCE IN SOUTHERN AFRICA

T0352728

CASS SERIES ON POLITICAL VIOLENCE

Series Editors:
DAVID C. RAPOPORT
University of California, Los Angeles

PAUL WILKINSON
University of St Andrews, Scotland

VIOLENCE IN SOUTHERN AFRICA

edited by

WILLIAM GUTTERIDGE
Research Institute for the Study of Conflict and Terrorism

and

J. E. SPENCE
Royal Institute of International Affairs

FRANK CASS
LONDON • PORTLAND, OR

First published in 1997 in Great Britain by
FRANK CASS AND COMPANY LIMITED
Newbury House, 900 Eastern Avenue, London IG2 7HH, England

and in the United States of America by
FRANK CASS
c/o ISBS, Inc.
5804 N.E. Hassalo Street, Portland, Oregon 97213-3644

British Library Cataloguing in Publication Data

Military power : land warfare in theory and practice
1. Military art and science – United States 2. Military art and science –
Great Britain
I. Reid, Brian Holden II. The journal of strategic studies 355

ISBN 0 7146 4665 2 (cloth)
ISBN 0 7146 4200 2 (paper)

Library of Congress Cataloging-in-Publication Data
A catalog record for this book is available from the Library
of Congress.

This group of studies first appeared in a Special Issue on
'Violence in Southern Africa' in
Terrorism and Political Violence Vol.8, No.4 (Winter 1996),
published by Frank Cass & Co. Ltd.

Printed in Great Britain by
Antony Rowe Ltd.

Contents

Preface

It is a privilege to be able to offer our readers our first special issue on violence in Southern Africa. We were fortunate in recruiting two of Britain's most distinguished Africanists to serve as guest editors, and I am sure that our readers will agree that they have created a fascinating and important series of studies on conflict and violence in a region of the world which is still woefully neglected by both European and North American academics and specialist institutes.

The contributors have provided a rich variety of material covering all the recent major conflicts in the region, comparative studies (Abiodun Alao and Jakki Cilliers), and analyses of violence specific to countries and regions (Keith Somerville, Chris Alden, Alexander Johnston and Judith Hudson), and an original and perceptive examination of the intractable criminal violence in South Africa, a phenomenon which is often linked to political violence and which at its most severe has serious political and economic implications.

It is particularly striking that none of these studies is of purely historical interest. Each author shows that the major outbreaks of violence have left terrible problems of reconstruction, reconciliation and peace building. Indeed, as Judith Hudson's essay on the violence in the townships demonstrates, the threat of a resurgence of major violence still casts a shadow on the most successful peace process in the most advanced country in the region, South Africa. Hudson and the other contributors all stress the crucial linkage between the conditions for long-term peace building and stability and the need for rapid economic growth to generate employment opportunities for the increasing population. The problems created by widespread political violence are not simply a technical problem for the reformed policing and criminal justice system: they can threaten the 'embryonic civil society' to which the editors refer in their introduction. Hence the international community cannot afford to ignore the bitter harvest of decades of violence, physically manifested in the enormous landmine problem in Angola, the simmering violence in KwaZulu-Natal, and the bitterness and suspicion which obstructs reconciliation and political development in countries such as Mozambique and Zimbabwe. This valuable collection fills a major gap in the literature on contemporary conflict, and is a poignant reminder that recent political political gains could all too easily be put at risk by fresh outbreaks of political violence.

PAUL WILKINSON
20 December 1996

Introduction: Violence in Southern Africa

WILLIAM GUTTERIDGE and J.E. SPENCE

Since the end of the Cold War Africa has been a continent of mixed fortunes: First, Russia's decline as a superpower has ended Africa's role as an arena for East–West competition and the continent's resulting marginalization has been reinforced by western preoccupation with the spectacle of state disintegration in eastern and central Europe and the former Soviet Union. Those African states which had looked to the Soviet Union for arms, aid and general ideological support found themselves friendless as Moscow's domestic problems multiplied and its commitment to the Third World 'allies' correspondingly waned. Second, the relative ease with which communist regimes collapsed and reform initiatives got under way exposed both the vulnerability and the intellectual and economic bankruptcy of those African regimes which still espoused Marxist-Leninist principles.

The European Union, too, has become relatively inward-looking, concerned with the complexities of the Bosnian crisis, arcane debate about the merits of a single currency and the scope for further integration – 'widening or deepening' – if and when the Union succeeds in incorporating its poorer and weaker neighbours to the east. The latter, in effect (and their number includes the former Soviet Union), appear more attractive candidates for western investment, aid and technical assistance than do their poverty-stricken counterparts in Africa south of the Sahara. Indeed, 30 years of economic mismanagement, corruption, and one-party statehood or military dictatorship had by 1990 produced a mood of disillusion about the continent's future verging on despair at the spectacle of states collapsing under the pressure of prolonged civil war and ethnic division.[1]

Yet western indifference to Africa's future has not meant complete abandonment, especially in view of the initially encouraging outcome achieved in many African states following the collapse of communist governments in eastern Europe. The demonstration effect of 'people's power' and the emergence of an incipient civil society underpinned by opposition groups (students, trade unions and churches) forced free elections on discredited regimes anticipating the creation of a new political order. Yet the price of continued western commitment to Africa has been high, for the growth of popular discontent reinforced a trend begun a decade earlier by the World Bank, the International Monetary Fund and major donor governments in the West: impatient with the poor performance of many African economies, external agencies insisted on major economic reform as the price of continued aid and debt rescheduling. The result was the acceptance by the great majority of African states of structural adjustment programmes which promised long term benefits at the price of short term pain. But the pain endured and the result was even greater popular resentment of government ineptitude and yet more pressure for political reform. This, in turn, led in the late 1980s to external emphasis on the need for 'good governance' which, according to a World Bank Report, involved making political systems properly accountable, encouraging pluralistic features such as public debate and a free press. Thus, governments in the West – the United Kingdom and the United States in particular – began to insist on 'political conditionality' as well as economic reform as the price of further support. Douglas Hurd, Britain's Foreign Secretary, argued in 1990 that 'in future aid policy would favour democracies: countries tending towards pluralism, public accountability, respect for the rule of law, human rights and market principles, should be encouraged'.[2]

Whether external strategies can manipulate the pace of change in a positive and ultimately beneficial direction is open to argument. One astute observer, Stephen Riley, has argued that 'there is...an inconsistency in ... requiring both domestic reform and continued economic adjustment and austerity. It is unlikely that the newly enfranchised citizens will actually vote for further austerity. Juggling the competing demands of external donors and an active citizenry is likely to remain difficult, despite the "techno–politicians"'. Riley is surely right in stressing that 'some democratic states may thus fall to revived authoritarianism or at least military *coups d'état* as a consequence'.

Perhaps the scale of the problems confronting many African governments are simply too vast for externally generated solutions to affect the outcome significantly in a positive sense. As Riley points out:

> These new regimes have to balance the demands of their external predators against the pressing needs of their newly enfranchised citizens...[yet]... life expectancy for black Africa as a whole averages just over fifty years. The United Nations has estimated that by the middle of the 1990's 400 million Africans will be living in poverty, 260 million of them women. These are not encouraging conditions for the stability of the new democratic governments...they also have to cope with the residue of the policy headaches of the 1980s: economic decline or stagnation, war, famine, refugees, environmental degradation, population pressures, food shortages, AIDS and other health problems, and policy reforms such as structural adjustment, privatization and market liberalization.[3]

Yet western willingness to impose standards of political and economic behaviour on African states struggling with the birth pains of a second independence has not been matched with an equal willingness to intervene when statehood threatens to collapse in the wake of civil war. The failure of the US-backed UN force to restore peace in Somalia effectively discouraged any further attempts a peace-making elsewhere, with the result that Liberia, the Sudan and Rwanda have been racked with protracted civil strife. True, the UN backed at peace-making mission (ECOWAS Monitoring Group, ECOMOG) undertaken by the Economic Community of West African states (ECOWAS), but its efforts to restore order and revive a semblance of civil and political administration have so far proved fruitless. In Zaire, the state has not yet collapsed; President Mobutu backed by his army remains in power, but his refusal to heed external calls for reform has left the country's administration paralysed and an economy – despite extensive mineral resources – in ruins.

The international community has proved reluctant to restore 'failed' states to some degree of viability despite the promise of a 'new world order' based on the principle of universal collective security as defined by President Bush in triumphalist mode following the successful conclusion of the Second Gulf War in 1991. Strategic and economic interests have dictated a selective pattern of post-Cold War intervention and there is the added constraint that expelling external aggressors across frontiers (as in Kuwait in 1991) more neatly meets the traditional criteria of a successful intervention (political will, availability of resources, limited objectives and the possibility of rapid disengagement) than is the case with peace-enforcement operations in civil wars where combatants have to be forcibly disarmed and the intervening party may well then find itself committed to a prolonged task of social and economic reconstruction. Significantly, President Bush, in his farewell address on 5 January 1993, substantially modified his definition of the 'new world order' and the means required to underpin it, that is, 'the selective use of military force for selective purposes with other nations making military and economic contributions whenever their interests are at stake'.[4] In these circumstances, the best war-torn states can hope for is UN-supported humanitarian intervention designed to alleviate the suffering of civilian populations in the short term and the assistance of contact groups of neighbouring states, the function of which is to employ diplomatic skills designed to halt the fighting and prepare the way for a 'peacekeeping' mission to police a precarious truce.

Some commentators have proposed more radical solutions: Douglas Hurd, when British Foreign Secretary, speaking at the General Assembly of the United Nations, mused about the possibility of restoring 'benign imperialism' to collapsed states. Similarly, Ali Mazrui suggested 'external re-colonisation under the banner of humanitarianism'. He went on to argue:

> countries like Somalia and Liberia where central control has collapsed
> may invite an inevitable intervention.... although colonialism may be
> re-surfacing it is likely to look rather different this time around. A
> future trustee system will be more genuinely international and less
> Western than it was under the old guise. Administering powers for the
> trusteeship territories could come from Africa and Asia, as well as
> from the rest of the membership of the UN.[5]

Interesting as these proposals are, there is little evidence that the
international community has the will or the means to conduct such an
enterprise. And this applies to African states in particular whose regional
organization – the Organization of African Unity (OAU) – is a weak vessel,
lacking the political and military resources, and the logistical back-up
required to intervene successfully in civil wars.

Southern Africa – An Exception to the General Rule?

Yet those who have despaired of Africa's regeneration have rightly taken
some comfort from the extraordinary transition that occurred in South
Africa between 1990 and 1994. The partnership forged between F.W. de
Klerk and Nelson Mandela successfully steered the country to a new and
fully democratic dispensation and they did so by displaying courageous and
imaginative leadership and, in the process, the willingness to defy the more
obdurate elements of their respective political constituencies. The result was
an 'historic compromise' involving the establishment of a Government of
National Unity (GNU) embracing the three major political actors – the
African National Congress (ANC), the essentially Afrikaner National Party
(NP) and the Inkatha Freedom Party (IFP) – and this despite the fact that the
transition was punctuated by outbreaks of political violence in the Black
townships of the Witwatersrand and the Province of KwaZulu-Natal.

South Africa's re-entry into respectable international society also
brought hope to its immediate neighbours in the region. For more than a
decade several of these states – Lesotho, Angola, Mozambique, Zambia and
Zimbabwe – had been exposed to a South African strategy of destabilization
designed to undermine their support for ANC exiles. The latter, in turn,
were attempting to mobilize indigenous support by means of the 'armed
struggle'. The problems these poorer and weaker states faced were
compounded by economic dependence in varying degrees on their powerful
neighbour. To reduce this dependence, a Southern African Development and
Co-ordination Conference (SADCC) was established in 1981, but, if
anything, the dependence increased as trade statistics amply demonstrate:

'the value of intra-SADCC trade is approximately 4 per cent of the total trade of SADCC countries; 25 per cent of total trade is with South Africa... it is the severe imbalance of trade between South Africa and the region: 5.5:1 in favour of South Africa'.[6]

Thus when the 'new' South Africa joined SADCC (subsequently named the Southern African Development Community – SADC) in 1994, there was a genuine expectation that the region as a whole would benefit from the 'engine of growth' the new member represented. Furthermore, there was the prospect that the economies of the member states would ultimately move towards greater regional integration and, by so doing, follow the example of states elsewhere in establishing regional groupings (e.g. NAFTA, EU, APEC and MERCOSUR). This tendency towards state aggregation is regarded as a means of countering the declining utility of state sovereignty under pressure from the impact of globalization. In other words, the southern African region, by increasing the level of inter-governmental co-operation in the short term, and over the long run maximising the opportunities for integration, might well escape the marginalization that threatens so many small and under-resourced states elsewhere on the continent.

This account of the African predicament will – it is hoped – provide an appropriate background to the theme of *Violence in Southern Africa* examined in this special issue of the journal *Terrorism and Political Violence*. Paradoxically, a regime that seems better placed than its counterparts elsewhere on the continent to survive the threat of marginalization has endured a variety of violent modes of struggle ranging from civil wars in Angola and Mozambique and wars of liberation in Namibia and Zimbabwe to low intensity urban and rural conflict in South Africa. By contrast, the decolonization process in much of Africa south of the Sahara in the post-war period was relatively peaceful – the exceptions being Eritrea and Kenya during the Mau-Mau phase. It was once fashionable to posit a positive cause and effect relationship between 'revolution' and state and nation building, on the grounds that the 'struggle' produced a catharsis, a purging of the body politic, and in the process transformed a divided society into a coherent and dynamic state capable of meeting the needs of its people and asserting itself in the international system. This is a dubious proposition, and hardly borne out by the experience of Nigeria in the wake of civil war in the 1960s.

And in this context both Keith Somerville and Chris Alden provide a detailed and salutary analysis of the Angolan and Mozambican conflicts in their contributions to this volume. Neither has ended in the transformation of state and society; rather, both have left a legacy of death and destruction that will take decades to repair. The precarious truce that currently exists in Angola between UNITA and the MPLA government, and the uneasy co-existence of Renamo (the defeated party in the 1994 elections) and the ruling Frelimo Party in Mozambique are fragile structures created by the mutual exhaustion of all the actors involved in earlier struggles and a recognition that the costs of continuing conflict exceeded the costs of compromise and peace-making. And the uncertainty surrounding the future of both countries has important implications for the region as a whole and SADC in particular. The objective of greater inter-governmental co-operation, let alone full-scale functional integration, will remain all the more difficult to achieve unless and until a legitimate and stable government is established in Angola, and Mozambique makes significant headway with the task of social and economic reconstruction.

Moreover, the extent to which South Africa can aid the integration process has to be qualified in two important respects: first, there is an understandable fear on the part of its poorer neighbours about the possibility of a hegemonic role for South Africa by virtue of its greater economic and political muscle. In his contribution to this special issue, Jakkie Cilliers graphically illustrates the dependence of these states on South Africa:

> South Africa's economy is nearly four times as big as that of all the other 11 SADC members combined... This absence of parity could lead to the establishment of a hierarchy and domination amongst cooperating partners.

Moreover, in 1992, South Africa exported some R17.35 billion worth of goods to its neighbours, but imported only R4.12 billion from them; it has 23,000 of southern Africa's 42,000 kilometres of railway line; 58,000 of 87,000 kilometres of paved roads, and over 5.1 million of the region's 6 million motor vehicles. South Africa handled nearly 16 times more tonnage of goods through its harbours than those of the rest of the region and it creates 75 per cent of sub-Equatorial Africa's total installed electricity capacity.

Even before the new government took power in May 1994, President Mandela recognized the political implications of this dependence, arguing that South Africa would have to treat its neighbours with 'sensitivity and restraint'.[7]

The second qualification is the constraining influence of domestic pressures on the government as it struggles to restructure the local economy and meet the pressing needs of its citizens. The latter constraint might seem – at first sight – to cancel out any incentive for South Africa to exert unwelcome influence in the region, but its leaders have long memories of the apartheid regime's destabilization strategy. Indeed, in this context it is significant – as Somerville reminds us – that South African efforts to mediate in Angola, following the 1992 election, were rebuffed by the

Luanda government after the discovery that the South African Defence Force was still involved in supplying arms to UNITA. Similarly, South Africa was not invited to participate in the UN peacekeeping force attached to Angola in 1994 following the truce between the warring parties.

It is in this context that Cilliers' analysis has continuing relevances. He rightly argues:

> South Africa's destiny is intertwined with that of the regions. South Africa shares more than 1000 kilometres of porous, unguarded, sometimes even unmarked borders with its neighbours – borders giving access to increased numbers of illegal immigrants, drugs, arms, contraband and stolen vehicles.[8]

Thus, the creation of a new security regime is essential to cope with transnational threats to the region's stability; indeed, it could be argued that just as the establishment of NATO in 1949 provided Europeans with the confidence to proceed with the work of economic integration, so a similar outcome is essential in the case of South Africa. Both Alden and Cilliers examine this prospect in detail, and one may fairly conclude that the outcome in terms of regional co-operation is likely to be some bilateral inter-governmental agreements in areas where a common interest exists (and security is the obvious example), and region-wide economic co-operation where this is possible on a functional basis involving common exploitation of the transport linkages, power supplies and water resources. This process will, admittedly, be slow and haphazard, on the principle that regional structures will only emerge once the substance of day-to-day economic and social transactions across borders multiplies to a level where regulation by regional institutions is required to create fair terms of trade.

Abiodun Alao's account of the relative weight of the 'armed struggle' in bringing independence to Namibia and Zimbabwe and ending apartheid in South Africa likewise has relevance for the future prospects of the southern African region. He emphasizes that in ease case 'dialogue and negotiation began after the warring sides in each realised that some form of compromise was inevitable...in all three... as each made political concessions to cater for the interests of the white minority'. Thus, competing actors in all three societies learned the value of compromise in protracted constitutional negotiations and this assists their current diplomatic and political efforts to find common ground for the creation of a network of regional structures. In promoting this objective, the leadership of all three states has this advantage, that the relationship between South Africa and its neighbours will certainly be very different from that which prevailed during the apartheid era when a profound ideological gulf made self-conscious and fruitful co-operation very difficult, if not impossible. At the very least, in the new post-apartheid era, relations will be governed by straightforward economic and political interests; clashes may well occur on issues such as migration from the poorer state to its richer neighbour, but at least there is an acknowledgement that co-operation rather than competition – as in the past – is the only basis on which to make progress.

As for South Africa's wider continental role, its economic and military capability, together with the moral authority of its State President following the country's successful transition to democratic government, has raised expectations at the OAU, for example, that the new government would conduct a constructive and dynamic policy designed to help raise the continent's economic performance and assist in the task of conflict resolution. Yet the Mandela government, following the failure of 'cautious diplomacy' to secure the reprieve of the Ogoni dissidents in Nigeria in November 1995, has resisted calls to be the 'saviour' of Africa. This applies particularly – as Cilliers argues – with regard to peacekeeping operations beyond its borders, especially where this threatens to draw the country into 'intractable conflicts and commitments'. This is hardly surprising given the formidable domestic agenda inherited by the Mandela government and – in particular – the priority attached to merging the security forces of the old regime and the military wings of the liberation movements into a coherent and efficient South African National Defence Force (SANDF). Nor can the government ignore the current and probably indefinitely continuing debate about the appropriate size of South Africa's military capability, given that resources are limited, with many competing claims in the area of economic and social reconstruction to consider.

Yet another constraint against a grandiose continental strategy is the persistent level of violence in South Africa itself in the post-apartheid era. It is true that the 'political' violence of the kind that disfigured the transitional process has markedly declined since 1994; the white right-wing threat has faded as has conflict between the ANC and the IFP in the black townships of the Witwatersrand. In this context Judith Hudson provides an account of the causes and consequences of township violence in the 1990s, arguing that the calm that currently prevails is precarious; indeed she sounds a sober note of warning in stressing that a viable long-term solution depends upon the area's economic and social regeneration.

> Thus there is a need for caution. Development disrupts the balance between and within communities, it is a highly politicized activity which has the potential to be divisive. Conflict over resources is common on the Reef, and the allocation of resources is a highly politicized activity in South Africa. Those with a stake in what development efforts seek to change may resist development initiatives with potentially explosive consequences. There is still the possibility

that violence in this area may flare up, tensions caused by development could be the spark.

Indeed, there are no quick solutions to this conflict. Having legitimate local government structures in place is indeed very important, but several challenges still confront the area. Perhaps the most important of these is economic growth and the generation of employment to provide for an increasing population. The top priority of development...must surely be the creation of wealth and jobs as fast and in as great a number as possible...

Equally intractable, as Alexander Johnston demonstrates in his contribution, is the violence in KwaZulu-Natal. This has continued unabated for nearly a decade with some 4,000 lives lost between 1987 and 1990 in a bitter, low-intensity conflict between the United Democratic Front (UDF), an ANC surrogate, and the IFP. Some 8,000 people died in the period between 1990 and 1995 after the ANC was unbanned. In the first months of 1996 at least as many Defence Force units were deployed on internal security duties across South Africa as in the late 1980s. Johnston's analysis examines the causes of this violence in detail and ends on a cautious note pointing to recent efforts to halt the killing. Failure in this context will continue to be a major obstacle to the Province's development and discourage the foreign investment which the country as a whole so badly needs. Equally, failure to curb the high incidence of crime in South Africa will inhibit progress as Mark Shaw demonstrates in his wide-ranging account.

This survey of the role of violence in southern Africa has looked at the impact of war and civil disorder upon state and society in a region characterised by uneconomic development where statehood is fragile (Mozambique) or bitterly contested (Angola). And, as we have seen, the legacy of violent conflict in both countries will require immense effort and resources to repair a battered infrastructure by governments whose legitimacy has yet to be firmly established. By contrast, Zimbabwe and Namibia have survived their 'wars of liberation'; statehood in both is uncontested, although both face formidable problems of development requiring leadership willing to accept the full discipline of the market economy. The outlook for the region as a whole might well improve if their powerful neighbour, South Africa, prospers.

The Mandela government has this advantage, that it has inherited a tradition of strong statehood and an embryonic civil society, together with well-established parliamentary and judicial structures. These advantages were, paradoxically, an inheritance from the past, but precisely because they are autochtonous there is the prospect of sensible adaptation and evolution as circumstances dictate under the new political dispensation. Blessed with abundant natural resources, human skills and an experienced business community, South Africa has the capacity to contribute to the region's further development, but much will depend on how far the government succeeds in redressing the evils of apartheid and the propensity to violence in the black urban areas and the valleys of KwaZulu-Natal. This negative inheritance from the past will no doubt preoccupy the Mandela government and its successor well into the next century, but the hope must be that the region will ultimately benefit from whatever positive spill-over results from greater foreign investment, the liberalization of the South African economy and the skills of an emerging class of technocrats and entrepreneurs in the black community. Failure in this context will risk repeating the stultifying experience of African states elsewhere and contribute to an even greater, indeed ultimately tragic marginalization of the continent as a whole.

NOTES

1. For an extended treatment of this theme see J.E. Spence, 'Africa in the Contemporary International System', in Armand Clesse, Richard Cooper and Yoshikazu Sakamoto (eds), *The International System After the Collapse of the East-West Order* (Dordrecht: Martinus Nijhoff 1994) pp.675–87.
2. Stephen Riley, 'Africa's New Wind of Change', *The World Today* 7 (1992) p.679.
3. Riley, p.680.
4. Quoted in *Financial Times*, 6 Jan. 1993.
5. Ali Mazrui, 'The Bondage of Boundaries', *The Economist*, 11–17 Sept. 1993.
6. In 1990 the EC accounted for 27.3 per cent of South African exports while the USA (4 per cent), Japan (6.4 per cent) and Africa (6.7 per cent) were the next most important customers. Similarly, the EC (44.7 percent), the USA (11.4 per cent), Japan (9.8 per cent) and Africa (1.6 per cent) supplied the bulk of South Africa's imports. Sheila Page and Christopher Stevens, *Trading with South Africa: The Policy Options for the EC* (London: Overseas Development Inst., Special Report 1994).
7. Nelson Mandela, 'South Africa's Future Foreign Policy', *Foreign Affairs* 72/5 (Nov.–Dec. 1993) p.88.
8. The issue of crime and lawlessness in South Africa receives separate treatment in this volume in the final contribution, from Mark Shaw, 'South Africa: Crime in Transition', pp.156–75.

Angola – Groping Towards Peace or Slipping Back Towards War?

KEITH SOMERVILLE

When President José Eduardo dos Santos and UNITA leader Jonas Savimbi met in May 1995 and pledged to work for reconciliation and a political solution to Angola's seemingly interminable civil warfare, it appeared as though a new chapter had been opened in Angola's history. But nearly two years have passed since that historic meeting with only the slowest and most grudging progress made on breaking down political and military divisions and attempting to forge a new nation from the shattered remains of then old. This essay deals with the major ethnic, cultural and political divisions that have made Angola the cockpit of southern Africa and the scene of constant internal conflict since the start of the liberation struggle against the Portuguese colonial army in 1960. For all but three of the last 26 years, the country has been at war and over two years of unstable peace has not diminished the forces that divide the country. The divisions between the Mbundu and *mestiço* peoples of the Luanda region and both the Bakongo along the Zaire border and the Ovimbundu supporters of UNITA in the centre and south are as wide today as they were at the height of the civil war and Angola's future as a peaceful and united state is far from assured.

'I have told him he is the president of my country and therefore my president. I want to cooperate in the consolidation of the peace process wherever he feels comfortable with me and where my party says I will be useful.' These two sentences spoken by the UNITA leader Jonas Malheiro Savimbi on 6 May 1995 after a meeting in Lusaka with President José Eduardo dos Santos of Angola may turn out to be the most important words spoken about Angola in the last 20 years. By accepting in public that dos Santos was the legitimate president and that he (Savimbi) was prepared to work with him, Savimbi may have gone far enough down the road of reconciliation for the peace agreement signed by the MPLA-led Angolan government and UNITA in Lusaka on 20 November 1994 to be implemented.

One still has to counsel caution, though. The November 1994 deal brought to an end two years of bitter war that followed UNITA's rejection of the September 1992 elections. They were the first multiparty elections ever held in Angola and were themselves the culmination of a 16-month transition process after 17 years of warfare, which followed Angolan independence from Portuguese colonial rule. The last 14 years of Portugal's involvement in Angola had been spent at war, too, as three Angolan liberation movements (the MPLA, FNLA and UNITA) fought a low-level guerrilla war to achieve independence. That war, like the following two periods of civil war, was militarily inconclusive but forced major political changes which eventually brought about freedom for Angola from colonial rule but not from years of war and human suffering.

But why has Angola proved so prone to the use of military rather than political instruments to solve its national crises? Even now, with the prospects for peace and reconciliation riding high following the historic meeting between Dos Santos and Savimbi in Lusaka, one must recognize that the prospects for real reconciliation and the discovery of common political ground between the combatants of the MPLA and UNITA are far from good. The UN Special Envoy to Angola, Alioune Blondin Beye, has tried consistently to strike an upbeat note about Angola's peace prospect, but even he was cautious after the meeting of the two leaders in Lusaka; he told reporters in Pretoria on 9 May 1995 that after Lusaka, 'I would not say that mistrust had disappeared, but the wall of mistrust has been pushed back.'

It is hardly surprising that mistrust exists between the MPLA and UNITA after a total of 19 years of war between them and one aborted and much disputed peace process. But the mistrust is so deep-seated, leading to the failure of the Angolan nationalist movements to work together at the time of independence in 1975, that this account of conflict in Angola must start with a close examination of the roots of nationalism in Angola, the effects of colonial rule on the diverse communities which were enclosed within the present-day borders of Angola by the European scramble for African colonies in the late nineteenth century and the polarisation of post-independence Angola. This examination will weave in the strands of southern Africa regional conflict and the wider superpower confrontation which have influenced the forms and scale of conflict in Angola, but the main emphasis must be on the indigenous roots of the conflict.

One Angola, One Nation or No Angola Three Nations?

Throughout Africa one of the hardest tasks facing the political leaders who emerged as heads of state and government, when their territories emerged into the harsh world of statehood from colonial rule in the late 1950s and early 1960s, has been nation-building. With a handful of exceptions (and Somalia, as one of those, proved that ethnic uniformity is no guarantee of peace and units), the new states of Africa were a patchwork of ethnic communities which had coexisted peacefully or otherwise in the pre-colonial period, but which were thrown together as states whose boundaries followed no logic other than that of the greed of European powers in the Partition of Africa. Pre-colonial conflicts or trade relations apart, they had little in common apart from their experience of colonial occupation.

But even their experience of colonialism was hardly uniform – coastal communities had a longer and often deeper relationship with the colonizing power than inland communities; strong, resistant polities were either destroyed (as in the case of the Herero in Namibia, the power of the Ashanti in Ghana and the Zulu military monarchy in South Africa) or used as instruments of indirect rule (as was the case with the Tutsi ruling class in Rwanda and Burundi or the Baganda in Uganda and the northern Nigerian Muslim rulers); some groups developed into small traders, providers of labour for colonial authorities or a source of recruits for the colonial armed force or police, while others were marginalized and had little direct contact.[1]

The majority of territories which achieved independence did so following the growth of nationalist movements led by Western-educated political elites who were able to generate nationalist opposition to colonial rule among mainly urban populations. David Throup has rightly pointed out that 'African nationalism had few roots in local societies, in some countries being primarily an attempt by the Western-educated elite to capture control of the colonial state. Essentially an elite enterprise, in contrast to the popular appeal of ethnic sub-nationalism, territorial nationalisms were fragile constructs, liable to fragment ... once competition for the limited resources of virtually all Africa's new states began with independence.'[2] This dichotomy between elite aspirations for the African state and sub-elite concentration on clan, community or regional loyalties meant that governments and state institutions, even where political leaders retained a belief in nation-building and truly national development, became increasingly remote from much of the population. The crisis of national and state legitimacy developed, compounded by corruption, nepotism and mismanagement, led to political conflict over the control of resources and of central state institutions as the source of development funds.[3]

The territories where colonial powers resisted the tide of African nationalism were not immune from the lack of a wider sense of national identity or from the transitory or fragmentary nature of a territory-wide nationalism. Despite the hopes of some liberation theorists, notably Frantz Fanon, the fight for liberation did not automatically forge a sense of national solidarity; 'violence in Africa has begotten violence – not freedom, not dignity, not socialism, not nationhood'.[4]

Angola was certainly not immune from crisis of African nationalism and the effects of sub-national loyalties. Prior to Portuguese intervention and then occupation, Angola did not exist as a single entity. Rather the region now called Angola was occupied by a diverse group of ethnic communities, some organized in kingdoms and others on a looser basis. When the Portuguese first set foot in Angola in the fifteenth century they found the Kongo kingdom of the Bakongo people to be the most powerful polity. Based in the area of the current Angola-Zaire border near the Atlantic coast, the kingdom had its own political and trading structure and levied tribute from neighbouring peoples. The Kongo monarch was a spiritual as well as temporal ruler.

To the south of the Kongo kingdom lay the Mbundu – a people ruled by a monarch whole title was *ngola a kiluanje*, from whom the Portuguese took the name Angola for the whole region they eventually occupied. The Mbundu resisted attempts by the Kongo kingdom to assert its hegemony.

Farther south and away from the Atlantic coast, the Ovimbundu people inhabited the central plateau area, while to the east lay scattered populations in what is now Moxico province and Cuando Cubango. The only other polity of note was the Lunda kingdom in north-east Angola and Zaire along the upper reaches of the Kasai river. It was an increasingly centralized kingdom, but its descendants played only a peripheral role in Angolan nationalist politics unlike the Bakongo, Mbundu and Ovimbundu.

The arrival of the first Portuguese in 1483 was followed by the opening of trade, economic and religious contacts between the Kongo kingdom and the Portuguese. Eventually, the Portuguese became involved in the internal politics of the Kongo and used this to gain increasing control over the kingdom. The development of the slave trade proved divisive among the Bakongo and between them and their neighbours, as the kingdom moved from selling its subjects to the Portuguese to raiding neighbours to provide slaves. This increased the level of Kongo-Mbundu conflict. During the sixteenth century the Mbundu resisted Portuguese incursions, but by 1576 the invaders had seized territory along the coast and established Luanda as their base.

Despite initial Mbundu and Kongo resistance, both kingdoms crumbled in the face of Portuguese pressure and amid the divisive influence of their own involvement in the slave trade. As the resistance weakened and the Portuguese foothold became more entrenched, the Mbundu in particular became more and more receptive to Portuguese culture, to playing an auxiliary role in the colonial trade system and to intermixing with the invaders to give birth to a creole population led by 'the swarthy sons of conquistador fathers and Mbundu mothers ... they became the commanders of the colonial armies, the interpreters in the finance houses, the leaders of the caravans of textile porters into the interior'.[5] The military and trade tradition continued into the twentieth century.

The Rise of Three Nationalist Movements

The diverse ethnic background of Angolans and their differing experiences of colonial rule led to the formation of a colonial state made up of three distinct component parts in the north of the territory and then the more isolated south, centre and east of the country – the latter regions only being brought under Portuguese control in the twentieth century. The three northern regions were the Cabinda enclave, the old Kongo kingdom and the Mbundu/creole/Luanda region. They effectively developed in separate ways with the Portuguese colonial state as the only real unifying factor. The Bakongo looked more to the Belgian Congo (Zaire) and its capital, Leopoldville, for their cultural and economic livelihoods than to Luanda, Cabinda was geographically and ethnically separate and Luanda was the centre of Portuguese influence and the only region where there was real assimilation of language, culture and ideas of European-style nationalism from the Portuguese. A further source of differences between the regions came from the missionaries who set up their churches, schools and clinics in Angola – different groups went to the different regions, increasing the gulf.

As David Birmingham points out, by the time of the rise of nationalism throughout Africa in the twentieth century,

> Angola lacked a cultural, economic and administrative unity on which the aspirations of black politicians could be focused ... In between the north and the south lay the Luanda corridor, the most conventional part of the colony, related economically and administratively to the colonial capital to which it was linked by historical ties ... and by the Kimbundu vernacular language [the language of the Mbundu] ... When confrontation between black and white broke out in the 1950s ... politics were homogenised at a regional level, to create a single political party. The Luanda community and its outlying allies of the corridor were unable, however, to form a national alliance with the political traditions of the Leopoldville-oriented north or the plateau sub-region of the south.[6]

Thus it was that the three main political movements which have been dominant in Angola since the advent of modern nationalism there in the early 1950s developed from the three basic constituencies in Angola – the Bakongo, the Luanda alliance of creoles, assimilated black Angolans and the Mbundu, and the Ovimbundu of the central plateau and south of the country. The three movements developed their support from these constituencies – the FNLA from the Bakongo, the MPLA from the Luanda alliance and UNITA from the Ovimbundu – though they did not specifically exclude other groups (the MPLA, in particular, setting out from the start to recruit on a national basis). Over the 40 years from the advent of modern nationalism in Angola to the present, the movements have remained surprisingly cohesive and faithful to their original support bases. Ideological loyalties have come and gone and there have been factional struggles based on both ideology and personal ambition, but there has been no major change in the core group of each movement.[7]

The FNLA was the first movement to emerge and make any international impact. Its origins were among Bakongo in both northern Angola and across the border in the Belgian Congo. A group of Bakongo nationalists, some of them descendants of the old Kongo monarchy, in the mid-1950s began to agitate for the restoration or the Kongo kingdom. In May 1956, these Bakongo activists wrote to the US State Department putting forward their view that the Kongo kingdom was historically separate from Angola. Two months later, they formed the União das Populacões do Norte de Angola (UPNA – Union of the People of Northern Angola). It was not founded as a movement to represent Angolans as a whole and limited its activities to campaigning for Bakongo rights. Its leader was Holden Roberto. In 1958, Roberto represented the movement at the All-African People's Congress in Accra, where he was elected to the steering committee for the next congress. However, there was not a universal welcome in Accra for the UPNA's ethnically and regionally-based programme. Roberto was persuaded to change its name to the União dos Populacões de Angola (UPA – the Union of the People of Angola) and to make an effort to bring non-Bakongo into the movement and its leadership. The result was that a few token non-Bakongo gained middle-ranking positions, including a young Jonas Savimbi, but with Roberto as the undisputed leader.

Some military training and material support were given to the UPA by independent African states, including Algeria. After Congo's independence, the UPA set up its headquarters in Leopoldville (Kinshasa) and Roberto developed a close relationship (later cemented by marital ties) with Joseph Mobutu Sese Seko, the dictator-to-be in the Congo. The UPA was later named the FNLA as an attempt to create a more modern and less ethnically-based nationalist movement, though the movement remained an essentially Bakongo organization. It had a small guerrilla force but was relatively inactive in military terms, despite receiving military training and arms from China.

The MPLA developed from leftist and nationalist movements in Luanda and the neighbouring provinces of Bengo, Cuanza Norte, Cuanza Sul and Malanje. Its founders and early leaders were educated black Angolans, members of the old creole military and trading clans and *mestiços*. They drew their support from the Mbundu, from urban dwellers, from among educated Angolans inside and the country and in Portugal and from the mestico community. But the founders of the movement set out to form a national movement. They had a strongly socialist or Marxist inclination and close links with the Portuguese Communist Party.[8] It was the combination of the leftist ideology of MPLA leaders, their base among the more ethnically varied and cosmopolitan peoples of Luanda and the coast and the links the leadership built up in Lisbon with nationalists from other Portuguese colonies (Mozambique, Cape Verde and Guinea Bissau) that ensured the development of a nationalist platform that sought to transcend ethnic, racial, linguistic or regional barriers and appeal to all those who lived within the borders of the Portuguese colony.

Thus the MPLA was immediately differentiated in ideological terms from the FNLA and was seen by it as hostile because of its attempt to appeal to all Angolans, including Bakongo, and because of its implicit opposition to ethnically-based politics. After a failed rising in Luanda in 1961, a handful of MPLA activists managed to reach the Dembos forest north-east of the capital from there and carried out a low-level war right up until the 1974 revolution in Portugal. The MPLA also infiltrated guerrillas through Zaire in the early 1960s and then into Cabinda via Congo (Brazzaville) and later into eastern Angola via Zambia.

The third major movement, UNITA, and the one that now rivals the MPLA for control of Angola, was a one man show from the start. Its founder, Jonas Savimbi, had been foreign secretary of the FNLA and of the short-lived government-in-exile formed by Roberto and the FNLA and, for a time, recognized by the OAU. But Savimbi, one of the few non-Bakongo to rise within the ranks of the FNLA, was disenchanted with what he saw as the ethnic and personality based politics of the movement and he left it in 1964 after a major clash with Roberto. After a brief flirtation with the MPLA, Savimbi returned to his home area of central Angola and in 1966 established UNITA. Savimbi had taken some non-Bakongo (and mainly Ovimbundu) FNLA supporters with him when he left Roberto and these formed the base of the new organization. A primary aim, Savimbi said, of the new group was to get away from the squabbling, exile-based politics of the FNLA and MPLA and to base the struggle inside Angola. UNITA was established, like the MPLA, as a national movement. However, the problems of recruitment and mobilization in a country at war meant that UNITA was chiefly able to recruit within its immediate area of operations in the Ovimbundu-populated central highlands (notably Huambo and Bié). It carried out a low-level guerrilla campaign in the highlands, though this was obstructed by arguments with Zambia (UNITA's main African supporter and its route for supplies and externally-trained guerrillas to enter

Angola) after UNITA attacked the Benguela railway (which served
Zambia's and Zaire's copper mines as well as the Portuguese in Angola).

The implicit conflict between the movements rapidly became explicit in
the mid-1960s. Their ethnic, personality and ideological differences were
made worse by their sources of African and external support. The FNLA
was based in Zaire and from the early 1960s received support from Mobutu
and a little from the United States via the CIA. The MPLA was eclectic in
its external links, receiving support from the Soviet Union, Cuba,
Yugoslavia, Sweden and, for a short whole, China. The FNLA's strong links
with Zaire led to the expulsion of the MPLA from Zaire and the
development of close links between the MPLA leadership and the
succession of radical governments in neighbouring Congo (Brazzaville).

During the period that the MPLA tried to infiltrate guerrillas into
northern Angola from Zaire, the FNLA attempted to intercept them, on one
occasion eliminating an entire MPLA guerrilla unit. There was less direct
conflict between the MPLA and UNITA, though as MPLA units spread their
operations from the eastern province of Moxico, they began to encroach
upon what UNITA considered to be its area of operations. There was
hostility between the movements' guerrillas and the MPLA consistently
accused UNITA of colluding with the Portuguese in their counter-
insurgency efforts – a charge denied by UNITA but one which served to sow
mistrust between them during the liberation war.

Although the MPLA made some military progress in the sparsely-
populated areas of eastern Angola and the small unit in the Dembos forest
remained an irritant for the Portuguese, at the time of the 1974 revolution in
Portugal the three Angolan movements were a long way from defeating the
colonial power militarily. However, they had built up their forces
sufficiently for them to try to seize power once the Portuguese decided that
the time had come to cut their losses and negotiate independence for
Angola.

The talks on a Portuguese withdrawal involved the three movements,
though rarely cooperating or seeking identical goals. At one stage, right-
wing groups within the Portuguese government held talks with the FNLA
and South Africa in an attempt to arrange a deal that would ensure that the
MPLA was excluded form power in an independent Angola. Portugal was
increasingly torn over the future of Angola – with the right siding with the
FNLA and UNITA and the left favouring the MPLA. Unlike Mozambique
and Guinea Bissau/Cape Verde, where the Portuguese had to deal with just
one movement, in Angola they had to deal with three hostile groups. The
Portuguese named 11 November 1975 as the exit date and attempted, with
support from members of the OAU (particularly Zambia, Zaire, Nigeria,
Tanzania and Kenya), to mediate between the three groups. The result was

the Alvor accord of January 1975 (later supplemented to no greater effect by the Nakuru agreement of June 1975), which established a national unity government made up of representatives of the MPLA, FNLA and UNITA. They worked uneasily with the Portuguese in Luanda to organize a transition to independence.

But the transition process became a civil war. When the Portuguese revolution turned the situation in Angola on its head, the three movements continued to strengthen their armed forces. The FNLA obtained large supplies of arms from China (along with 450 Chinese military instructors) for its Zaire-based forces and was given arms and the support of Zairean military units by Mobutu. In late 1974 the CIA also became interested in the FNLA as it sought to obstruct an MPLA takeover in Angola. The MPLA, which went through severe factional conflict in the 1972–74 period, was unprepared for a struggle for power. Its enigmatic leader, Agostinho Neto, had fought off attempts to oust him, but at the cost of one large faction (the so-called eastern group under guerrilla leader Daniel Chipenda) breaking away from the MPLA and joining the FNLA. This weakened the MPLA but, in late 1974, it began to rebuilt its forces and it elicited ever increasing supplies of arms from the Soviet Union in the face of the evident FNLA build-up (the USSR seems to have been particularly concerned at growing Chinese involvement in the region). UNITA tried to get more foreign aid but, with the exception of small deliveries from China, was largely unsuccessful. UNITA was closer to the FNLA than to the MPLA but at this stage was not firmly allied to Roberto's group. The arms build-up boded ill for the Alvor accord and continued to escalate in early 1975 as the unity government proved increasingly unworkable.[9]

The arms race turned into a civil war when the FNLA launched an invasion of northern Angola in February 1975. Backed by Zairean armoured and paratroop units, the FNLA forces drove south from the Zairean border towards Luanda. The MPLA sought to defend its areas of control from the FNLA attack, but came under severe pressure between March and October 1975, losing a string of northern and coastal towns to the FNLA. Neto's forces also came into conflict with UNITA in Luanda. The MPLA suspected UNITA of siding with the FNLA and its forces expelled UNITA from Luanda. Savimbi then set up his headquarters in the central plateau town of Huambo and, with South African support, attempted to seize southern and central Angola and then march on Luanda from the south. South Africa entered the war in mid-1975 skirmishing with the MPLA along the Angola-Namibia border, but launched a full-scale invasion in co-operation with UNITA in October 1975.[10]

By October 1975, the MPLA had received substantial quantities of Soviet arms, including armoured vehicles and multiple rocket-launchers. It had also asked Cuba to supply military instructors. These had arrived in mid-year and were training MPLA forces near Luanda and at the southern coastal town of Benguela where they came into direct conflict with the advancing South African/UNITA column. The steady advance of both the FNLA/Zairean and UNITA/South African columns endangered the MPLA forces and threatened their hold on the capital, Luanda, as independence day approached. Neto appealed to Cuba for more help, including combat troops. These were supplied, along with increased deliveries of Soviet arms.

There is no evidence of a Soviet role in deciding on the commitment of the Cubans, but clearly, once the Cubans were dispatched, the Soviet leadership ensured that they and the MPLA had the arms they needed to repel the two columns and then achieve a military victory over the invading forces and the MPLA's domestic opponents. The Cubans arrived soon enough to halt the offensives before 11 November – enabling Neto to have himself installed as president in Luanda at the head of an MPLA government.

As an estimated 10,000–12,000 Cuban combat troops and some $200 million worth of Soviet arms (including MiG-21 aircraft and T-34 and T-55 tanks) began to arrive to strengthen the MPLA, a counter-offensive began. The FNLA/Zairean forces crumbled in northern Angola and soon fled back over the border into Zaire. To the south of Luanda, the Cuban/MPLA forces had a harder fight on their hands, but on 14 March 1976 the South African forces abandoned their final positions at Gago Coutinho and withdrew across Angola's southern border into South African-occupied Namibia.[10]

The MPLA now set about establishing control across the whole of Angolan national territory – bolstered not only by the presence of the Cuban troops but also by recognition from the OAU. But its task was a difficult one. During the independence war it had retained the loyalty of its Luanda and Mbundu constituency and had established a guerrilla presence and small liberated areas in eastern Angola, but had not penetrated far into the central plateau region or Bakongo areas along the border with Zaire. Propaganda by UNITA and the FNLA and the mere fact that the MPLA was a new movement to these areas meant that control of the territory did not mean support from its population or the end of lingering loyalties to the FNLA or UNITA. Years of peace and economic reconstruction combined with sensitive political policies would have been required to pull Angola from civil war into the formation of a united nation. Instead, Angola was to suffer another 15 years of war and periodic invasion or raids by South African forces.

Guerrilla War and South African Destabilization

The military defeats suffered by the FNLA and UNITA did not mean political annihilation or the loss of all their external support. The FNLA moved back into Zaire and continued to receive the backing of President Mobutu. He and his US supporters were hostile towards the pro-socialist, Soviet-backed government now installed in Luanda. Mobutu (and both the Americans and Chinese) would have preferred to have seen Roberto as president or as a leading force in a coalition government which excluded the MPLA. The CIA and the Chinese were both willing to continue funding and arming the FNLA. This meant that there was a continuation of fighting in the Angolan provinces bordering Zaire – though it was at a low enough level not to be a serious military or political threat to the MPLA's control of Angolan territory. FNLA military activity only lasted for two years after independence.

The FNLA was effectively prevented from operating militarily by Mobutu in 1978, following a *rapprochement* between Angola and Zaire. The agreement was put together following two invasions of Zaire's mineral-rich Shaba province by former Katangese gendarmes who had fought first for the Portuguese colonial army and then for the MPLA. They were based in northern Angola and launched invasions of Shaba via Zambia in 1977 and then again in 1978. Moroccan, Belgian and French forces (and US logistical aid) helped Mobutu regain control of the invaded areas. The threat to this economically important region and the concern of other states in the region led to the Zaire-Angola agreement, under which each side agreed to refrain from giving support to the activities of opposition movements.

UNITA proved a more difficult opponent. It retained strong support from South Africa and a safe rear-base in Namibia. South Africa was opposed not only to the socialist ideology and external supporters (the Soviet Union and Cuba) of the MPLA government but also to its alliance with the Namibian liberation movement, SWAPO. The independence of Angola gave SWAPO the opportunity to establish military bases and training camps in a territory adjacent to Namibia. Until then, SWAPO had operated chiefly from Zambia, infiltrating its guerrillas into the thin neck of Namibian territory (the Caprivi Strip) which runs between Zambia and Botswana.

From Namibia, UNITA was able to start a guerrilla war in southern and later central Angola. It was provided with arms, training and logistical support by South Africa, which carried out its own raids into Angola and maintained a covert unit (32 or Buffalo Battalion, recruited from South Africa special forces and former FNLA guerrillas) in southern Angola to attack SWAPO units and disrupt MPLA administration of the region.

Even with South African support, UNITA was unable to defeat the Angolan army (FAPLA). FAPLA, for its part, was able to restrict UNITA's area of operations but not to defeat the guerrillas or prevent them from mobilizing some support from among the Ovimbundu. Apart from regular counter-insurgency operations, FAPLA conducted annual sweeps in the September–December dry season to try to expel UNITA from Angola. These failed because of the huge areas of territory to be covered, the lack of Angolan expertise in coordinated, large-scale counter-insurgency warfare and South African intervention to assist UNITA. The scale of South African intervention remained modest in the late 1970s, but during the 1980s developed in scale. This was partly a result of the increasing South African perception of the nationalist/Soviet threat in southern Africa (much inflated in the minds and propaganda of the government and military commanders in Pretoria) and partly because of the election in the United States, Britain, and West Germany of conservative governments which favoured a more confrontational policy towards the Soviet Union and those perceived to be its allies. South Africa took the change in Western policy as the green light for its 'total strategy' against the ANC and its regional supporters.

From 1981 onwards, South Africa launched a series of major incursions into southern Angola to support UNITA, attack SWAPO and create a buffer zone in southern Angola under its or UNITA's control. This enabled UNITA to establish its headquarters at Jamba (in south-eastern Angola), to spread its operations further north into the central plateau area, and it tied up Angolan military units in the areas adjacent to the buffer zone. After a major invasion in 1983, the South African army remained in occupation of much of Cunene and part of Cuando Cubango province until the final South African withdrawal in 1989.

The South African presence, the growing strength of UNITA (estimated at 50,000–70,000 guerrillas in 1988) and the political failure of the MPLA to gain support in traditional UNITA areas meant that by the mid- to late-1980s, Jonas Savimbi's movement had effective control of parts of southern and central Angola, had prevented the use of the Benguela railway and was tying up massive resources by continuing a costly war (the MPLA built up a debt of $4 billion to the Soviet Union for arms deliveries and paid out approximately 40 per cent of its income annually to prosecute the war). UNITA, even with South African support, was unable to defeat the MPLA or force it to agree to political negotiations, while the MPLA was incapable of regaining control of its southern provinces from South Africa or of countering the guerrilla warfare waged by UNITA. The resumption of US financial and military support for UNITA (particularly the delivery of Stinger anti-aircraft missiles) strengthened the movement's military capabilities and its diplomatic strength. It also received support from Morocco and Ivory Coast.

UNITA was able, with South African and then also Zairean support, to spread its area of operations north of the Benguela railway and into the diamond-producing regions of Lunda Norte province. Savimbi developed close relations with Mobutu and was able to use Zaire as a platform from which to launch guerrilla operations in north-eastern Angola, to get diamonds out to foreign buyers to help finance the war and to get US arms supplies in to its guerrillas. This augmented the direct military and logistical help from South Africa. The Angolans still had Cuban military support (by 1987 there were an estimated 30,000 Cubans based in Angola – chiefly protecting economic and other installations around Luanda and northern Angola and training the government armed forces) and was receiving sophisticated heavy weaponry from the Soviet Union. By the late 1980s, Angola had taken delivery of MiG-23 aircraft and the latest Soviet tanks, and Soviet technicians had built a sophisticated air defence system in southern Angola (based on the town of Lubango but covering south and east Angola).

The development of air defences was vital for the Angolan army because of South Africa's air superiority in southern Africa. During major anti-UNITA offensives in 1985–87, the South African Air Force (with ground support from 32 Battalion and special forces units) had intervened to save UNITA from military defeat in the south-east of the country. On the point of victory with a potentially unstoppable offensive against the UNITA HQ at Jamba, the FAPLA armoured columns had been smashed by South African air and ground units along the Lomba river near the town of Mavinga.

As a result of such South African interventions, the building up of its own air combat capabilities became a major military priority for the government of President dos Santos (who had succeeded Neto, following the latter's death in 1979). Unwilling to see one of its main allies in Africa at the mercy of the South Africans, the Soviet Union had provided linked radar and surface-to-air missile systems, the technicians to install them and training for the Angolans in the use of the air defence network. The Cubans may also have played a role in training and in the operation of the system.

The test of Angola's newly-acquired military power came in late 1987 and early 1988 in a way that had a decisive impact on the military equation in Angola and on the balance of power in southern Africa as a whole.

From Cuito Cuanavale to Bicesse

By mid-1987, the Angolans were confident that they had the military strength to succeed where they had failed before in pushing UNITA out of southern Angola.[11] They were also aware of the subtle changes in Soviet foreign policy under Mikhail Gorbachev which could eventually have meant that substantial quantities of up-to-date Soviet arms would no longer be available. Moscow was by then beginning to stress negotiations between the superpowers as a means of solving regional disputes. As a result of having the military means and fearing for what the future might bring, the dos Santos government prepared for the largest offensive against UNITA that it had ever launched. Backed up by the air defence system, which stretched from Lubango through the town of Menongue to the military base at Cuito Cuanavale, the Angolan army advanced from Cuito Cuanavale towards the UNITA liberated zone around Jamba.

Early successes were achieved against UNITA, which still lacked the conventional strength or organisation to fight large-scale actions. But again, the South Africans intervened with ground and air support for UNITA. The government forces were pushed back to Mavinga and defeated there again, and retreated towards Cuito Cuanavale. Sensing an opportunity to smash the new air defence network, clear southern Angola of FAPLA units and give UNITA a huge military boost, the South Africans threw heavy artillery and armoured units into the battle with a massive attack against Cuito Cuanavale. Thousands of UNITA guerrillas, backed by SADF infantry, tank units and air cover, laid siege to Cuito Cuanavale.

The Angolan army, with strong air support, dug in and was able to fend off the combined SADF/UNITA attacks for several months and to inflict heavy casualties on their opponents. Most importantly they kept open Cuito's airstrip and shot down several South African combat aircraft (the South Africans refused to give figures for their personnel or aircraft losses but at least 20 aircraft were destroyed). In December 1987, aware that the SADF was reinforcing its units in southern Angola, President dos Santos warned that he would ask the Cubans to become involved. Until then, the Cubans had avoided a combat role in Angola and only been deployed in the north of the country. President Fidel Castro immediately agreed to deploy his combat forces in the south and on 7 December, a Cuban combat division led by General Ochoa Sanchez (who had commanded the Cuban forces in Angola in 1975–76) was on its way to Cuito Cuanavale.[12]

The Cuban arrival and the danger of the rainy season trapping South African units in southern Angola pushed the South Africans into a series of desperate attacks on the besieged town. Hundreds of UNITA guerrillas were killed in the attacks, a South African tank unit became trapped in a minefield and the combined Angolan/Cuban forces gained almost total air superiority. Cuban forces were also dispatched to areas between Cuito and the coast and pushed right up to the border with Namibia. The South Africans were forced to pull back some of their units and to open a dialogue with the Angolans and Cubans to arrange some form of disengagement in the region.

Although the SADF had not been defeated decisively, the loss of control of the air over southern Angola, the ability of the Angolans to withstand the

South African offensive and the domestic political effects of heavy human and matériel losses in Angola forced Pretoria to negotiate. The Angolan government was now keen to talk as the war was putting a heavier than ever strain on its economy and it could now see an advantage in diplomacy as it could negotiate from a position of comparative military strength. The possibility of changes in the Soviet diplomatic position over regional conflicts could also have influenced Angolan decision-making. The two sides were urged to meet round the table rather than across the battlefield by the United States and the Soviet Union, who were keen to test their new-found cooperative spirit.

The talks that ensued lasted from May until September 1988. They did not involve SWAPO or UNITA but were between the Angolan government, the South Africans, the Cubans and the United States, with the Soviet Union as an observer. The Angolans made a concession by agreeing to consider the Cuban presence in Angola as part of the equation, while South Africa was willing to discuss a withdrawal from both Angola and Namibia. Previously, the Angolan government had refused to discuss the Cuban troops alongside the issue of Namibian independence; this linkage had been a longstanding South African and US condition for progress on the independence of Namibia.

The results of several rounds of talks in London, Brazzaville and New York was the signing of an agreement on the phased withdrawal of the Cubans from Angola (to be completed by July 1991), the withdrawal of all South African forces from Angola, and the total and phased withdrawal of Pretoria's forces from Namibia. The agreement brought about a total South African and Cuban withdrawal and the independence of Namibia on 21 March 1990.

But the agreement did nothing to reduce the hostility between the MPLA and UNITA. UNITA was not party to the talks and the final agreement had not addressed the civil war in Angola. After the withdrawal of the South Africans, who left behind massive stores of ammunition, weapons, fuel and other war matériel for UNITA, the movement continued its fight against government forces. The Angolan army, in its turn, launched offensive after offensive against south-eastern Angola. Although the United States and the Soviet Union were committed to finding a peaceful solution in Angola they were not willing to see their allies in the region defeated and both continued to deliver weapons and other military supplies to UNITA and FAPLA. President Mobutu tried to mediate between dos Santos and Savimbi and actually brought them together in the Zairean town of Gbadolite in June 1989 at a meeting of African heads of state. But the peace deal he tried to broker collapsed within days and the ceasefire the two sides had agreed lasted just two days.

The war went on as before, with FAPLA unable to destroy UNITA or stamp out its widespread guerrilla attacks and UNITA unable to pose a conventional military threat to the government. UNITA forces were active from Cuando Cubango in the far south-east to Cabinda in the north-west (where the government had for years been fighting a low-level conflict with guerrillas of the Front for the Liberation of the Cabinda Enclave, FLEC, who wanted independence for the oil-rich enclave). Eventually the government and UNITA fought themselves almost to a standstill. Neither side was making any further military inroads against the other. They therefore turned Carl von Clausewitz on his head by turning to political means to achieve what had eluded them on the battlefield – victory over their opponents. The MPLA had the prospect of a more difficult situation on the battlefield as the withdrawal of the Cubans approached, while UNITA was keen to exploit the government's apparent exhaustion and the relatively favourable diplomatic situation with the Soviet Union urging the MPLA to talk. But both sides retained their total commitment to the defeating rather than co-operating with their enemies.

With strong encouragement from the USA, the USSR and Portugal, peace talks stated between the MPLA and UNITA in 1990. They centred on a ceasefire, demobilization of the opposing armies and the establishment of a multiparty political system. The main sticking points were the formation of a new national army, the nature of the post-election government, the political future of Jonas Savimbi and the administration of UNITA-held areas during the transition from war to elections. The talks dragged on for over a year, with neither side trusting the other or being prepared to compromise. In the meantime, the MPLA shed its commitment to Marxism-Leninism, scrapped the single party system and allowed the formation of opposition parties (many of them offshoots of the MPLA which were suspected of working to give the impression of a multiplicity of parties while in fact still being loyal to the MPLA).

As the talks continued, so did the war. By early 1991 more lives had been expended but neither side had gained an advantage on the battlefield. The same could be said of the talks, but there was heavier and heavier pressure on the two sides to reach an agreement. Angolan diplomats in Dar es Salaam told the author in February 1991 that their government was angry that the Soviet Union appeared to want peace at any price and was pushing dos Santos harder than Washington was pushing Savimbi to compromise and reach a deal. Reaching a deal was particularly tough because of a basic disagreement – the MPLA wanted a ceasefire first and political agreement later, while UNITA refused to agree to any cessation of hostilities ahead of agreement on all outstanding political issues. But eventually agreement was reached and an accord signed at the Portuguese holiday resort of Bicesse on 31 May 1991.

From Bicesse to Lusaka: The Ballot Box and the Battlefield

Under the Bicesse accord UNITA and the MPLA agreed to an immediate ceasefire, the demobilization of their forces, the formation of a new 40,000-strong army (to be half UNITA and half FAPLA), an arms embargo on both sides, the formation of a joint political-military commission to oversee the transition period, the deployment of UN observers, elections in September 1992 and a role for Portugal, the USA and the USSR as guarantors. There was no provision for a major UN military presence in Angola (unlike Namibia, where 10,000 persons were deployed in the transition period) to oversee the ceasefire and the disengagement/ demobilization of the rival armies. A UN team, known as UNAVEM II, was deployed but with insufficient funding ($132 million), little logistical support and, by election time, only 840 civilian and military observers in a country five times the size of Britain and with 5,280 polling stations. The inadequacy of the international commitment to Angola became apparent as the transition process progressed.

There was, however, a feeling of optimism about Angola, which accounts for the poor international respose. The Cold War was over, the Namibian independence process had worked smoothly, and in South Africa Nelson Mandela had been released and the ANC unbanned and constitutional negotiations were underway to draw up a new, democratic and non-racial political framework. Furthermore, the early months of the Bicesse implementation process were amazingly successful. The ceasefire held, there was a steady movement of combatants to assembly areas, UNITA was able to start transforming itself into a civilian, political movement after 25 years as a primarily military organization, and the joint commission appeared to work. There were, it must be noted, frequent accusations by both sides of violations of the accord, but these did not slow the disengagement or the move towards political rather than violent competition. Early complaints by UNITA, the MPLA, and smaller Angolan parties were treated by the peace guarantors, the UN and Western diplomats in Luanda as teething troubles, though the UN personnel made little secret of their resource problem and the impossibility of monitoring demobilization and the handing in of weapons by both sides.[13]

For most of 1991 and the beginning of 1992, implementation of the accords continued amid growing signs that the political confrontation between the MPLA and UNITA would be bitter and that there was little room for compromise between them. Despite this, many commentators thought that the elections would end in a coalition government between the MPLA and UNITA and that they would effectively divide political power and Angola's oil wealth between them.[14] This impression was reinforced by Savimbi when he told an audience in London in April 1991 that he wanted to ensure that under a future constitution no single party would have a monopoly of power.[15]

But the words of Savimbi and his opponents in the MPLA were very different as they addressed political meetings inside Angola. Savimbi attacked the MPLA, accusing it of massacring the Ovimbundu, of constant violations of the peace accord, of selling Angola to foreign interests and of being themselves foreigners in Angola who spoke Portuguese rather than Angolan languages. Savimbi also accused the MPLA of plotting to kill him and he delayed his return to Luanda until September 1991. He was greeted by a crowd of some 50,000 on his arrival a big disappointment for UNITA as it had been predicting a turnout six times that size. Dos Santos and the MPLA launched equally bitter attacks on UNITA – referring to their HQ at Jamba as a place of death.

By the beginning of 1992, things were turning sour. Demobilized government soldiers were not being paid or fed and many took their weapons and deserted, becoming armed robbers who preyed on the local population; UNITA was refusing to allow government administrators access to its territory and even the UN had trouble monitoring UNITA areas; and the joint commission was beginning to lose its grip, its meetings ending up in arguments between the MPLA and UNITA delegates. Attempts to form an electoral commission to start organizing the polling were obstructed by UNITA's refusal to cooperate and the movement also refused to involve itself in a multiparty conference on the preparations for the elections.

The major problems, though, was the pace of demobilization and the formation of the new army. As September 1992 and the elections drew near, only 1,500 of the projected 40,000 members of the new army had been sworn in and only 8,000 more were being trained. Even more worrying was the fact that just 45 per cent of government troops (of which there were 94,000 plus tens of thousands more in local armed militias) had been demobilized and only 24 per cent of UNITA's 70,000 guerrillas. There was no effective means of guarding the weapons that had been handed in and many of the heavier weapons held by both sides had been hidden. UNITA accused the government of merging its elite units with the police paramilitary forces, while the MPLA said that UNITA was hiding much of it army and committing constant violations of the accord. Both sides accused the peace guarantors of ignoring the serious problems facing the country as the elections approached.

Although preparations were underway to hold the elections at the end of September, voter registration was slow and there was not real verification of registration in UNITA-held areas. The minor parties, including the FNLA (which had registered as a party under its old leader, Holden Roberto, to contest the elections in the Bakongo inhabited provinces along the border with Zaire), accused both the MPLA and UNITA of harassment. To calm people's fears, in September the peace guarantors persuaded the MPLA and UNITA to issue a statement promising to work for reconciliation after the election and to form a coalition government, whatever the result of the vote. The chief US liaison officer in Luanda said this was not an attempt to pre-empt the vote but to reassure voters that the election would take place peacefully and that is result would be respected by all parties.[16] At the same time, Jonas Savimbi was constantly telling his supporters that the MPLA was trying to rig the elections and that if this happened he would not accept the result. At the time, this was treated as election rhetoric, rather than a serious statement of intent.

The elections went ahead at the end of September 1992 with few obvious problems, in surprising peace and with a huge turnout by the voters. There was much self-congratulation among the guarantors and on 3 October, the chief US liaison officer, Jeffrey Millington, and the UN mission chief Margaret Anstee both praised the conduct of the elections; Millington said that Angolans could be proud of their behaviour during the elections and of the smooth operation of the electoral process. But as soon as the early results showed a clear lead for the MPLA, UNITA cried foul. The UN agreed to delay the announcement of the results until all votes had been counted, but UNITA did not wait and started accusing the MPLA of cheating and the UN and other observers of accepting MPLA dishonesty. Savimbi repeated his pre-election threat that he would not recognize the results if he believed them to be fraudulent. The UN and the guarantors continued to hold the election to have been free and fair, something unacceptable to Savimbi. The situation was made worse when the UNITA army commander, General Ben-Ben, announced the withdrawal of UNITA personnel from the integrated armed forces. On 11 October, violence broke out in Luanda when armed UNITA members fired on police units, areas of Luanda where UNITA had set up offices became effective no-go areas for non-UNITA people and weapons were brought in by the movement.

Attempts were made to mediate by the US Assistant Secretary of State, Herman Cohen, by the South African Foreign Minister, Pik Botha, and by the UN. All mediation failed, Both being told to stop his efforts by President dos Santos when evidence emerged that the SADF was continuing to supply arms to UNITA. Finally, on 17 October, the UN had to announce the elections' results. The MPLA had gained 53.74 per cent of votes for the National Assembly with UNITA coming in second with 34.10 per cent; while dos Santos beat Savimbi by 49.57 per cent to 40.07 per cent in the presidential vote (as no candidate had received 50 per cent a second round of voting would be required for the presidency). The voting pattern across Angola was very clear – non-Ovimbundu areas and urban areas voted in

general for the MPLA and, in very small numbers, minor parties;
Ovimbundu areas generally voted for UNITA, with very heavy UNITA
majorities in areas to which the UN, observers and the government had been
denied access; and in the Bakongo regions along the border with Zaire,
voting was split between FNLA, MPLA and smaller parties.

UNITA refused to accept the results and another mediation effort by
Margaret Anstee and UN Under-Secretary Marrack Goulding failed to avert
conflict. On 31 October 1992, further clashes erupted in Luanda between
UNITA and police units and UNITA attempted to seize control of the
airport. The MPLA began to arm its supporters and launched a general
offensive against UNITA in the capital. UNITA was soundly defeated and
expelled. The movement suffered very heavy casualties as the MPLA and
police attempted to wipe out the UNITA presence. Among those killed were
the UNITA Vice-President, Jeremias Chitunda, and several senior members
of the movement's political leadership. UNITA foreign secretary Abel
Chivukuvuku was captured by the government. UN officials reported that
the MPLA and its supporters used the outbreak of fighting in Luanda to kill
every UNITA supporter they could find.[17]

The MPLA's success in expelling UNITA from Luanda was not matched
elsewhere in Angola. The latter, rapidly mobilizing tens of thousands of
troops, was able to launch a countrywide offensive and by mid-1993 had
captured 60–70 per cent of Angolan territory, including at least three key
provincial centres. In six months it achieved far more militarily than in the
previous 16 years of war. There was considerable circumstantial evidence
that UNITA had kept intact large military formations and had not
surrendered heavy weapons. Its forces had suffered little from desertions
(unlike the MPLA which had been decimated by the desertion of conscripts)
and they retained a strong will to fight, believing the version of events given
by the UNITA leadership that the movement had been cheated of its
'rightful' election victory. MPLA forces had been demobilized to a greater
extent, had suffered a heavy desertion rate and were no longer a mentally
prepared for the continuation of the war as UNITA guerrillas.

In the first few months of resumed warfare, UNITA gained control of
provincial capitals and towns which they had failed to capture during the
1975–91 war. These included N'dalantando in Cuanza Norte, Caxito in
Bengo (60 km from Luanda) and Uige, capital of the province of that name
and centre of the coffee industry. By March 1993, the MPLA was in an
extremely precarious situation. It had been unable to rebuild its military
strength while at the same time containing UNITA attacks, while UNITA
was in the ascendant and was receiving arms from South Africa and
financial support through the sale of diamonds smuggled out of north-
eastern Angola and sold in Zaire or Antwerp.[18] Despite the political changes

underway in South Africa, elements within the South African armed forces were supplying arms to UNITA. These were flown into UNITA-held territory by South African transport aircraft and by former Soviet Antonov planes hired by South African air transport companies linked to South African military intelligence. The supply flights were tracked by Botswana's defence force and by the Zimbabwean authorities. They started shortly after the elections in 1992 and continued until mid-1993.[19]

There was a gradual improvement in the MPLA position in mid-1993, with the recapture of Caxito and successful resistance to UNITA attacks in the key central and southern towns of Menongue, Luena and Cuito. However, on-shore oil production had been halted by UNITA's capture of Soyo and UNITA's diamond income was assured by its continued control of the diamond-producing areas of Lunda Norte.

The UN and southern African states still continued their mediation effort sand the MPLA seemed keen on finding diplomatic means of ending the fighting. A meeting was arranged for Addis Ababa in early 1993, but was aborted when UNITA failed to turn up. Six weeks of talks in Côte d'Ivoire (ending in May 1993) failed to produced agreement on a ceasefire, the exchange of prisoners, the holding of the second round of presidential elections, the apportionment of cabinet portfolios for UNITA (they had been offered four ministries), the appointment of provincial governors and the formation of the national army. There seemed to be little or no common ground between the combatants and UNITA was unwilling to negotiate seriously while it felt that it had the opportunity to extend its physical control of territory – a UNITA viewpoint which was strengthened after it captured the key central town of Huambo (the effective capital of the Ovimbundu area) in March 1993.

But the MPLA's apparent willingness to negotiate, its image as the injured party and its control of oil exports eventually turned the tide. After the MPLA said it was willing to sign a ceasefire accord at the abortive Abidjan talk of April–May 1993, President Clinton announced US recognition of the Angolan government and the UN adopted an increasingly critical stance towards UNITA. In September 1993, UNITA intransigence over talks led to the imposition by the UN Security Council of an arms and fuel embargo against UNITA (the Bicesse arms embargo no longer applied). Although the following month UNITA announced that it still recognized the Bicesse accord and it would respect the outcome of the 1992 elections, the movement made no attempt to end hostilities or start serious negotiations.

By late 1993, the lifting of the arms embargo against the Angolan government, international sympathy for the dos Santos government and success with conscription campaigns had enabled the MPLA government to improve its military capabilities while retaining a strong diplomatic hand.

Its forces began to launch offensives against UNITA-held areas and to recapture territory. Arms were imported from Russia and Brazil and from commercial suppliers, and the armed forces regained the capability to fight conventional battles. The government began to recapture towns and areas of northern and central Angola. A major offensive was then launched from the central and southern coastal strip to threaten UNITA's control of central Angola and to retake the symbolic town of Huambo.

By early 1994, UNITA had resumed talks with the MPLA and the UN. A continuous negotiation process started in the Zambian capital Lusaka that went on as the MPLA offensives gained pace. There was a growing feeling that although Jonas Savimbi showed no sign of compromise and in fact was hardly seen in public, the negotiation process would gain a momentum of its own and that months of daily contact between the UNITA and MPLA representatives would break down suspicion. If this did occur, it was a slow process and remained peripheral to the main differences between the combatants. However, major advances by the MPLA (including the relief of the siege of Cuito, the recapture of the majority of provincial capitals and, after a bloody battle, the expulsion of UNITA and Savimbi from Huambo) put UNITA in an increasingly precarious position. It was internationally isolated (the election of an ANC-led government in South Africa deprived Savimbi of support from that quarter, leaving him dependent on Zaire) and on the retreat on the battlefield. It faced the loss of all urban areas and provincial capitals and of much of the countryside too. There was no prospect of its total destruction but it had to come to terms with the prospect of more decades of guerrilla warfare without the diplomatic and logistical support it had enjoyed in the 1980s and early 1990s.

On 31 October 1994, with its back to the wall militarily, UNITA agreed in Lusaka to set a date for a ceasefire and to initial a political accord allowing for UNITA participation in government (still with only four ministerial portfolios) and for the appointment of provincial governors (UNITA, having lost physical control of Huambo, conceded that the MPLA could appoint the governor of Huambo province). On 15 November, a cessation of hostilities was agreed pending a full ceasefire. The Lusaka protocol was signed on 20 November by UNITA's secretary-general, Eugenio Ngolo Manuvakola, and the Angolan foreign minister, Venancio da Moura. But there was little optimism about the agreement. UNITA had signed under duress and the MPLA was not in the ascendant militarily. There was every indication that the government had been willing to see delays in the signing to allow it to capture more territory and that even after the ceasefire it would use every opportunity to extend its area of control. The Angolan army chief of staff, João de Matos, emerged as the major military adviser and source of influence over President Dos Santos.

The only really positive point of the new agreement was that the United Nations committed itself to sending 7,600 peacekeeping troops (including soldiers from Uruguay, Portugal, Brazil, Bangladesh and India and logistical support from Britain). At one stage, it was hoped that South Africa would play a major role in the UN military operation but the Mandela government declined to do so after the Angolan government expressed doubts about the advisability of former SADF units returning to Angola under UN auspices. There was the added complication that many former SADF or 32 Battalion personnel from South Africa were employed by the Executive Outcomes company, which was supplying military aid (at a price) to the Angolan government and it was accused by UNITA of providing a mercenary army to bolster dos Santos's forces. After repeated complaints by UNITA and some foreign pressure, Executive Outcomes announced in early 1996 that it had withdrawn from Angola – though in fact many personnel stayed on to work for the myriad security companies which sprang up to provide armed protection for companies and even non-governmental organizations operating in Angola.

After Lusaka

A ceasefire was agreed and put into effect with the understanding that political negotiations would continue to make the basic peace accord into a workable political deal. To be decided were the role to be played by Savimbi, the extension of government administration to areas held by UNITA, disengagement of forces, demobilization and the formation of a national army combining government and UNITA personnel. But in the 18 months between the ceasefire and the writing of this article there has been only slow and grudging progress towards implementing the Lusaka agreement. The agreement was not signed by Savimbi himself and in his few public comments between the signing and his appearance in Lusaka in May 1995, he was critical rather than supportive of the agreement. It was only during his meetings with dos Santos in the latter part of 1995 and early 1996 that he began to adopt a more positive attitude towards the agreement and towards his potential role as a Vice-President.

Opening the UNITA congress at Bailundo on 7 February 1996, Savimbi was at best ambivalent about what had been achieved, at one point referring to the accord as 'a piece of paper with no worth' and at another stage as being 'full of lies'.[20] More ominously, the congress saw the replacement of the UNITA officials who negotiated or signed the Lusaka deal. Manuvakola lost his position as secretary-general, being replaced by the more hardline Paulo Lukamba Gato, while Isias Samakuva and Jorge Valentim (both prominent in the Lusaka talks) disappeared from the front rank of UNITA officials, although after the May talks, Samakuva re-emerged as the UNITA representative on the joint peace commission with the Angolan government. However, there appeared to be a growing split with UNITA between Savimbi and the political leaders on the one hand and the military leadership on the other. Generals Arlindo Chenda Pena Ben-Ben and Demosthenes Chilingutila emerged as the most sceptical members of the UNITA military command. It was not certain whether Savimbi was playing up the scepticism of the military about the peace deal as a negotiating tactic or whether there was a real split emerging within UNITA. The military wing of the movement was most certainly unhappy with making political compromises and particularly with agreeing to a rapid demobilization of the army.

However, the political advances made through the Dos Santos-Savimbi meetings led to the start of the assembly process on 20 November 1995, under which UNITA forces commenced gathering at assembly points designated by the UN and the joint commission; the government was then due to restrict its forces, including paramilitary police units, to designated barracks. The assembly process was first delayed by the lack of cooperation between UNITA and the government, the hold ups in deploying UN forces at the assembly points, the widespread presence of landmines (laid indiscriminately during Angola's 33 years of war) and the lack of control exercised by the government in Luanda over its military forces and its provincial leaders. Then, in late 1995, UNITA said that the government had launched a major offensive in northern and north-eastern Angola. The objective was said to be towns in the region that remained in UNITA hands, areas near the Soyo oil terminal and some of the diamond producing areas. The UN criticized Angolan government troop movements and it appeared as though a major breakdown in the peace process could occur. UNITA suspended its demobilization. The government denied that it was undertaking an offensive and accused UNITA of using delaying tactics. Senior officers within the armed forces made it clear that they had no trust in UNITA's promises to demobilize and refused to start confining troops to their barracks until UNITA had completed its first phase of demobilization.

The stalemate, during which time the government military actions ceased and both the UN and the United States put pressure on UNITA to resume demobilisation, lasted for several months. UNITA failed to keep to the timetable for assembling just over 16,000 of its guerrillas by early February. But further pressure, particularly from the Clinton administration, and threats by the UN to reconsider its mandate eventually pushed UNITA into resuming the assembly process. By late March 1996, some 17,000 UNITA guerrillas were in assembly camps and the Angolan army, albeit reluctantly, agreed to start confining units to their barracks.

By late May 1996, the number of UNITA personnel confined had reached 30,500 (just over half the target of 60,000) and government troop confinement was continuing. This led the hawkish Angolan army chief of staff, General João de Matos, to admit that the conditions of the integration of the armed forces could be met and that the integration process could soon get underway. However, for once the military progress was outstripping political events and Savimbi was still confusing the situation by appearing to draw back from Lusaka commitments and from his statements during his meetings with dos Santos. On 15 May, the French newspaper *Le Figaro* published an interview with Savimbi in which he talked of the need for a transitional government (including all legal parties) to be in place from November 1996, for UNITA to retain control of some of the diamond-producing areas of Lunda Norte province and for an end to police and army threats to those UNITA forces which had been disarmed. The government reacted angrily, pointing out that the idea of a transitional government and the retention of the diamond areas were both in contravention of Lusaka and of the agreements reached in Gabon. However, the first 14 officers from UNITA were sworn in as members of the new army on 3 June by Chief of Staff de Matos.

The limited political progress and the continuation of demobilization moved the peace process on from the unstable ceasefire which had been in place between the November 1994 deal and March 1996. Yet sporadic fighting has continued across the country and the ceasefire lines between the competing forces have been unstable in the extreme. Delays in deploying the UN peacekeepers have meant that there has been limited monitoring of the repeated clashes in provinces such as Huila, Huambo and Lunda Norte and little has been done about accusations by both the government and UNITA that their opponents have launched regular armed attacks on them. These alleged and recorded violations have not developed into general warfare but the military situation remains unstable, even given the relative success of demobilization and the start of integration in June 1996.

Many of the clashes that have taken place have their origins in local conditions – with military commanders on both sides attempting to gain advantage. In Lunda Norte – the diamond producing region of the country – there has been almost constant conflict between the government forces and UNITA and between the government forces and heavily-armed illegal diamond miners. There have even been intimations of the growth of a separatist movement in the province, whose inhabitants are chiefly from the Lunda and Chokwe ethnic groups and voted heavily for the regionally-based Partido da Renovação Social (PRS) in the 1992 elections.

The chances of peace in the long term are also endangered by the lack of faith demonstrated by the government armed forces (notably the Chief of

Staff, General de Matos) in the peace deal and their evident desire to resume the war. De Matos clearly believes that his FAA forces are in a position to defeat UNITA militarily; he opposed the signing of the 1994 peace agreement as his forces were enjoying a period of success against UNITA. There is also the problem posed by the 'warlordism' evident among MPLA provincial leaders. They are loyal in a general sense to the dos Santos government, but use their positions for economic exploitation of the disruption to the economy caused by the war, and use their military and police forces to enforce their corrupt rule on a local basis.

On the positive side of the balance, diplomatic pressure from southern African states (particularly South Africa, Zambia and Zimbabwe), containing UN involvement and the positive effect of the pledging of nearly one billion dollars in aid at the Brussels donors' meeting of September 1995 have all worked to keep the peace process going and to give both sides material incentives to continue with it. Jonas Savimbi is now accepted by southern African leaders as part of the political process in the region and has been received for political discussions in Pretoria and Harare. This public recognition of his role and status is a not insignificant element in convincing him and UNITA that he has a major political role to play and is not politically isolated (as he was during the last stage of the civil war).

What still remains to be done is the full implementation of demobilization, the guaranteeing of the safety of UNITA leaders in Luanda and other MPLA strongholds, the development of free movement of goods and people around the country and the integration of UNITA into government through Savimbi's installation as Vice-President and the taking up of the four cabinet posts allotted to UNITA. Demobilization and the formation of the new army are the key to the success of the whole process. The military commands of both sides do not support the peace agreement but have so far gone along with their political masters. If this continues then there is a greater chance that the demilitarization will progress better than in 1991–92 – when there were no UN military forces in Angola to monitor effectively demobilization and the surrender of heavy weapons. While both sides will undoubtedly try to keep back some force and weapons as insurance policies against the suspected bad faith of the other side, the prospects are slightly better now than four years ago.

The current target is to assemble the 200,000 plus troops in their barracks or assembly points and then form an integrated force of 90,000 (equally drawn from the two armies), demobilized soldiers in an economically disintegrating and administratively chaotic state. The presence of over 100,000 demobilized soldiers could be a politically and socially destabilizing element.

But in the short, medium and long term, the viability of the peace deal and the political settlement will be governed by the extent to which the two major parties can overcome the history of separate social and cultural development, mutual hostility and decades or war to find some common political ground. Short-term solutions may be found which will temporarily bring a cessation of hostilities, but lasting peace and political accommodation will need more than handshakes between the leaders. The continued presence of UN troops (and the threat that if the peace process becomes stalled that they will have their mandate withdrawn) could also swing the balance over the next year or so, but once they are withdrawn the onus will be on the Angolans to find solutions to their national problems.

It may be that such solutions will not be found in the centralized, unitary state structure which has been the accepted form of government in Angola and throughout most of Africa in the post-colonial period. Power-sharing has worked to smooth the transition process in South Africa and could provide the basis for a prolonged period of transition from war to peace in Angola. In the longer term, decentralization of power could provide the answer if the dominant political forces (notably the MPLA and UNITA) are willing to forego centralized power in the interests of national peace. The search for a federal solution may prove more fruitful (it could hardly be less fruitful) than the quest for undiluted national power undertaken by the MPLA and UNITA since 1975. As David Welsh has written, in sub-Saharan Africa the examination of political systems based on decentralization and increased power for local and provincial governments could be the way 'to grope towards political accommodation'.[21]

If the prospects for such an accommodation are still distant and dim, there is plenty for Angolans and the international community to do in the meantime to improve the immediate material conditions for reconciliation and reconstruction. The demobilization campaign must go alongside a more concerted and better funded programme of landmine clearance. There are an estimated 10–15 million mines in Angola, sown around contested towns and in the rural areas of most provinces. Some 80,000 Angolans have been disabled by landmines. Mine clearance is being carried out by charitable organisations from Europe such as Halo Trust, the Mines Advisory Group and Norwegian People's Aid, and to some extent by government forces. But there are years of work ahead to clear rural roads, the approaches of major towns and valuable agricultural land. Clearance is vital if food production is to be increased, free movement ensured and the return home of hundreds of thousands of displaced people assisted. These tasks are vital to end dependence on food aid and to end the food shortages facing an estimated three million Angolans.

Serious economic reconstruction cannot be attempted until the rival armies have been demobilized and a political settlement is seen as viable.

But in the immediate future the guarantee of free movement, the UN presence, a gradual resumption of food production and serious efforts to combat corruption are necessary to end the economic hardship experienced by the majority of Angolans and convince them – particularly those being demobilized from the rival armies – that they have more to gain from peace and reconstruction than from a continuation of war or of the phoney peace that has been in existence since the signing of the November 1994 peace deal. The extent of the economic hardships and corruption were finally admitted by President dos Santos on 3 June 1996 when he sacked the entire government, including Prime Minister Moco, and charged the parliament Speaker, Fernando Van Dunem, with forming a new government that could bring the country back from the verge of economic collapse. If the political leaders are intent on peace at last, then the support of the mass of the population for peace and the acquiescence in the process of those being demobilized or being integrated into the new army are vital to overcome the evident opposition of the military commanders on both sides.

NOTES

1. See Keith Somerville, *Foreign Military Intervention in Africa* (London: Pinter 1990) Ch.1, p.8.
2. David Throup, 'The Colonial Legacy' in Oliver Furley (ed.) *Conflict in Africa* (London: Tauris Academic Studies 1995) Ch.12, p.245.
3. Ibid.
4. Douglas Rimmer, 'The Effects of Conflict II: Economic Effects, in Furley (note 2).
5. David Birmingham, *Frontline Nationalism in Angola and Mozambique* (London: James Currey 1992) Ch.1, pp.8–9.
6. Birmingham (note 10) Ch.2, pp.26–7.
7. Keith Somerville, 'The Failure of Democratic Reform in Angola and Zaire', *Survival* 35/3 (Autumn 1993) p.56.
8. See Keith Somerville, *Angola: Politics, Economics and Society* (London: Pinter 1986) Ch.1, pp.25–8, for further details of the formation of the MPLA.
9. A.J. Klinghoffer, *The Angolan War* (Boulder, CO: Westview Press 1980) pp.82–3; and John Stockwell, *In Search of Enemies* (London: André Deutsch 1978) p.52.
10. Klinghoffer (note 9) p.14 gives the date as June; addressing the South African parliament in Jan. 1976, then Defence Minister P.W. Botha said that 43 South Africans had been killed in action in Angola between 14 July 1975 and 23 Jan. 1976, *Guardian* 26 Jan. 1976.
11. *Africa Confidential*, 27 May 1987.
12. Maputo radio home service in Portuguese, 7 Dec. 19897 and *Independent*, 14 Dec. 1987.
13. Author's discussions with Anita Coulson (the BBC's correspondent in Luanda during the 1992 elections), Jeffrey Millington (US liaison officer in Luanda in 1991–92) and UNAVEM head Margaret Anstee.
14. *Africa Confidential*, 30 April 1991.
15. Speech at Royal Inst. of Int. Affairs, London, 30 April 1991.
16. Telephone interview with Jeffrey Millington, Luanda, 6 Sept. 1992.
17. Author's discussions with UN officials and Mats Berdahl of the Int. Inst. of Strategic Studies.
18. Information supplied to the author by De Beers.
19. Interview with Botswana's Foreign Minister, Dr Gaositwe Chiepe, and information supplied

by David Martin, Director of the Southern African Research and Documentation Centre, Harare.
20. Voice of the Resistance of the Black Cockerel (UNITA radio), 7 Feb. 1995; see also *Africa Confidential*, 17 Feb. 1995.
21. David Welsh, 'Domestic Politics and Ethnic Conflict', *Survival* 35/1 (Spring 1993) p.79.

Political Violence in Mozambique: Past, Present and Future

CHRIS ALDEN

Mozambique has experienced political violence for 30 years. After subjection to colonialism and a liberation struggle, even independence brought with it further destruction in the form of counter-revolution and external aggression. The 1992 peace agreement between Frelimo and Renamo marked the beginning of a process of reconciliation which, with the intervention of the United Nations, culminated in the country's first ever elections in October 1994. While the official establishment of a multi-party democracy in Mozambique appears to solve the outstanding political problems of the last decades, the inheritance of a brutal past and the failure to address its legacy threatens to subvert the recent political gains.

For 30 years, Mozambique has experienced a virtually unbroken cycle of political violence. After subjection to the ravages of colonialism and the attendant rise of a liberation struggle, even independence brought with it the scourge of counter-revolution and external aggression. The signing of a peace agreement between the government and the opposition in 1992 marked the beginning of a process of reconciliation which, with the intervention of a substantial United Nations peace support operation, culminated in the country's first ever free elections in October 1994. The withdrawal of the United Nations, coupled with the establishment of a multi-party democracy in Mozambique, provides a new opportunity to build conditions for lasting peace and stability. Despite these propitious developments, the inheritance of a brutal past and the failure to address its legacy, coupled with massive economic and social problems stemming from the war, threaten to undermine Mozambique's hard fought political gains.

From the Liberation Struggle to the Counter-Revolution

Mozambique, though nominally a Portuguese colony for over 400 years, was not effectively brought under European control until the early part of the twentieth century. This vast territory, comprising 783,000 square kilometres and a multiplicity of ethnic groups, was subject to a rudimentary form of colonialism by a metropole which itself was a bastion of extremes of conservatism and underdevelopment. At the dawn of what was the independence era for much of Africa north of the Zambezi river, colonial

Mozambique seemed to be a political anachronism matched only by its fellow Lusophone territories and the apartheid-dominated neighbour, South Africa.

The Mozambican liberation movement was created from a group of indigenous anti-colonial groups in Dar es Salaam in 1962. Called Frelimo (Frente de Libertação de Moçambique), the fractious alliance was led by an American-educated Mozambican named Eduardo Mondlane. From the outset, Mondlane found himself mediating between two opposing perspectives within the organization. One, associated with Lazaro Nkavandame, saw the struggle primarily in terms of securing the expulsion of the Portuguese. The other faction, promoted by avowed leftists like Marcelino dos Santos, favoured the subsuming of nationalist ideals to those of scientific socialism. Dissident elements went on to found small and short-lived rivals liberation organizations, but these were never to offer serious competition to Frelimo. The divisions in the liberation struggle, thought to have been essentially eradicated with the ascension of Samora Machel and a radical-oriented clique in 1970, were to re-emerge with the onset of independence and the encouragement of external forces.

The armed struggle that was to ultimately topple the colonial government began on 25 September 1964 in Cabo Delgado province.[1] The next ten years saw the growth of guerrilla insurgency in the northern provinces, coupled, ironically, with the rising tempo of economic expansion and development in the central and southern half of the country.[2] The Portuguese military committed thousands of troops from both metropolitan Portugal and the colonies in pursuit of its counter-insurgency aims, including a growing number of black Mozambicans attached to regular and special forces battalions. Implementation of a 'strategic hamlets' programme in the north, coupled with the relative weakness of Frelimo's military capacity, effectively quarantined the overall impact on the territory.

Nonetheless, the failure to halt the incipient revolution had a dilatory effort on the Portuguese state already encumbered by numerous political problems. On 25 April 1974, a cabal of radically-minded officers, the Movimento dos Forças Armadas, took control of the government and proceeded to open independence negotiations with the various anti-colonial movements.[3] In the case of Mozambique, Socialist leader Mario Soares held talks with senior Frelimo officials, culminating in the signing of the Lusaka Agreement. The terms of the accord called for recognition of Frelimo as the sole liberation movement in Mozambique and a short transitional governance period, effectively abdicating Portuguese responsibility for the colony's future political status. By the time the Portuguese flag was lowered on 25 June 1975, Frelimo appeared to have uncontested political control of the new nation.

Independence and Socialist Commitment

The new government lost no time introducing domestic and foreign policies that took scientific socialism and international activism, particularly with reference to the white minority regimes in Southern Africa, as its inspiration.[4] It promulgated a series of edicts banning strikes, curtailing religious activity, as well as nationalizing of certain sectors of the economy and social services, land, and legal services.[5] Reacting to the changing political and economic climate, the settler population dwindled from a high of over 200,000 to less than 30,000 by 1977. International capital, for which the bellicose rhetoric of socialism seemed only to harbinger future constraints on business activities in Mozambique, beat a hasty retreat out of the country.

In the agricultural sector, Frelimo introduced a programme of *socialização do campo* (socialization of the countryside), calling for the promotion of state-run production and the collectivization of agriculture based on the Soviet model.[6] Government-sponsored resettlement projects, purportedly to ease the administration of resources and facilitate 'politicization' of the peasantry who made up over 80 per cent of the population, soon began to take on the appearance of forced relocations.[7] With their traditional beliefs and established hierarchies deliberately singled out for elimination by Frelimo as a legacy of 'feudalism', the peasantry began to actively resent and even resist the new state. In the industrial sector, Frelimo pressed for the expansion of domestic manufacturing and selected heavy industry 'prestige' projects in an effort to modernize the Mozambican economy. Unable to raise the requisite capital, Frelimo resorted to squeezing the agriculture sector to assist in financing its programmes, putting further pressure on the already beleaguered farmers. By 1981, with three quarters of Mozambique's industrial sector under direct state control, the cash and skills strapped industrial sector began to collapse. The situation was exacerbated by a series of natural disasters and the loss of the skilled settler sector, and Mozambique's GNP fell from an estimated US$2.1 billion in 1981 to $1.2 billion in 1985.[8]

External Intervention and Counter-Revolution

The new government moved swiftly to implement a foreign policy rooted in regional solidarity by introducing sanctions in 1976 against neighbouring Rhodesia, thereby cutting traffic between the land-locked state and the vital port of Beira. While the Zimbabwean African National Union (ZANU) used its bases in Tete province to infiltrate the settler state, bringing further pressure to bear on the embattled Smith regime, the Rhodesians countered by engineering direct military incursions into Mozambican territory as well as establishing an armed guerrilla movement (the Mozambican National Resistance, or MNR) composed of black Mozambican paramilitary units and, later, joined by dissident elements within Mozambican society.[9] Operating out of Rhodesia, the proxy forces wreaked havoc upon (ZANU) guerrilla camps and selected economic targets within the central provinces of Mozambique before being put out of action by the signing of the Lancaster House agreement in 1979. The cost to Mozambique of the implementation of sanctions against Rhodesia was high: $550 million in lost trade, port revenues and miners' remittances.[10]

While Zimbabwe moved towards independence, the build up of a significant presence of African National Congress (ANC) members within the country increasingly became a sore point with South Africa, particularly as ANC infiltrations and acts of sabotage in that country began to have a direct impact.[11] The South African government, which had taken over responsibility for the MNR in the waning days of the Rhodesian state, housed the organization at a military base in the Northern Transvaal and embarked on extensive recruitment, training and re-equipping so that within two years its numbers had jumped from 500 guerrillas to 8,000.[12] Disaffection with Frelimo policies, felt strongest in the central region dominated by Mozambicans of Ndau origin, provided a continuing source of passive support for anti-government actions in the country.[13] Now called Renamo (the Portuguese acronym for the MNR),[14] the counter-revolutionary organization unleased a ruthless campaign of intimidation and violence in the countryside, immobilizing government security forces and crippling the already debilitated Mozambican economy.[15] Health clinics, schools, party headquarters as well as traffic moving between cities and towns all were targeted for attack by Renamo. Amid warnings from the South African government to desist from supporting the ANC, the South African Defence Force launched a series of raids into Maputo and the outlying suburbs beginning in 1981.[16] Caught between the destructive power of the Renamo insurgency and further threats of conventional assault by the SADF, the government illusion of invulnerability from the realities governing regional security was shattered.

With only limited East Bloc economic and military support forthcoming,[17] the Frelimo leadership recognized that significant changes in its domestic and foreign policies were imperative if the state was to survive intact. A succession of secret meetings between Mozambican and South African officials were held, culminating in the highly-publicized signing of the Nkomati Accord on 16 March 1984. The agreement called for the closing of ANC offices and curbing of ANC activities within Mozambique in exchange for the suspension of South African support for the Renamo guerrillas.[18] Complementing this move were modifications in the agricultural and market pricing policies, bringing relief to the shackled farming sector.

The promise of peace embodied in the Nkomati Accord never came to pass. When the discovery of the Vaz diaries in a remote Renamo base in 1985 revealed that elements within the South African military establishment were continuing to provide support for Renamo, the embattled government in Maputo suspended the Nkomati Accord's joint security commission. Despite the issuance of a collective statement of principles by Frelimo and Renamo in October 1985, representing a last ditch effort to salvage South African sponsored diplomacy aimed at reconciling the two adversaries, the détente initiative collapsed.[19] South African-Mozambican relations reached a nadir with President Machel's untimely death in a mysterious plane accident over South African territory a year later.

The simultaneous ousting of Renamo from its safe haven in Malawi in October 1986, instigated by regional political pressure, saw several thousand guerrillas descend upon the countryside. A new cycle of destruction began, with the mutilation of villagers and forced recruitment of child soldiers added to crimes committed by a desperately impoverished government army.[20] While Renamo failed in its endeavour to cut the country in two (staved off by Zimbabwean and Tanzanian troops), it successfully established itself in all 11 provinces and, from these bases of support, continued its campaign. By 1990, an estimated 600,000 Mozambicans had died of unnatural causes, 1.7 million more had fled to neighbouring countries, tens of thousands were internally displaced, and famine and war threatened still more death.[21] With over 1,000 health clinics and 2,773 primary schools destroyed,[22] the transport network incapacitated by indiscriminate attacks and the sowing of landmines, the country had moved perilously close to total disintegration.

Suing for Peace

Changes in erstwhile support from the Soviet Union and eastern Europe, coupled with the prospect of a continuing military stalemate with Renamo, caused the government to consider introducing further radical measures to secure its survival. The new strategy for rehabilitating war-torn Mozambique was to embark on significant economic and political reforms domestically while engaging in a novel diplomatic initiative aimed at ending the armed conflict through negotiations.

In 1987, the government launched its plan for the movement away from a socialist economy to that of a market economy. The introduction of the Economic Recovery Programme (PRE), a structural adjustment plan which sought to increase production in the agricultural sector, rehabilitate existing industrial capacity and place Mozambique's financial institutions on a sound footing, based upon the limited policies promulgated in the previous three years.[23] Signalling its commitment to broaden economic reforms to include the political sphere, Frelimo renounced its status as 'Marxist-Leninist vanguard party', opened its membership ranks and promised to hold direct presidential elections. A new constitution was drawn up in 1990, guaranteeing separation of powers, direct presidential elections and a limitation on presidential terms, allowing for multi-party elections, introducing 'habeas corpus' and press freedoms.[24]

With the encouragement of Western influences, talks were reopened with South Africa over the renewal of the joint security commission in August 1987. This was followed by a meeting between State President P.W. Botha and President Chissano in Tete province in September 1988 in which the two leaders called for the 'reactivation and reinforcement' of the Nkomati Accord.[25] These discussions paved the way for the shipment of US$4.5 million of South African military equipment to protect the Cabora Bassa dam and a modest increase in trade relations.[26]

Building upon these initial measures,[27] Chissano gave his consent for discussions to be held between Mozambican church officials and representatives of Renamo in 1988. In July 1989, he dramatically reversed the government's most sacrosanct position and authorized the initiation of preliminary negotiations with Renamo. Originally held in Nairobi under the sponsorship of Kenya's President Daniel Arap Moi and Zimbabwe's President Robert Mugabe, the protracted negotiations were shifted to Rome with the Sant' Egidio Community serving as mediators. Protracted talks, centring on the unilateral promulgation of the new constitution, the status of political parties, and provisions for demilitarization, culminated in an abortive ceasefire agreement in December 1990. The collapse of this initiative, fuelled by mutual distrust between the Mozambican parties, was followed by an extensive effort to secure peace through adherence to a series of protocols. After lengthy mediation and spurred on by the advent of another severe drought, the government and Renamo signed the General Peace Agreement formally ending hostilities on 4 October 1992.[28]

The United Nations Interregnum

The entry of the United Nations (UN) into the peace process ushered in a new phase of international engagement in Mozambique. While the UN position at the negotiations had been that of an observer, with the onset of the General Peace Agreement (GPA) it was thrust into the role of chief facilitator of the peace process. The difficulties encountered in implementing the terms of the GPA, encumbered by the UN's own operational deficiencies, were to hinder the peacekeeping mission throughout its tenure in the country. The GPA called for UN participation in the areas of the monitoring of the ceasefire, providing humanitarian assistance and monitoring of the elections. It established a timetable for the implementation of the major components of the peace agreement, with the full demobilization of both armies to be completed by April 1993 and the elections to be held in October 1993.[29] Substantial delays, primarily a product of continuing enmity between the government and Renamo, obliged the UN to shift the timetable to one full year later.

The guiding purpose of UN involvement in the peace process was to foster and promote adherence to the conditions deemed necessary by the negotiators in Rome to establish a lasting peace in Mozambique. To realize the objectives of the GPA, the UN was given a central role in the key institutions of transitional authority in the country. The Commission of Supervision and Control (CSC), chaired by the Special Representative of the Secretary General, was charged with the settlement of disputes between the Mozambican parties, any question of interpretation of the GPA and a coordinating role for the subsidiary commissions to be established. Below the CSC were three subordinate commissions established to deal directly with the immediate issues surrounding the demilitarization of the conflict. These were the Cease-Fire Commission, the Commission for the Reintegration of Demobilising Military Personnel and the Joint Commission for the Formation of the Mozambican Defence Force.

Demilitarization

The demilitarization of conflict, that is the establishment of the conditions for 'social peace', was a priority issue for the new UN mission in Mozambique (referred to by its acronym, ONUMOZ). Complicating the situation was a determination to avoid a central flaw in the Angolan peace process, the failure fully to demobilize troops in advance of the elections. In order to carry out these arduous responsibilities, ONUMOZ put together a structured programme which drew upon the military and humanitarian resources of the international community. These resources were brought to bear on the range of demilitarization activities, including the monitoring of the ceasefire, the demobilization and reintegration of troops and the creation of a new national army.

The first component of the demilitarization programme was the introduction of the 7,500 strong UN peacekeeping force to monitor the withdrawal of Zimbabwean and Malawian troops from transport corridors within Mozambique. With the UN experiencing significant delays in acquiring the requisite military units for the mission as well as problems in obtaining a status of forces agreement from the government, the operation got off to a rocky start. Having finally resolved these problems by June

1993, ONUMOZ began to engage in the business of monitoring of the ceasefire between the government and Renamo. The majority of ceasefire violations put before the Cease-Fire Commission were centred around movement of troops rather than accusations of shooting incidents or attacks and the Commission was able to handle these to the satisfaction of both parties within its established procedures.[30]

To achieve the full demobilization of the estimated 63,000 government troops and 20,000 Renamo troops, the UN mission developed a comprehensive programme which combined the short term goals of troop demobilization with the long terms goals of social reintegration. Mozambican soldiers were instructed to go to one of the 49 designated Assembly Areas where a team of three UN military officers and one civilian officer would register the soldiers, arrange for disarmament and storage of their weaponry, process selected soldiers for the new national army and, finally, oversee the formal demobilization and transport of ex-soldiers. Educational activities geared towards informing the soldiers about the specific terms of the GPA and especially those which affected them directly were part of a general programme during the soldiers' cantonment. Finally, once formal demobilization had taken place, the International Migration Organization was to provide transport for the ex-soldiers and their dependents to a destination of their choice.

Bickering between the government and Renamo which accompanied the peace process, with both sides using participation in demobilization as a bargaining chip, resulted in considerable delays in assembling their troops. It was not until 30 November 1993 that 20 of the 49 Assembly Areas were actually opened to receive troops; the other 29 had became operational by February 1994. Significant oversights in the GPA, including the failure to account for government militias and the police, hung over the process and sowed further distrust. Slow identification of those soldiers who were to join the new military from those to be demobilized, coupled with the clandestine demobilization of Renamo's notorious child soldiers, caused additional delays.[31] The prolonged pace of the demobilization process, aggravated by inflated expectations of the process from the Mozambican troops, resulted in the outbreak of a series of disturbances at the Assembly Areas. Unruly soldiers engaged in attacks on UN officials, the taking of UN hostages in the camps and blocking major roads or looting in neighbouring towns.[32] Successful efforts to mediate were punctuated by the introduction of government police or troops, sometimes resulting in injuries and death. By 1 September 1994, 37 reported incidents had occurred in Renamo Assembly Areas and 40 in government Assembly Areas.[33] Despite these problems, ONUMOZ elected to commence demobilization in March 1994. UN officials hurried to complete demobilization before the planned starting

date for the election campaign, declaring the process to be over on 15
August. The final total of registered soldiers was tallied at 64,130
(government) and 22,637 (Renamo), though both sides retained troops and
weaponry outside of the formal demobilization process.[34]

The last stage of demobilization, introducing measures for the long term
maintenance of the ex-soldiers, was taken up by the humanitarian
component of ONUMOZ and consisted of the Information and Referral
Service (IRS) and the Reintegration Support Scheme (RSS). The IRS was
conceived as a mechanism for providing demobilized soldiers with access
to information on the job market as well as basic information on aspects of
the reintegration programme. The RSS was to provide demobilized soldiers
with 24 months of subsidies in the form of cash disbursements given at
local branches of the Banco Popular de Desenvolvimento. Supplementing
these programmes was the allocation of vocational kits consisting of
agricultural tools, seeds and food rations for up to three months to
demobilized soldiers upon departure from the Assembly Areas. It was
hoped that these provisions would allow former combatants the time
necessary to find employment in their districts and in the process, begin to
integrate more fully into the local community.

The final component of demilitarization was the creation of a new
national army, the Forças Armadas de Defensa de Moçambique (FADM).
At the time of the Rome Agreement it was envisaged that the new army
would consist of 30,000 soldiers, equally divided between former
government and former Renamo troops.[35] The establishment of training
centres for the new army, staffed by military instructors from Britain,
France and Portugal, was to educate the Mozambicans in the curriculum of
Western militaries. It was through this process that the core of a new
national defence force, instilled with professionalism and a commitment to
the new democratic state, would develop.

After some false starts, 550 soldiers were sent to a camp in Nyanga,
Zimbabwe, where British officers provided instruction on aspects of military
training which the Mozambicans themselves were expected to pass on to their
own troops back home. The thorny question of command of the new army
was resolved in January 1994, with dual authority vested in the government's
Brigadier General Lagos Lidimo and Renamo's Lieutenant General Mateus
Ngonhamo. Delays in the supply of new equipment and the renovation of
inadequate training facilities, coupled with the prolonged process of
identifying new soldiers, forced the compression of training into six weeks.
Unhappiness over the prospect of being forced to continue in the military
brought about strikes and desertions.[36] By the time the elections had started,
80 top officers were appointed to command the newly-created infantry
battalions while fewer than 10,000 soldiers had completed their training.

Humanitarian Assistance

The humanitarian component of the UN mission was primarily directed towards the crucial areas of emergency relief, refugee and internally displaced repatriation and demining. The United Nations Office for Humanitarian Assistance Coordination (UNOHAC), comprising all of the international aid agencies, non-governmental organizations (NGOs) and relevant government departments, was the instrument for the implementation of these programmes. With over one million Mozambicans outside of the country and large numbers of internally displaced persons, the prospect of uncontrolled migration within the country raised the spectre of starvation, disease and social chaos which the international community sought to avert. UNOHAC presided over food relief and health projects organized by the World Food Programme and the World Health Organization, as well as a host of national and international NGOs. An extensive refugee resettlement and internally-displaced persons resettlement project was managed by the UN High Commission for Refugees and the International Migration Organization respectively. And the clearance of land mines, of which an estimated two million[37] were scattered throughout the country, set off an increasingly contentious row between UNOHAC, the international donor community and national and international NGOs over sub-contracting procedures, the timeliness of the effort and its cost.[38]

Elections

The role of the UN in the election process in Mozambique consisted of monitoring the registration of voters, the conduct of the campaign itself, and the counting of votes. The election was to be direct for the office of President for a five-year term on the basis of a simple majority (or second ballot if necessary) and indirect for representation to the 250-member National Assembly for a five-year term, selected on the basis of proportional representation. The Mozambicans themselves, through the National Election Commission (CNE), would administer all of the logistical components of the election including that of voter education and registration, the establishment of polling stations, and the counting of votes. Establishing a legal framework for the election and ensuring that all of the officially registered parties had equal access to the media were also part of the CNE's brief.

Although the election itself had been postponed until October 1994, the process nevertheless underwent a series of crises. The Multi-Party Conference held in April 1993 failed to resolve issues involving the composition of the various district, provincial and national electoral commissions, as well as the status of overseas voters, and were only overcome through concerted interventions by Boutros Boutros-Ghali and the UN Special Representative.

The Electoral Law was passed by the Mozambican National Assembly and the CNE belatedly took up its duties in January 1994. Seventeen parties took part in the election, though their capacities were severely circumscribed by the brevity of the campaigning period, limited access to the media and over financial support.

As the election neared, Renamo leader Afonso Dhlakama increasingly resorted to linking further progress in the peace process with the securing of funds for his organization. The ONUMOZ commitment to both the spirit and the terms of the Rome Agreement meant that the Special Representative found himself engaged in seeking financial support for Renamo from the international community.[39] Concern within the international community that Mozambique was poised to degenerate into an Angolan-like disaster caused Western governments to embark on an unsuccessful effort to pressure the Mozambican parties into accepting a government of national unity.

Although voter registration did not begin until 1 June 1994, over 5.2 million persons endured considerable hardship and registered for the franchise.[40] The election campaign itself was conducted in an atmosphere of growing tension, fuelled by Renamo's declaration that it would view anything less than victory in key central provinces as a sure sign of fraud.[41] As it transpired, Dhlakama's temporary withdrawal from the election hours before it was to take place, a move which galvanized Western and regional diplomats, did not seriously disrupt voter turnout. With approximately 85 per cent of the electorate participating, Chissano won the presidency with 53 per cent of the vote against Dhlakama's 33 per cent while Frelimo secured 129 of the 250 seats in the National Assembly and Renamo won 112.[42] None of the smaller parties achieved the 5 per cent minimum support set by the constitution to obtain a place in the National Assembly. The Special Representative declared the results to be fair and, despite some carping from Renamo quarters, the results were accepted as valid.[43]

Prospects for Peace in Mozambique

The departure of the UN mission was, in many ways, as potentially disruptive as its intrusion into Mozambican affairs. The distortions to the economy, causing for example accommodation prices to soar to astronomical levels, were only matched by the interference in the political sphere, which saw effective sovereignty slip into the hands of ONUMOZ and the international donor community. The new government, heir to the conflict and its resolution (and indeed, a participant), is burdened with the multiple legacies of the war, socialism, and regional and international intervention. Above all, the spectre of violence, no longer political but rather criminal in origin, hangs over the new democratic state.

Economic Conditions

Addressing a conference in 1995, President Joaquim Chissano declared: 'We cannot have sustainable government if there is no economic base.'[44] The economic situation in the country remains crucial to the overall stability of the political and social environment. While overall figures on the government's Programme for Economic and Social Recovery give the impression of a robust economy (GDP grew 19.2 per cent in 1993), the rising rate of inflation, pegged at over 70 per cent annually in 1994, and the estimated 65 per cent unemployment figure belie such an optimistic perspective.[45] The level of abject physical destruction in the country, from roads and buildings to farmland and industry, and the virtual absence of an educated or trained population provide a further caution. At the same time, some developments augur well for Mozambique's long term revival. The utilization of the transport corridors and ports, especially Beira, by landlocked countries has increased measurably since the signing of the GPA. In 1994, over 50 per cent of Zimbabwe's containered exports went through the relatively inexpensive port at Beira (as opposed to South African ports), though it was clear to foreign trade officials and businessmen that the capacity of the port facilities needed further upgrading and the problem of 'en route' tolls needed to be addressed.[46] The revival of Beira would firmly re-establish a commercial and industrial hub that could serve as base for development in the central provinces.

The fostering of these conditions depends, at least in the short and medium term, on the level and direction of foreign assistance to Mozambique. At the same time, as the world's most aid dependent state, Mozambique must exercise tremendous caution in designing, and approving development plans.[47] One of the key sources of future revenue for the government is the sale of power from the crippled Cahora Bassa hydro-electric project in Tete province. To this end, the European Investment Bank and European Development Fund have pledged ECU40 million and ECU20 million respectively to rehabilitate Cabora Bassa.[48] The development of the natural gas fields at Pande in Inhambane province is another area capturing foreign attention. At the World Bank Consultative Group meeting in March 1995, US$780 million was pledged (excluding debt relief) to assist Mozambican development. The Mozambican Finance Minister, in keeping with the prevalent international financial practice, outlined an austerity programme which took further aim at government spending and called for further privatization of parastatal concerns such as the Moatize coalfields. Included in the new budget was a 37 per cent reduction in military spending, bringing it to 1.6 per cent of total GDP (though overall spending on security is one quarter of the total budget), while education and health were increased by 22 and 44 per cent respectively.[49] Mozambique's battered transport network will receive a boost in the form of US $100 million to repair 10,000 kilometres of road.[50]

Another important component of economic rehabilitation is the encouragement of foreign direct investment in the country. Mozambique has experienced significant gains in this area, with foreign direct investment rocketing to US $16.5 million in 1994, three times the total in the previous year. Significantly, Portuguese interests have eclipsed South African and British foreign direct investment in 1994, buying up the majority of newly-privatized government concerns. Related to this phenomenon is the growing attention given to agriculture. The Natal and Transvaal Agricultural Unions, as well as an Italian-South African association, have conducted talks with the Mozambican government over farming opportunities in Mozambique. Spurred on by fears of land reform in South Africa (as well as a dislike for the ANC), the white farmers and the Afrikaner political leader General Constand Viljoen have signed an agreement with Maputo to open up farmland to white interests in the Save region. This has been coupled to a US$16 million South African initiative, backed by the SANDF and the private company Mechen, to begin demining the potential farmland for which 2,000 South African farmers have applied.[51]

At the heart of the land issue lies the contentious matter of tenure. For the vast majority of Mozambicans, some form of subsistence agriculture remains the single most prevalent occupation. Dispossessed under colonialism, forced to collectivize under socialism, driven from the land by famine and war, the Mozambican peasant appears on the brink of becoming marginalized yet again. Despite the promulgation of laws guaranteeing entitlement to smallholders, the last few years have been witness to a massive sell-off of natural resources which took no account of legality. According to an authoritative study, by January 1994 20 million hectares of land – representing a quarter of Mozambique's total land area – had been granted on a concessional basis or had been outright sold to foreign interests.[52] Aggravating the problem is confusion over entitlement to the land stemming from counter-claims originating from the colonial era, independence and the war itself. Financial and administrative mismanagement at the provincial and district level, as well as rampant corruption amongst government officials, have contributed to this firesale of Mozambican resources.[53] The creation of a landless peasantry is a potentially explosive development for the new democratic state.

Political Conditions

As in any country emerging from a traumatic period of conflict, the economic climate is hostage to the political situation. In this regard Mozambique is no exception and, for this reason, Chissano's unwillingness to give Renamo governorships or significant positions in any of the five provinces in which it won a majority of votes is a continuing source of controversy. Both the United States and the European Union have criticized the President for his stance, suggesting that some of the political crises facing the new state would have been averted had Dhlakama had a greater public role. At the same time, the state has yet to allocate the resources necessary to assure the independence of the legislature and the judiciary. The establishment of what has been characterized as a 'crisis cabinet' – composed of old Frelimo stalwarts and ex-military officials (such as the former Minister of Defence Alberto Chipande) – which seems to wield effective power in the new government is for some an indication that Frelimo will try to continue to rule the country on its own.[54]

Uncertainty still surrounds the position of Renamo under the new dispensation. Dhlakama has to date resisted government's offers of a substantial (by Mozambican standards) salary and official perks, while continuing to call upon Chissano to recognise his status as official Leader of the Opposition, a position which would give him the right to address the parliament.[55] At Renamo's first post-election conference in February 1995, the paucity of trained officials was made apparent as senior figures moved into parliament only to be replaced by lesser qualified personnel. Renamo itself is in some measure of disarray, partially a function of the Frelimo government's strategy of denying it access to sources of authority while concurrently attempting to divide the leadership from its support base. Renamo's blatant pleas for funding, calling alternatively for foreign support or a share of government revenues, overshadowed any attempt to define a post-election programme which would signal its relevance to contemporary Mozambican politics.

The longer-term components of the demilitarization programme are experiencing problems, though these still remain manageable. The government's bid for direct control over the foreign-funded subsidiary package for ex-soldiers, allegedly as a means of courting the veterans' vote in the forthcoming local elections, was blocked by the international donor community.[56] At the same time, the fund itself is short US $4.29 million, owing to the unexpected numbers of soldiers choosing to demobilize rather than stay in the army.[57] The formation of an association for demobilized soldiers actively petitioning for issues concerning ex-combatants presents an interesting case of emergent civil society which could, paradoxically, work against the very reintegration goals of the UN's demobilization programme.

Adding to the government's woes is the problem of dissent within the military. Three major mutinies have occurred in 1995, one in the heart of Maputo itself at the Escolar Militar, provoking responses ranging from government payouts to police shootouts. Complaining of their low salaries and poor living conditions, soldiers have taken hostages and fired on passers-by. Threatened by a march on parliament in April this year, the government was forced to deploy its special forces to thwart further attacks. Complicating the situation, former Renamo officers in the new army have voiced concern over their isolation from army decisions and threatened to withdraw altogether from the FADM.[58] Finally, with the FADM still short of its new target of 15,000 personnel, the government has launched a recruitment drive to make up the shortfall.

Outside of dissension in the military and among demobilized soldiers, violence and criminality have risen in post-election Mozambique. Over 100 undeclared arms caches have been discovered containing 22,000 functioning weapons; if the proliferation in illegal arms transactions in neighbouring South Africa is any indication, there remain vast quantities of weapons still available in Mozambique.[59] In a crime symptomatic of this breakdown in the recently achieved law and order, even the new Chief of the General Staff, Lagios Lidimo, was shot by car thieves while driving in Maputo.[60] A police assault on Renamo officials in Tete underscored both the lack of reconciliation between Frelimo era figures and concurrent problems with the ill-disciplined police force. Responding to a growing chorus of criticism, the Minister of the Interior fired 98 policemen and announced the establishment of a three-year training programme for the police, funded by the French government, aimed at instilling professionalism in the force.[61] Nevertheless, the proliferation of small arms both within Mozambique and across the region continue to contribute to rising crime, posing a constant danger to peace and stability.

Regional Relations

Relations with South Africa, crucial to the economic and political well-being of the new government in Maputo, are stabilizing. Chissano's visit to South Africa in March 1996, following a series of meetings in Mozambique with Nelson Mandela, saw the signing of bilateral agreements in a range of areas. Most pertinent was the agreement to coordinate policing activity designed to cut down on illegal immigration and trafficking in arms, drugs and stolen goods. In fact, repatriating Mozambican migrants to South Africa is one of the first foreign policy issues which the ANC-led government has taken a firm stance. With only 90,692 Mozambicans returned to their country of origin of an estimated 200,000 illegally residing in South Africa, Pretoria has been increasingly adamant about stemming the flow of migration.[62] According to the head of the Catholic NGO Masungulo, over 80 per cent of the Mozambicans forcibly repatriated in the Ressano Garcia area are back in South Africa within 24 hours.[63] Neighbouring Zimbabwe, the other regional pole of influence, plays an increasing part in the economy of the country (see above) matching its political position. A small anti-government insurgency movement, originally linked to Renamo, retains bases in Mozambique and is being watched closely in Harare while the growing number of Zimbabweans purchasing land along the border and Beira corridor has raised concerns in Maputo.

Looking Forward

In the end, for stability and growth to prevail in Mozambique, *peace building*, the transition point between peacekeeping and development, must move from its preliminary stages concerned with demilitarization and elections to the long term dimensions of economic rehabilitation, the cultivation of a vibrant civil society and other nation-building activities.[64] The willingness of the international community to support this transition, through selective financial assistance, foreign investment, institutional support and capacity building both inside the government and in the wider society, will have a determining influence on the success of the new dispensation. Balanced against this role is the corrosive impact on Mozambican sovereignty caused by its dependency on international assistance and, increasingly, the state's indiscriminate pandering to the interests of foreign capital at the expense of its citizens.

The reconciliation between Frelimo and Renamo, whether through a genuine commitment to peace or through sheer exhaustion may prove easier to achieve than building the economic and social base of the nation. Armed banditry, borne of hunger, unemployment and habit, threaten the new democratic dispensation in the same way that civil war once brought the old government to its knees. The inability of the nascent legal system to enforce existing statutory legislation on land tenure, coupled with the phenomenon of a dispossed peasantry, is in itself alarming. Coupled with the monumental social problems of the reintegration of ex-soldiers, the unregulated circulation of weaponry and the return of over a million refugees, it is not far-fetched to suggest that the criminal violence of today – mediated through growing social disaffection – could well end up as the political violence of tomorrow. For the time being, the government can rightly claim the legitimacy bestowed upon it by the 1994 elections. Whether it retains the loyalty of its newly enfranchised citizenry remains to be seen.

NOTES

1. See Thomas Henriksen, *Revolution and Counterrevolution: Mozambique's War of Independence, 1964–1974* (NY: Greenwood 1983). Also see Eduardo Mondlane, *The Struggle for Mozambique* (London: Penguin 1969) for an insider's account of Frelimo's formation and its early years. For documents from that era see Ron Chilcote, *Emerging Nationalism in Portuguese Africa* (Stanford, CA: Hoover 1972).

2. Henriksen (note 1) pp. 138–9.
3. See Douglas Porch, *The Portuguese Armed Forces and the Revolution* (Great Britain: Redwood Burn 1977).
4. Joseph Hanlon, *Revolution Under Fire* (London: Zed 1984) pp.93–131.
5. Colin Legum (ed.) *Africa Contemporary Record: Annual Survey and Documents 1975–1976* (London: Rex Collings 1976) B274–78.
6. Hanlon (note 4) pp.95–8.
7. Ibid. pp.128–31; also see C. Geffray, *La cause des armes au Mozambique* (Paris: Karthala 1990) pp.49–92.
8. Erfried Adam 'Mozambique: Reform Policy – A Way Out of the Crisis', *Aussenpolitik* 39/2 (1988) p.184.
9. Ken Flower, founder and director of the Rhodesian Central Intelligence Office, describes Rhodesia's role in the establishment of the MNR/Renamo. K. Flower, *Serving Secretly: Rhodesia's CIO Chief on Record* (Johannesburg/London: Galag/John Murray 1987) (appendix) pp.300–2.
10. Harold Nelson (ed.) *Mozambique: A Country Study,* 3rd ed. (Washington, DC: American U. 1985) p.135.
11. Robert Jaster, *The Defence of White Power: South African Foreign Policy Under Pressure* (London: Macmillan 1988) pp.119–20; D. Geldenhuys, 'Some Foreign Policy Implications of South Africa's "Total National Strategy", *Special Study* (Braamfontein: SA Inst. of Int. Relations (March 1981) pp.23–4.
12. M. Hall, 'The Mozambican National Resistance (Renamo): A Study in Destabilization of an African State', *Africa* 60 (1990) p.40.
13. The Ndau, as did some other Mozambicans outside of the southern provinces, claimed that the southern domination of Frelimo translated into active discrimination against their interests.
14. Flower (note 9) p.262.
15. For a comprehensive study of Renamo see Alex Vine, *Renamo: Terrorism in Mozambique* (London: James Currey 1991).
16. Jaster (note 11) pp.119–20.
17. A turning point was the failure of Mozambique's application for membership of Comecon in 1981 and, especially when viewed against Soviet support for Angola and Ethiopia, and the low level of military commitment.
18. See G. Erasmus, 'The Accord of Nkomati: Context and Content' *Occasional Paper* (Braamfontein: SA Inst of Int. Affairs Oct. 1984) pp.15–21.
19. *Southern Africa Report* 2/41 (1984) p.10.
20. For a detailed account of the atrocities committed by both sides against the civilian population, see Human Rights Watch, *Conspicuous Destruction: War, Famine and the Reform Process in Mozambique* (Washington DC: Human Rights Watch 1992).
21. Ibid. pp.103–4; UN High Commission for Refugees, *The State of the World's Refugees: The Challenge of Protection* (London: Penguin 1993) pp.108–9.
22. Ibid. p.27.
23. *Economist Intelligence Unit* 1990–1991 (London: Economist 1991) p.10.
24. *Mozambiquefile* Dec. 1990, pp.7–8; Mozambique Information Office, *News Review* 183/4, 2 Aug. 1990.
25. 'Botha, Chissano Meet in Mozambique', *Washington Post,* 13 Sept. 1988.
26. L. Maveneka, 'Marching with Pretoria', *Southern African Economist* (April/May 1989) p.18. Joint Mozambican and South African co-operation on the replacement of more than 500 damaged pylons for the Cabora Bassa project was denounced by Renamo and, within two months' time, a further 891 pylons were destroyed by its guerrillas.
27. Mozambique Information Office 'News Review' No.120, 21 Dec. 1987.
28. For a detailed study of the negotiations, see Cameron Hume, *Ending Mozambique's War: The Role of Mediation and Good Offices* (Washington, DC: US Inst. of Peace 1994).
29. For an outline of the timetable see *General Peace Agreement 1992* (Amsterdam: African–European Institute 1992) pp.34–6, 42–4, 48–50, 56–64.
30. Interview with Col. Pier Segala, Cease-Fire Commission, 14 Sept. 1994.

31. *Sunday Times* (UK), 6 Nov. 1994. Only 3,632 child soldiers were in fact discovered at the Renamo bases though numerous Renamo soldiers were only just above the internationally sanctioned age of 15.
32. CCF, 'Problems/Incidents in Assembly Areas and Other Areas' (Maputo: ONUMOZ Sept. 1994).
33. Ibid.
34. *Africa Confidential* 35, 23 Sept. 1994, pp.3–4.
35. *General Peace Agreement 1992* (Amsterdam: AWEPAA/African-European Inst. 1992) p.30.
36. AWEPA, *Mozambique Peace Process Bulletin* 10, July 1994, p.5.
37. This figure has been considerably reduced in subsequent years, though all estimates are speculative. Human Rights Watch, *Landmines in Mozambique* (Washington, DC: HRW 1994) p.14.
38. C. Alden, 'The UN and the Resolution of Conflict in Mozambique', *Jnl of Modern African Studies* 33/1 (March 1995) pp.121–3.
39. Interview with Aldo Ajello, Special Representative to the UN Secretary-General, Maputo, 16 Sept. 1994.
40. *Africa Confidential* 35/19,23 Sept. 1994, p.3.
41. *Weekly Mail and Guardian*, 21–27 Oct. 1994.
42. *Washington Post*, 11 Nov. 1994.
43. G. Harrison, 'Elections in Mozambique', *Review of African Political Economy* 63/22 (March 1995) p.116. The election cost US $63.5mn to run. *Marchés Tropicaux* (Paris), 24 Dec. 1994.
44. *Facts and Reports* 25:J, 26 May 1995.
45. Hans Abrahamsson and Anders Nilsson, *Mozambique: The Troubled Transition* (London: Zed 1995) pp.116–17; Minister of Labour, Mozambican Television, 13 Jan. 1995.
46. *Indian Ocean Newsletter* No.654, 14 Jan. 1995.
47. Abrahamsson and Nilsson (note 45) pp.131–46.
48. Indian Ocean Newsletter No.674, 3 June 1995.
49. Ibid. No.663, 18 March 1995.
50. Radio Maputo, 15 May 1995.
51. *Indian Ocean Newsletter* No.664, 25 March 1995.
52. G. Myers, 'Competitive Rights, Competitive Claims: Land Access in Post-War Mozambique,' *Jnl of Southern African Studies* 20/4 (1994) pp.609–10; H. West and G. Myers, 'A Piece of Land in a Land of Peace? Start Farms Diversification in Mozambique', *Jnl of Modern African Studies* 34/1 (March 1996) pp.29–30.
53. B. O'Laughlin, 'Past and Present Options: Land Reform in Mozambique,' *Review of African Political Economy* 63/22 (March 1995), p.105.
54. *Indian Ocean Newsletter* No.654, 14 Jan. 1995.
55. Having run for the executive position, Dhlakama is not eligible to sit as a Renamo MP.
56. *Indian Ocean Newsletter* No.665, 1 April 1995. It is alleged that the government wanted control of these funds as a means of wielding patronage over the ex-soldiers in advance of the local elections.
57. US $31.9mn is required for the Trust Fund, of which $8.9mn has been received and $27.6mn has been pledged by the donor community. AWEPA, *Mozambican Peace Process Bulletin*, Feb. 1995.
58. *Indian Ocean Newsletter*, 27 May 1995.
59. *Africa Recovery*, Dec. 1994, p.14.
60. *Africa Confidential* 36/8, 14 April 1995.
61. Radio Maputo, 12 May 1995.
62. *Indian Ocean Newsletter* No.659, 18 Feb. 1995; G. Ansell, 'A New Swart Gevaar?', *African Agenda* 1/2, pp.27–9.
63. Ibid.
64. Boutros Boutros-Ghali, 'Supplement to An Agenda for Peace', *An Agenda for Peace 1995*, 2nd ed. (NY: UN 1995), pp.19–22.

A Comparative Evaluation of the Armed Struggle in Namibia, South Africa and Zimbabwe

ABIODUN ALAO

The end of apartheid in South Africa marked the end of the armed struggle in Southern Africa, a struggle that accounted for the transformation of five countries in the region. The objective of this study is to examine the armed struggle in three of these countries – Namibia, South Africa and Zimbabwe. Although the nature of the historical evolution of these countries made them to be different from the Lusophone territories of Angola and Mozambique, there were significant differences in the ways the armed struggle was conducted in each. Areas of convergence and divergence in the armed struggle are identified as well as those areas where the armed struggle left lasting legacies.

The Past is Another Country

The attainment of majority rule in South Africa has received its fair share of attention.[1] But it has also resulted in changes in attitude and focus. For example, the historical hatred many people had for the erstwhile apartheid regime rapidly changed into affection for the new South African leadership. Sanctions imposed on the country gave way to 'investigations of avenues' for investment. Even academics were not spared this sudden re-diversion of focus, as many began 'looking into the future' of the new South Africa and the implications of the new found 'regional fraternity' for the countries in the region.[2] While the euphoria that justifies this 'forward looking' tendency is understandable, one should not overlook the fact that the attainment of majority rule in South Africa completed a phase whose history would need to be pathologically examined before it could be properly buried. This is that of the armed struggle.

The southern African sub-region has had enduring and often controversial links with foreign domination. It was in the region that colonial domination of Africa made an early debut, when the Portuguese established a foothold on the territory that later became Angola; it was in Namibia (South West Africa) that the international trusteeship of a mandated territory resulted in a complicated decolonization; it was also in southern Africa that the continent experienced its first, and only declaration of unilateral independence; it was in the region, too – in Angola and

Mozambique – that a hasty decolonization policy by a colonial power resulted in two civil wars that each lasted more than 15 years; and finally, it was in the sub-continent that apartheid began and ended. And the attainment of majority rule in South Africa further reinforces the need to re-examine some of the facets of colonial and foreign domination of the region.

This essay attempts a comparative evaluation of the armed struggle in Namibia, South Africa and Zimbabwe.[3] Although the intention is to investigate what the struggles in these countries have in common and where they differ, it is also intended to identify in the process aspects of the armed struggle that have played, or could yet play important roles in the future of the region. This is all the more necessary now that the sub-continent stands at the threshold of many opportunities and challenges. The article opens with a comparative explanation of the circumstances that created the need for armed struggle. It then compares the historical and military evolution of the groups that took up arms in these countries. This is followed by a comparative evaluation of the tactics and achievements and the extent of external involvement in these wars. Other comparisons considered include the reactions of the incumbent minority governments to the armed struggle; the activities of the black individuals and political parties who 'betrayed' the armed struggle to support the minority regimes; and finally, the negotiated settlements that ended the armed struggles in the three countries. Where necessary, digressions are made to compare the revolutionary wars in these countries with those in the Lusophone countries of Angola and Mozambique.

The 'Justifications' for the Resort to Arms

The situations that necessitated the adoption of armed struggle in Namibia, South Africa and Zimbabwe were similar, as they had to do with the exploitation and the dehumanization that came with foreign conquest. Political sociologists have classified societies that emerge after an exotic culture has made initial impact with its indigenous values into two categories: colonial and settler.[4] Thomas Hodgkin defined a colonial power as 'a state which, through whatever constitutional arrangements, enjoys effective control over a dependent African territory'.[5] In this equation, there is 'a recognised relation of dependence and subordination' between the colonial power and the colonial territory. On the contrary, however, a settler society is defined as one having:

> major emphasis on racial differences, ... the racial identity of the dominant group, and the permanence of its settlement, [as well as] social cleavage, cultural diversity, and ethnic hostility.[6]

In the latter case, race becomes a major determinant of power differential and privilege. Michael Macara notes that the desire by the settler societies to make permanent their stay involves transferring the belief systems, societal institutions and traditions of the metropole into the new society, a process which invariably leads to less effective imperial control over the administrative structure of settler societies.[7]

All the three countries discussed here were settler societies, with South Africa presenting, perhaps, the most extreme manifestations of settler oppression. The gross structural imbalance in the ways blacks and whites lived in South Africa has been the focus of several studies, such that a summary of the situation would suffice here. White privileges alongside black deprivation characterized all aspects of life: land ownership, economic resources; pay and access to occupations; welfare services; provision of health services; etc.[8] A few figures: 80 per cent of the land was allocated to the whites who formed less than 14 per cent of the population, while the black 75 per cent had just 13.7 per cent of South Africa's land; 95 per cent of managerial occupations were occupied by the whites, with blacks in this category less than one per cent, while in the labourer cadre, the figures were reversed with blacks occupying 85 per cent and whites one per cent. The income distribution, even as late as 1987, was 27 per cent for blacks and 62 per cent for whites; the official mortality rate was 66.8 and 74.3 respectively for white male and female, with 55.1 and 62.5 for blacks. Expenditure on education per student was R.368 for blacks and R.2,299 for whites. These inequalities were further compounded by laws which perpetuated separate development along racial lines.

The political and racial situation in Rhodesia was much closer to that of South Africa. Here, 8 million blacks scratched out a living at subsistence level or below while 250,000 whites enjoyed unparalleled privileges, including the possession of half of the available land, virtually all its business and industries. The situation was no different on the education, health care and housing fronts; while whites enjoyed opportunities equivalent to those in western Europe, blacks were confined by law to black townships and barren rural 'tribal trustlands'. Job opportunities available to blacks were limited in quality and in quantity. Again, there was no minimum wage for blacks until 1979, when it was set at $20 per month.[9] The political disenfranchisement of blacks meant the perpetuation of this racist arrangement.

In Namibia, about 1 million blacks, forming 88 per cent of the population, lived in abject poverty, while the whites, constituting about 12 per cent of the country's population, appropriated the nation's enormous wealth. Blacks depended largely on subsistence agriculture and poorly-paid contract labour work, while, as in South Africa and Zimbabwe, whites occupied most managerial and professional positions. Of the Namibian land area 43 per cent was reserved for occupation by the whites, while a further 17 per cent, including the coastal diamond mining zone, was set aside for direct South African government control.[10] The remaining 40 per cent of the land was left for blacks. Politically, Namibia was administered as part of South Africa,[11] and from 1964, the government accepted the Odendaal Report that recommended the 'Bantustanization' of Namibia.[12]

The above summary shows that in all the three countries, there were entrenched political, economic and social structures of dominance. These structures not only stripped the local population of any social, political and economic rights, but also left their fate in the hands of settler regimes that were not only racist but also fundamentally authoritarian. The effect this had on all the countries was the same: the emergence of black political parties determined to redress this imbalance.

The Birth and Development of the Military Wings of the Armed Struggle

Once the 'settlers' in the three countries made blunt their determination to establish minority rule in their respective states, reactions from the local inhabitants became more organized. In all three, the first manifestation of this organized reactions to settler oppression was the formation of unions and pressure groups. Some examples: in Namibia, the Lüderitz Port Workers Union was formed in the late 1940s. In Zimbabwe, the Southern Rhodesia African National Congress, formed in 1934, was essentially a pressure group, while the Cape Native Convention, formed in South Africa in 1887, was in the same category. Initially, the aims of these organizations were limited to obtaining better deals from their respective governments in terms of pay, and in getting relief from racial discrimination. The Namibian Lüderitz Port Workers Union organised two strikes of Ovambo workers in 1952 and 1953. The Southern Rhodesian African National Congress tried to persuade the government to adopt reforms, while the Cape Native Convention tried to argue against the creation of the Union of South Africa. These associations later gave way to real political parties, which articulated their demands for political participation in clearer and stronger terms. When these were banned, the political parties in all the countries went underground, and some into exile, from where they organized riots and sabotage against economic installations. These were to serve as antecedents to full scale armed struggle. The excerpt below, taken from an ANC document, captures the feelings that resulted in the graduation from street riots and sabotage to full revolutionary wars in all three countries:

The riots, the street-fight, the outbursts of unorganised violence, individual terrorism: these were symptoms of the militant spirit, but not pointers to revolutionary techniques. The winning of our freedom by armed struggle – the only method left open to us – demands more than passion. It demands an understanding and an implementation of revolutionary theory and techniques.[13]

The armed struggle in Zimbabwe, the first of the three to achieve its objective, began effectively in 1961, when the Zimbabwean African People's Union (ZAPU) emerged out of the hitherto proscribed National Democratic Party (NDP).[14] The party later broke into two, and a splinter group formed the Zimbabwean African National Union (ZANU) in 1963.[15] The split had several implications for the country's war of liberation. One, which is important for this analysis, was the ethnic politics it evoked. By the time the two political parties were established, it became clear that ZAPU was dominated by the Ndebeles, the smaller of the two major ethnic groups in Zimbabwe, while ZANU comprised largely the Shona group. This created considerable disagreements, and despite the apparent unanimity of their intention, disagreement between them were often profound enough to set back the armed struggle.

Both ZANU and ZAPU had military wings which engaged the government security forces in a protracted war that lasted more than a decade. ZANU created the Zimbabwean African National Liberation Army (ZANLA), while ZAPU had the Zimbabwean People's Revolutionary Army (ZIPRA). These military wings, like the political parties, were largely structured along ethnic lines. ZIPRA, like ZAPU, drew its combatants from the Ndebele ethnic group, while ZANLA was made up largely of Shonas.[16]

The guerrilla war in Namibia provided an interesting contrast. Comparing the geographical nature of the country and its population with the war fought for its liberation, Paul Moorcraft opined that: 'never had so few fought so bitterly for so long and for so much territory as in this Africa's last colony'.[17] Organized opposition by Namibians to South African domination started in 1958, with the formation of the Ovamboland People's Organization. Two years later, this was renamed the South West African People's Organization (SWAPO). The members of the organization were predominantly recruited from the Ovambo ethnic group – a factor which SWAPO opponents often stressed in their efforts to portray the organization as being unrepresentative. The organization later formed the People's Liberation Army of Namibia (PLAN) to prosecute the war for the country's independence.

In both Namibia and Zimbabwe, the armed struggle had one early similarity. This was because of the two critical events which raised the stakes in the conflict. In Rhodesia, Prime Minister Ian Smith, in 1965, announced a Unilateral Declaration of Independence (UDI), which severed

Rhodesia from British colonial control.[18] This changed the political climate of Rhodesia, as it heightened the desire for African independence. Between the declaration in November 1965 and July 1966, there were 80 incidents involving sabotage (20 attacks on the railway system, 23 attempts to interfere with essential services, 32 petrol bomb attacks and five attacks involving explosives).[19] Also, between the pronouncement of the UDI and February 1966, there were 36 cases of malicious damage of crops and seven cases of attacks on animals.[20] The key development in the case of Namibia was the International Court of Justice's rejection in 1966 on technical grounds, of the case brought by Ethiopia and Liberia to challenge South Africa's occupation of Namibia. Although figures are not available, the court's ruling increased the momentum of the armed struggle. In fact, a few days after the ICJ's ruling, SWAPO announced that it had no 'alternative but to rise in arms'.[21]

The evolution of black political parties in South Africa dated back to the formation of the African National Congress (ANC) in 1912, and it is one of the ironies of southern African politics that the ANC, which fathered several similar organizations in the region,[22] was the last to accomplish its objective. This, no doubt, was largely because of the formidable and entrenched nature of the government it fought against. At the time of its formation, defining the nature of the struggle in South Africa was difficult. Describing it as a national liberation struggle would not be correct, as it would presuppose a foreign occupying colonial power. South Africa's situation was obviously different from Rhodesia, which many considered a not-yet-decolonized British colony. Finally, describing it as a struggle against apartheid may not be completely accurate because apartheid had yet to be fully 'legalised', although of course its practice was entrenched. All these made it initially difficult for the ANC to have a clear ideological framework for the prosecution of its struggle. This was a problem that remained for sometime in the party's long fight against minority rule.

African nationalism in South Africa, as in Rhodesia, was a 'contradictory phenomenon, with different, and at times, antagonistic with divergent trends and tendencies'.[23] In 1959, the ANC, like the ZAPU in Zimbabwe, split up over disagreement on the alliance the party made with left-wing whites and Indian organizations. The faction that opposed this alliance later broke away from the organization to form the Pan-African Congress (PAC).[24] Unlike the case of Rhodesia, however, there was no serious ethnic cleavage involved. The ANC and the PAC later took to armed struggle. The armed wing of the ANC, known as the *Umkhonto we Sizwe* (MK) (Spear of the Nation) was formed in 1961, under the leadership of Nelson Mandela, who was to become Southern Africa's most famous leader. The PAC's armed wing was known as the *Poqo*, meaning 'ourselves alone'. The party totally repudiated the ANC's relationship with non-Africans. The party made it clear that there was virtually no place for non-blacks in a future South Africa. Once the political parties in the three countries had formed their military wings, the battle lines were drawn.

On Tactics, Performance and External Support[25]

It is impossible here to provide a detailed account of the armed struggle in all three countries.[26] All that is attempted, therefore, is an examination of major themes to bring out similarities and differences in the struggles that took place in these countries. The armed struggles in Namibia, South Africa and Zimbabwe have much in common, such that it would be difficult to discuss one without making reference – even in passing – to others. In fact, the differences that existed were introduced by local ingredients, which gave each of the struggles its peculiar shape. No doubt, what accounted for the similarities is the historical evolution of the three countries as settler societies.

The first and perhaps most important similarity in the armed struggle was the form each took. In all the countries, but especially in Zimbabwe and Namibia, the armed struggle took the form of a guerrilla war. This is not surprising, giving their inferiority in numbers (at least initially) and in weapons. At the outbreak of the war in Zimbabwe, for example, only seven guerrillas took part. In fact, it was not until late June 1967 that the number of guerrilla insurgents in a single operation reached two digits.[27] By contrast, the military strength of their adversary was more than 5,000. The statistics in Namibia are similar – only 32 took part in the famous Ongulumbashe episode against a several thousand-strong South African force. At the start of the struggle in South Africa, the MK and the Poqo were numbered in hundreds. Although in subsequent years the numerical strength of the guerrillas in all three countries was to increase dramatically, their enormous inferiority at the outbreak of the struggle made the adoption of guerrilla tactics the only realistic option. Shortly before the declaration of the of the armed struggle, all the armed wings in these countries had sent people abroad for training in guerrilla insurgency. Egypt, Algeria, the Soviet Union and China provided such training.[28]

Circumstances, however, made these guerrilla struggles differ from country to country. In Namibia and Zimbabwe, the guerrillas soon acquired sufficient strength and firepower to prosecute a sustained and fairly well-articulated war against the minority regimes, but this was not the case in South Africa, largely because of the strength and force of the apartheid military machine and the absence of a stable external base. In all three countries the armed struggles were divided into phases, determined by internal developments in their respective countries and wider regional, indeed global, politics. The Namibian struggle has been divided into five phases.[29] Phase one (1959–66) covered the period from exile to the first strike in Ongulumbashe; phase two (1966–74) was the period of transfer of SWAPO headquaters to Lusaka; phase three (1974–78) involved the SWAPO offensive from Angola (following that country's independence); phase four (1978–84) covered the period when SWAPO's efforts had more impact on the SADF, making some parts of the country a no-go-area for the SADF; phase five (1985–88) ended with the Cuito Cuanavale débâcle. Each of these phases had military and political significance of its own.[30]

Zimbabwe's war was broken down into three phases. The first phase covered the period between the declaration of the UDI in 1965 and 1968, during which there were uncoordinated insurgent campaigns; the second phase (1968–72) involved more militant action; and the third phase from 1972 to 1979) when the war ended. South Africa's struggle, too, may be divided into five phases. Phase one covered the beginning of the armed struggle in 1961 to the arrest and detention of the MK leaders in 1963; phase two lasted from 1963 to the Soweto uprising of 1976; phase three concentrated on the period from 1976 to 1984, the era which saw a further clampdown in the aftermath of the Soweto riots; phase four covered 1984–86, when the increasing influence of the military in South African politics resulted in more internal repression of African nationalists and attacks on Frontline States; phase five lasted from 1987 to the release of Nelson Mandela in February 1990.

In all three countries, armed struggles were launched with support of the black ruled neighbouring states. In some cases, neighbours offered their territories as headquarters and launching grounds for their military offensives. In Zimbabwe, ZANLA and ZIPRA guerrillas launched their attack on the Rhodesian minority regime from Zambia and Mozambique respectively. Initially, all the attacks were launched from Zambia, but with the independence of Mozambique in 1975, geographical considerations and the establishment of a durable camaraderie between the ZANU leadership and the new FRELIMO leadership in Mozambique led the ZANLA guerrilla to transfer their military headquarters to Mozambique. In the same way, SWAPO first established its base in Tanzania in 1961, moving later to Zambia in 1968, and finally to Angola in 1976. All these countries served as bases for launching insurgent attacks on the South African presence inside Namibia. South Africa's experience in this regard was different. Although all the countries in the region allowed the ANC (and in some cases, the PAC) to establish a presence in their countries, they were equally conscious of the retaliatory measures South Africa could take if they allowed their countries to be used as bases for launching attacks on the

Republic. The only country that was initially relaxed in this respect was Mozambique, but this too, had to cease when South Africa unleashed unacceptable retaliatory damage on the country.[31] Moreover, SWAPO in Namibia and ZANU/ZAPU in Zimbabwe made use of their neighbours to a greater degree than the ANC and PAC in their forays into South Africa.

In Namibia and Zimbabwe, the initial performance of the guerrillas was lamentable. Some examples: in Zimbabwe, early attempts by the guerrillas to attack Rhodesian installations were unsuccessful. The April 1966 attempt to blow up a power pylon near Sinoia failed and all the seven men involved were killed.[32] In May, another seven guerrillas were again caught and shot after they had succeeded in killing a white farmer and his wife. More daring incursions made in 1967 were only a little more than suicide missions and most guerrillas were arrested or killed. Namibians did not fare better. In late August 1966, a South African police unit of 32 men attacked the Ongulumbashe SWAPO base inside Ovamboland. Although SWAPO saw the attack coming, they decided to stand up and fight. After a brief encounter, lasting less than five minutes, two insurgents were dead and nine were captured. This dismal performance was due more to inexperience than any other factor. This is a phenomenon that the three countries shared with the Lusophone countries of Angola and Mozambique.

There were initial practical difficulties with the armed struggle. This again was more apparent in Namibia and Zimbabwe. In Namibia, SWAPO suffered enormous political and logistical difficulties. Access to Ovamboland was exceptionally difficult, especially from the first SWAPO base in Zambia. Guerrillas were forced to make their way on foot via the 250 mile panhandle of the Caprivi Strip. Carrying heavy equipment for weeks across very sandy soil was arduous.[33] Zimbabwean guerrillas experienced the same problem, especially ZAPU forces operating from Zambia. The Zambezi river that marks the natural boundaries between Zambia and Rhodesia is 450 miles in length. With its 'untamed terrain, a heaven for wildlife, mosquitoes, tsetse flies, mopani bees and vultures',[34] the early Zimbabwean guerrillas faced major practical difficulties.

In all the countries considered in this article, there were also extra-African ramifications. In Namibia and South Africa, the politics of this extra-African connection derived from the Cold War. In Namibia, the Soviet Union supported SWAPO and considerable military assistance was given to the movement to prosecute the war of independence. The link between the Namibian war of independence and the conflict in Angola meant greater Soviet military support. This, inevitably, led the United States to perceive SWAPO's struggle for independence in Cold War terms, and it explained, at least in part, the military support the United States gave UNITA rebels in Angola. It also explained the sympathy Washington and its allies showed for

South Africa's position in the controversy over the implementation of UN Resolution 435 which called for Namibian independence.

The ANC's struggle evoked deeper and more intricate external involvement. First, like that of Namibia, the external involvement was shaped by the Cold War. In this connection, the ANC and the PAC obtained military support from the communist world, while South Africa was, throughout the conflict, a beneficiary of military, economic and psychological support from the Western world. Although there was open condemnation of apartheid by the Western alliance, there was also condemnation for the support the communist world gave South African guerrillas. For the West, the problem of apartheid could only be solved by peaceful negotiation.

The external support from the communist world for the armed struggle also had its own politics, which were no less intricate than the Cold War conflict. Here the Sino-Soviet rivalry came into play. The former Soviet Union supported the ANC. However, when the PAC broke away in 1959, the party sought and obtained support from China.

Zimbabwe's experience in this regard was different, as there was no distinct Cold War involvement in the struggle for independence, since none of the Western powers supported the Smith regime. Yet the Sino-Soviet rivalry made its impact on the guerrilla struggle. The Soviet Union supported the united ZAPU until its split in 1963. With the breakaway of ZANU and the subsequent formation of its ZANLA military wing, the new party sought and obtained military assistance from China.[35] This introduced a major factor that was endure in the politics of Zimbabwe, even in its post-independence years.

Another development common to all three countries was the attempt to mobilize mass support – in varying degrees, and with a varying degree of success – in the armed struggle. The guerrillas soon realised that active participation of the populace was essential for victory. Zimbabwe made the best use of this technique. The two armed wings, especially ZANLA, embarked on a massive indoctrination campaign to explain the justification of their struggle. This had a marked effect on guerrilla activity. Before the mobilization phase, it was not uncommon for individuals to give up guerrilla activists among them under pressure from the authorities.

Religion played an important role in the wars in all three countries. In Zimbabwe, where the influence of religion was most profound, the guerrillas relied enormously on spiritual mediums to give warning and advice on the prosecution of the war. How effective this was remains a matter of opinion, but what cannot be disputed is that it assisted the liberation cause, as it provided sufficient motivation for the guerrillas. Of the two guerrilla wings in Zimbabwe, ZANLA relied more on the use of mediums. So effective was this that the members of the Rhodesian security force adopted the use of spiritual mediums to justify their position in the war.[36] In later years, the SADF was to draw lessons from the Rhodesian experience, and the Directorate of Military Intelligence (DMI) attempted to use the South African traditional religions to establish a foothold in the black community. The South African Traditional Faith Healer Council (SATHC), with approximately 400,000 members and considerable influence with the rural and urban areas, was the best tool. Its secretary and permanent advisors were thus made members of the DMI. The council also received financial assistance from the government, and delegations of the council met with President P. W. Botha, Magnus Malan (Minister of Defence) and Adriaan Vlok (Minister of Justice) on several occasions.[37]

Responses to the Armed Struggle

Once the battlelines were drawn in all these countries and the armed struggles graduated from an initial passive resistance to full scale wars, the minority regimes in Namibia, Rhodesia and South Africa immediately initiated moves to counter guerrilla campaigns. The first important thing to note about these minority/illegal regimes was their perception of their struggle. In the regional context, the governments believed that they were fighting to preserve a heritage that was passed down to them from generations. As compared with the Portuguese, the white South Africans and Rhodesians believed they had a greater stake in the region. While the Portuguese could go (as they actually did eventually) when the going got tough and the cost was unjustifiable, the South Africans and Rhodesians believed there was no alternative but to fight it out with the guerrillas. A second perception derived from a wider global interpretation of the insurgent wars. They all believed that they were fighting communist infiltration in a region of strategic importance to the 'free world'. The regimes in question used this infiltration to win sympathy and support from the west.

The military option open to the governments in Rhodesia and South Africa, once the revolutionary fighters in these countries and Namibia adopted a guerrilla strategy, was counter-insurgency. In understanding the counter-insurgency method adopted by the government forces, some general features peculiar to counter-insurgency doctrine should be considered. Philip Schlesinger has identified three:

(a) they all had clearly formulated assumptions regarding world order;

(b) counter-insurgency theories took the legitimacy of the state for granted;

(c) revolutionary struggles are seen as the product of external manipulation rather than structural contradictions.[38]

The military operation in Rhodesia was the most complex. There are two reasons for this: first, put together, both ZANLA and ZIPRA presented to the Rhodesian Security Front a capability far more formidable than that possessed by the ANC and SWAPO in relation to the regimes in South Africa and Namibia respectively; second, by 1974, sympathy for the white minority regime had dropped considerably, with serious implications for the Smith minority regime in the prosecution of the war. From the early 1950s, white Rhodesian military leaders had begun to analyze guerrilla operations elsewhere. In fact, many Rhodesians had fought in the Malayan campaign of the 1950s.[39] They also studied other conflicts, for example, the Arab–Israeli Wars. In short, even before UDI, many white Rhodesians had anticipated a guerrilla struggle in the country, and had started taking steps to cope with its eventual outbreak.[40]

The military operation itself was extensively planned, even if not properly executed at different stages. At its peak, the strength of the Rhodesian Security Force (RSF) was about 46,000 men, including 15,000 men of regular status. Of these, 25,000 men could be mobilized at any one time.[41] There were two regular infantry battalions – the Rhodesian Light Infantry (RLI) and the Rhodesian African Rifles (RAF). These battalions were mixed, incorporating both white and black soldiers. There were also two counter-insurgency forces – the Grey Scouts and the Selous Scouts – both with a reputation respectively for speed of attack and an ability to stay in the bush for lengthy periods. Equally important was the Special Air Service (SAS), known for its aggressive long-range reconnaissance, military intelligence and small-scale assault tactics. All these were backed by an array of support units like the medical corps, pay corps, service corps, engineers and military police. The RSF concentrated on straightforward military suppression, while the SADF had a more diverse and elaborate perception of the guerrilla threat, and there were other reasons – beside counter-insurgency – for South African militarization. The National Security Management System, established in the 1980s, was an elaborate attempt to provide both intelligence on potentials flashpoints in the urban areas and at the same time win the 'hearts and minds' by collaborating with local government authorities to provide basic services to the black majority.

In the early stages of the South African campaign in Namibia, responsibility for 'peacekeeping' was given to the South African Police (SAP), and subsequently to the regional control of the SADF at the Grootfontein military base. In 1977, military activities in Namibia were centralized in Windhoek. This in turn prepared the way for the creation of a

South West African Territorial Force (SWATF) in 1980. However, from the late 1970s, the extent of South Africa's commitment to the war in Namibia can be understood against the background of Pretoria's wider involvement in the Angolan war. In May 1980, the SADF launched Operation 'Reindeer' – the first major incursion into Angola to destroy SWAPO bases inside the country. As Paul Moorcraft has pointed out, the operation marked SADF's entry into large scale semi-conventional warfare.[42] It consisted of three 'sub-operations': an airborne attack on a SWAPO base near Cassinga; a mechanized force attack on the north of the border; and an heliborne force attack on small bases east of Chetequera. South Africa's strategy was extensive and expensive.

The SADF tried to conduct a 'textbook' counter-insurgence campaign in Namibia.[43] Like the Rhodesian Army, the SADF, too applied lessons from Malaya, Vietnam and Algeria. Yet, while Pretoria adopted the military lessons direct from these case studies, it ignored the political lessons, at least for most of the 1970 decade. With the coming of the 1980s, South Africa diverted attention to the political front, where, like the Rhodesian, they created their own internal proxies. It was estimated that, by the 1980s, the cost of the Namibia war reached R4 million a day, and approximately 20,000–30,000 SADF and 22,000 SWATF were committed to the war.[44] It was thus not surprising that, when the turning point came in the Angolan war after the Battle of Cuito Cuanavale in 1987, it also signalled the beginning of Namibian independence.

Once South Africa recognized that its position in Namibia was untenable, its strategy changed to influencing the outcome of the election. It was here that the South African Directorate of Military Intelligence (DMI) played an important role. According to Williams, the DMI attempted to derail the independence process and to influence the outcome of an election.[45] In January 1989, General Jannie Geldenhuys, while addressing a group of senior SADF and SWATF officers in a Defence Force mess in Windhoek, instructed them to do all they could to prevent SWAPO from winning.[46] Other plans were to be more potentially catastrophic: the planned assassination of two senior SWAPO officials, Hamutenya and Danny Tjongarero; the contamination of the drinking water at the Dobra refugee camp in Namibia (housing several SWAPO returnees) with the cholera virus; the detonation of explosives at SWAPO meetings; and falsification of UN Transitional Assistance Group Signals to demonstrate that a SWAPO troop build-up was occurring on the Namibian border.[47]

South Africa's reactions to the activities of the ANC and the PAC were twofold: political and military suppression of the internal activities of the revolutionary forces and the destabilization of neighbouring states. Black activists caught were given long jail terms while some were in fact hanged.

There were also jailed black activists who died in police custody under suspicious circumstances.

The second method – the destabilization of the neighbouring states – is one that has attracted considerable attention from scholars.[48] In summary, the policy behind this strategy was to destabilize these countries to such an extent that harbouring the ANC and/or other similar organizations would become dangerous and unsupportable. The effect of these on South Africa and the entire region was the militarization of South African politics. In most cases, the strategies of the minority governments worked, at least in postponing their inevitable end. One other factor that assisted them in the prolongation of their rule was the activities of the blacks who opposed the armed struggle.

Collaborators or Pacifists?

In all the three countries, there were indigenous elements who, for a variety of reasons, opposed the adopted armed struggle and instead supported the minority regimes in the hope of a 'peaceful' solution to the conflict. Throughout the liberation struggle, these groups became controversial – evoking both admiration and condemnation from the minority regime and the revolutionary fighters respectively. To the minority administration, these people were regarded as pacifists, who wanted a peaceful end to the crisis in their respective countries, and thus minimize the casualties that might result from conflict. The minority governments thus regarded the vilification poured on these people as wanton, ill-informed and unfortunate. To the advocates of the armed struggle, however, these people were simply collaborators. While agreeing that there were bound to be differences over means of achieving the same end, the ease and the extent to which these people supported the minority regimes on key issues struck the armed fighters as bordering on treachery.

In all the countries, the black advocates and opponents of the armed struggle disagreed on three main issues: the terms and timing of independence, and the process. While the advocates of armed struggle wanted a complete handover of power, those who opposed the armed struggle were ready to accept a compromise, that is, a gradual transition with major concessions to the minority whites. With regard to timing, the protagonists of the armed struggle wanted independence immediately; for their opponents, independence was seen as a gradual non-violent process to be achieved on mutually agreeable terms. Finally, the advocates of the armed struggle believed that peaceful dialogue was ineffective and should be disregarded, while opponents still believed in the efficacy of dialogue, negotiation and compromise.

There were, however, differences in the process through which these groups of anti-armed struggle elements emerged, and in what they did to frustrate the cause of the armed struggle in their respective countries. To a large extent, these depended on the historical peculiarities of each of the countries, the strength and extent of the armed struggle and the pattern of international involvement in the politics of the independence struggle. In Zimbabwe, three individuals – Bishop Abel Muzorewa, Reverend Ndabaningi Sithole and Chief Jeremiah Chirau – represented the group that opposed the armed struggle. And it must be noted that at some stage in their nationalist careers, they had all taken part in the armed struggle, only to change their political views at a later stage. So compromised were these people that they were described by the whites as 'moderate' politicians.

The story of the arrangement between Ian Smith and the moderate politicians is well known; all that is required here is a summary of the similarities and differences between Rhodesia on the one hand, and Namibia and South Africa on the other hand. Largely because of pressure from South Africa, Ian Smith stepped down and conducted an election to ensure a 'transition' to majority rule. The constitution on which the election was held conceded key positions on security, finance and home affairs to the whites. The election which was boycotted by ZANU and ZAPU was won by Bishop Abel Muzorewa who become the first (and last) President of Zimbabwe/Rhodesia. He administered the country for almost two years before the pressure of increased guerrilla activities and wider global criticism forced him to concede another election with wider participation.

In Namibia, the South African government, having realised the inevitability of granting independence to Namibia, created the Democratic Turnhalle Alliance (DTA), to challenge the monopoly SWAPO had on the country. In origin, DTA was a constitutional conference, gathering a motley collection of South African selected delegates. The conference was unrepresentative and the outcome was flawed. SWAPO was banned from participating in the conference, while some political parties refused to participate. To fill these gaps, the South African government created political parties to take part in the conference. The constitutional conference produced a declaration of intent two weeks after its inauguration: ethnic representation at a tribal level; an overarching *de facto* white national government with its dominant ethnic group, the whites, capable of vetoing all decisions, Bantustan-style regionalism in rural areas and, in theory, multiple ethnic enclaves in urban areas.[49] A political party, supported by the South African government, later emerged from the proceedings.

The DTA, though it shared fundamental objectives with the 'pacifists' in Zimbabwe and South Africa, differed in one major way: it was the only one that was multiracial. Although most of those who attended the conference were blacks, and blacks formed the bulk of the political party when it was eventually formed, the secretariat of the DTA was controlled by whites. In fact the party leader, Dirk Mudge, was white. Perhaps what accounted for this was the nature of Namibia's political history and the impact this had on the nationalist evolution in the country. Unlike Zimbabwe and South Africa where the minority whites were effectively dominant and the battlelines drawn between two groups living within the same geographical area, armed struggle in Namibia was with a minority regime based outside the country. Against this background, the government in Pretoria had to establish a Namibia-based movement that would represent white interests but also one that would be able to ward off allegations of racism by incorporating blacks into its membership. In the end, the DTA was sworn in as the government of Namibia in July 1980, with Mudge as its chairman. The party ruled uncomfortably till 1983, when it collapsed. Remnants of it were, however, to survive till the 1990 independence election.

In the South African case, only the ANC and the PAC took up arms against the apartheid government. However, those blacks who were perceived as collaborators belonged to two different categories. First were those who supported the apartheid creation of the black homeland states; the second involved individuals who accepted minor political appointments as councillors and local chiefs from the apartheid government.

The creation of homeland states in the 1960s and 1970s was the major government strategy designed to ensure separate development of ethnic groups. Four black territories were granted nominal 'independence' by Pretoria. The major armed movements – ANC and PAC – opposed the creation and none of the four created 'independent' states achieved recognition outside South Africa. At their creation and for most of the period that followed, the ANC considered these states and their leaders as collaborators in apartheid South African strategy. The acceptance of such a fundamental alteration to the South African state put the leaders of these homeland states in opposition to the ANC. Although some homeland leaders later realigned themselves with the ANC, some fought the ANC's wish to have a united South African state with a powerful central administration to the bitter end. Lucas Mangope's Bophutatswana and Mangosuthu Buthelezi's Kwazulu homeland states were the most obvious examples. Others identified by the armed struggle as collaborators were those who accepted political appointments from the apartheid regime. These and others believed to be informants to the police became victims of township violence in the 1980s.

Yet another group of 'collaborators' existed in all three countries. These were the blacks that joined the security forces of the minority regimes. In Zimbabwe, these people belonged to two groups. There were those that joined the Rhodesian Security Forces; as mentioned earlier, these individuals served mainly in the Rhodesian African Rifles. The second group were those that joined the 'Auxiliaries', the military force created to sustained the white-backed Muzorewa government in power. In Namibia, many blacks, even among the Ovambos, joined the South African created South West African Territorial Force (SWATF), while the homeland states in South Africa created their own security forces. In the post-independence phases of all three countries, integrating these groups into a reconstituted national army became a major preoccupation of the new governments.

How Wars End

In Namibia, South Africa and Zimbabwe, the ultimate resolution of the armed struggle came through peaceful negotiation and transitional elections. Again in all, the international community played a significant roles in resolving the conflicts. In Zimbabwe, the first of the three to attain majority rule, Britain assumed the colonial authority it had lost following the UDI in 1965. A sub-committee set up after the 1979 Commonwealth Heads of Government summit in Lusaka, Zambia, provided the basis for a constitutional dialogue on Zimbabwe's future. These included: majority rule; participation of all the parties involved; a democratic constitution safeguarding the interests of the "minorities", and a free and fair election supervised by the British government with representatives from other Commonwealth countries. This paved the way for the Lancaster House Conference which eventually brought independence to Zimbabwe in April 1980.

Namibia's independence followed a similar process, as the United Nations, the successor of the League of Nations that mandated the territory to South Africa in 1919 administered the final decolonization rites. The end of the Cold War and South Africa's changing perception of its role in the region accelerated Namibia's independence. By 1988, the issue of the Cuban presence in Angola, had been satisfactorily resolved and the UN became responsible for organizing pre-independence elections. The process ended with the independence of Namibia in 1990 – a decade after Zimbabwean independence.

The South African armed struggle ended in a similar way. With the accession of F.W. de Klerk to the South African presidency in 1989, and his subsequent adoption of a South African version of *perestroika*, efforts to a reach political settlement began. In February 1990, de Klerk unbanned the ANC and other political parties, repealed major apartheid laws and released Nelson Mandela. Events subsequently moved fast and election was slated for April 1994. Apprehensions about white and black extremists derailing the peace process proved unfounded, and a new South Africa was born in May 1994.

Conclusion

In all the three countries, the dialogue and negotiation began after the warring sides in each realised that some form of compromise was inevitable. In Zimbabwe, although the guerrilla fighters had succeeded in frustrating the government, the Rhodesian Security Forces still possessed enough strength to deal decisively with the Frontline States, and thus affect the lifeline of the guerrillas.[50] In Namibia, while SWAPO had maintained its position as a credible liberation movement, further gains had been cut short by South Africa. In South Africa, although the guerrilla forces did not make any significant military gains, they came close to making the country ungovernable.

A second point of note is that, in all three cases, the guerrilla fighters made political concessions to cater for the interests of the white minority. With respect to Zimbabwe, the Lancaster House Conference devised a constitution with 20 seats reserved for the white minority in a hundred-seat parliament. Furthermore, this arrangement was to last for ten years. In Namibia, SWAPO had to cooperate in drafting the constitution with those political parties that had won significant minority representation in the election. This gave the DTA a role to play in post-independence Namibia. South Africa's case was more complex, as de Klerk had to go into the negotiation conscious of the fears of the whites for their safety in a black-ruled South Africa. Indeed, in 1991, he paused in his negotiations with the black political parties to get a mandate, via a referendum, from his white constituency. In the end, his National Party won major concessions, and in fact won enough seats to have representatives in the Government of National Unity.

Although a complete account of the armed struggle against illegal/minority regimes in southern Africa awaits its own historian, this essay has attempted to identify and discuss some of the features that appear common to the struggles in Namibia, South Africa and Zimbabwe. An attempt, too, has been made to identify some of the differences in approach to the armed struggle in each case.

NOTES

1. Virtually all aspects of the 'new' South Africa have received scholarly attention ranging from internal security and economic reconstruction, to the government's efforts at correcting the legacies of apartheid and South Africa's role in regional affairs. Some of the studies include: Carole Birch, *The New South Africa: Prospects for Regional Security and Stability* (London: Centre for Defence Studies 1994); Valerie Seward, *The New South Africa and Its Neighbours: The Challenges of Democratisation* (London: HMSO 1994); W.J. Breytenbach, *Bargaining in North/South Politics: Policy Options for a New South Africa* (Stellenbosch: Centre for Int. and Comparative Politics 1994); Alexander Johnston, Sipho Shezi and Garvin Bradshew (eds. *Constitution-Making in the New South Africa* (London: Leicester UP 1993).
2. In some cases, research began before the attainment of majority rule in South Africa. See, for example, Heribert Adam and Kogila Moodley, *The Opening of the Apartheid Mind: Options for the New South Africa* (Berkeley: U. of California Press 1993).
3. Two of the countries have had a varied nomenclature. In this article, South West Africa is occasionally used for Namibia, while Rhodesia and Zimbabwe are often used interchangeably.
4. For more on this, see Michael Macara, 'The Political Sociology of Racial Dominance, 1890–1971', Unpub. PhD Thesis, U. of Rhodesia, 1982.
5. Quoted from ibid, p.27.
6. L. Kuper 'Political Change in White Settler Societies: The Possibility of Peaceful Democratisation', in M.G. Smith and L. Kuper (eds.) *Pluralism in Africa* (Berkeley: U. of California Press 1969) pp.170–1.
7. Macara (note 4) p.27.
8. Ibid.
9. These figures are quoted from Lawyers Committee for Human Rights, *Zimbabwe: Wages of War* (NY 1986) p.17.
10. *Namibia*, Amnesty International Briefing, 1977.
11. The whites were granted representation in the South African Parliament in 1949.
12. The Odendaal Report was the outcome of a commission set up by South Africa to examine the situation in Namibia.
13. Declaration at the First Consultative Conference of the ANC in April 1969. As quoted from Sheridan Johns and Hunt Davis, *Mandela, Tambo and the ANC: The Struggle Against Apartheid, 1948–1990. A Documentary Survey* (Oxford: OUP 1991) pp.281–2.
14. The NDP emerged from the African National Congress (ANC) which was banned by the government in Feb. 1959, and which itself arose from the City Youth League (CYL) which James Chikerema, George Nyandoro and Edson Sithole formed in 1953.
15. For more information about the ZAPU split, see Joshua Nkomo, *The Story of My Life*, (London: Methuen 1984) pp.109–19; Nathan Shamuyarira, *Crisis in Rhodesia* (London: André Deutsch 1965) pp.173–93.
16. There were other political parties that emerged at one time or the other during the struggle for independence of Zimbabwe. I have disregarded most of them here because of their limited relevance to this article.
17. Paul Moorcraft, *African Nemesis: War and Revolution in Southern Africa, 1945–2010* (London: Brassey's 1989) p.101.
18. There are many studies on UDI, but perhaps the most comprehensive is Robert Good, *Rhodesia: The International Politics of the Rhodesian Rebellion* (London: Faber 1973).
19. See Abiodun Alao, 'The Defence and Security Implications of the Liberation War on Zimbabwe, 1980–1987'. Unpub. PhD Thesis, U. of London 1992.
20. Ibid.
21. Susan Brown, 'Diplomacy by Other Means – SWAPO's Liberation War', in Colin Leys and John Saul (eds.) *Namibia's Liberation Struggle: The Two Edge Sword* (London: James Currey 1995) p.20.
22. Some of these organizations include: the Basutoland Congress Party, the Malawi Congress Party and the Southern Rhodesia African National Congress.
23. Francis Meli, *South Africa Belong to Us* (Harare: Zimbabwe Publishing House 1988) p.137.
24. For the ANC's account of the split, see Nelson Mandela, *Long Walk to Freedom: The*

Autobiography of Nelson Mandela (London: Little, Brown 1994) pp.214–16.

25. Some of the books that have discussed aspects of the armed struggle include: for Zimbabwe: Henrick Ellert, *The Rhodesian Front War: Counter Insurgency and Guerrilla War In Rhodesia, 1962–1980* (Gweru: Mambo Press 1980); David Martin and Phyllis Johnson, *The Struggle for Zimbabwe: The Chimurenga War* (London: Faber 1981). For Namibia: Du Pisani, *A SWA/Namibia: The Politics of Continuity and Change* (Johannesburg: Ball 1986) and Peter Katjavivi, A History of Resistance in Namibia (London: James Currey 1988). For South Africa: Noel Manganyi and André Du Toit, *Political Violence and the Struggle in South Africa* (London: Macmillan 1990) and Robert Davies, Dan O'Meara and Sipho Dlamini, *The Struggle for South Africa* (London: Zed 1988).

26. It was believed that the ending of the armed struggles would result in a proliferation of publications on the subject. Shortly after independence, the Zimbabwean government launched an history project involving the three armed wings – ZANLA, ZIPRA and the Rhodesian Army – producing their separate accounts of the war. This has, however, suffered setbacks, one of which was the disappearance of several files of ZIPRA documents.

27. This occurred when 80 guerrillas attacked a Rhodesian installation in Wankie.

28. All these countries at this time had radical credentials. Egypt was then under Gamal Abdul Nasser, and the nationalization of the Suez Canal gave him a radical reputation. Algeria had only just completed its independence war against France.

29. This division was made by Susan Brown (note 21) pp.19–39.

30. For more on this, see ibid.

31. This was to result in the Nkomati Accord between South Africa and Mozambique.

32. These individuals were later regarded as heroes of the Zimbabwean struggle, and the date of their death was apotheosized as the central event of the war.

33. Moorcraft (note 17).

34. Martin Meredith, *The Past is Another Country, Rhodesia UDI to Zimbabwe* (London: André Deutsch 1981) p.67.

35. For more on the politics of Sino/Soviet rivalry in the Zimbabwean war of independence, see Alao (note 19) pp.45–9.

36. Discussions with former members of the Rhodesian Army.

37. See, Rockland Williams, 'Back to Barracks: The Changing Parameters of Civil-Military Relations Under the Botha and De Klerk Administration', unpub. PhD thesis, U. of Essex, 1992.

38. As quoted from ibid. p.200.

39. One of these was Lt.-Gen. Peter Walls, who was to become the last Commander of the Rhodesian Security Forces.

40. For more on this, see Lewis Gann and Thomas Henriksen, *The Struggle for Zimbabwe: Battle in the Bush* (NY: Praeger 1981) p.64.

41. Ibid. p.68

42. Moorcraft (note 17) p.219.

43. Ibid. p.195

44. Ibid. p.229.

45. Williams (note 37) p.221.

46. Ibid.

47. Ibid. p.222.

48. Some of these include: Joseph Hanlon, *Beggar Your Neighbour* (London: James Currey 1986); Susanna Smith, *Frontline States: The Right to a Future* (Oxford: Oxfam 1990); Phyllis Johnson and David Martin, *Apartheid Terrorism* (London: Commonwealth Secretariat 1989).

49. *Namibia in the 1980s* London: Catholic Inst. of Int. Relations/ British Council of Churches 1981, p.19.

50. Colin Legum, *Battlefronts of Southern Africa* (NY/London: Africana Publishing Co. 1988) p.127.

Politics and Violence in KwaZulu-Natal

ALEXANDER JOHNSTON

Political violence in KwaZulu-Natal has been the most serious threat to the integrity and stability of the post-apartheid settlement in South Africa. Although political violence declined to negligible levels in the rest of the country after the April 1994 elections, violent demonstrations and political killings have remained a feature of political conflict in KwaZulu-Natal. Rivalry between the ANC and the IFP has three main dimensions: a struggle to control territory: a struggle for the possession of 'Zulu tradition': and profound constitutional disagreement. Violence associated with this rivalry is exacerbated by acts of omission and commission by security forces, the prevalence of localized 'micro-conflicts', and the pathological social conditions which are apartheid's legacy.

Violence and the Threat to the 'Historic Compromise'

More than two years after the democratic election of 27 April 1994 which brought a legitimate national government to power in South Africa, political violence remains endemic in KwaZulu-Natal. Although casualty figures there fell after the election, as they did everywhere in the country, violence has remained at a higher level in this province than in others. In every month since April 1994, KwaZulu-Natal has contributed more than 63 per cent of the fatalities in political violence for the whole country. In several months it has claimed more than 75 per cent of the lives lost in this way.[1]

Since the political climate of the country changed so dramatically in February 1990 with the release of Nelson Mandela and the unbanning of the ANC, over 8,000 people have been killed in political violence in KwaZulu-Natal. However, high levels of violence were already being recorded there before 1990. Between the beginning of 1987 and mid-1990, around 4,000 people died,[2] principally in struggles between the United Democratic Front (UDF) and Inkatha.[3]

A revealing measure of this province's unenviable record is that it was the last region in which the old regime of white minority government lifted its state of emergency and the first province (to date, the only one) in which the new authorities have resorted to such measures.[4]

The overwhelming majority of politically-related deaths in South Africa have taken place in the two most populous provinces, Gauteng[5] and KwaZulu-Natal. Between 1990 and 1994, each topped the list of fatalities five times out of the ten half-yearly periods (January–June, July–

December). From July 1990 to June 1992, Gauteng consistently accounted for most deaths and from July 1992 to the end of 1994, with the exception of the second half of 1993, KwaZulu-Natal claimed this dubious distinction.[6]

Despite the periodic salience of violence in Gauteng, the conflicts of KwaZulu-Natal have attracted considerably more political, media and scholarly attention. This reflects a broad consensus that, compared with elsewhere, the violence there is endemic, intractable and potentially more destabilizing. This consensus is supported by the comparatively high, though reduced levels of political violence, which have continued in KwaZulu-Natal since 27 April 1994.[7]

The most serious element in this consensus is the belief that violence in KwaZulu-Natal has had (and continues to have) the potential to destabilize South Africa's painfully constructed 'historic compromise'. This compromise encompasses the negotiation and transition processes, the interim constitution, the 27 April 1994 election and the process for finalizing the new constitution. At every point, this evolving compromise has been obstructed and placed in jeopardy by the problems of fitting KwaZulu-Natal into its framework.

The IFP Challenge

Violence in KwaZulu-Natal is potentially destabilizing because it takes place in the context of intense political competition for the allegiance of the African majority. The focus of this competition is the Inkatha Freedom Party (IFP), the only political party which can rival the ANC in the arena of African popular politics. KwaZulu-Natal is, however, the only province where the IFP can claim a substantial foothold in this arena and it is this regional character which to a large extent defines the IFP's identity. It also deepens and exacerbates the IFP's rivalry with the ANC, inviting ominous ethnic and secessionist interpretations of the conflict.

The IFP's challenge to the ANC initially rested on the inter-action of three favourable circumstances. First, the potential for ethnic mobilization in African politics is much greater than in other parts of the country. By claiming that his party, and the KwaZulu 'homeland' statelet which it dominated, stood in direct line of succession from the nineteenth-century Zulu kingdom, the IFP leader Chief Mangosuthu Buthelezi has drawn on a rich source of political mythology. He has reinforced this by shrewd exploitation of the contemporary Zulu monarchy and other aspects of Zulu traditional life which have survived the depredations and adaptations of colonialism, white minority rule and modernization.[8]

Second, a geopolitical factor has encouraged the IFP's strategic position in the politics of KwaZulu-Natal. The territory of the KwaZulu homeland impinged more insistently on the borders of white cities and their satellite black townships than was the case with other black 'homelands'. This gave Buthelezi a base from which to challenge the ANC's surrogate, the UDF, in urban black areas. Indeed a major point of conflict between Inkatha and the UDF in the 1980s was the threatened incorporation of black townships into KwaZulu.

Third, the dynamics of white politics in Natal gave Buthelezi a purchase in white politics denied to any other black leader. Natal has no sizeable and concentrated Afrikaner population and the National Party has had no natural constituency there. The result was a mutually reinforcing alienation between Natal whites and the central government which disposed white elites in Natal to consider exploring accommodations with moderate black political forces. This gave Buthelezi valuable political space in which to resist the government's pressure to take independence for KwaZulu on the one hand, and to prosecute Inkatha's rivalry with the ANC on the other.

These three things allowed Inkatha to transcend the stereotype of homeland patronage politics. Patronage, through Inkatha's domination of the KwaZulu government, also played a part in its successful mobilization. Ethnicity clothed patronage in the mantle of popular politics, and patronage offered a material return for ethnic identification.

The movement thus created appeared to channel black aspirations within limits compatible with white vested interests. At the same time, it offered conservative blacks liberation from apartheid, without either the trauma of armed struggle and sanctions or the self-mutilating strategies of strikes and educational boycotts. Furthermore, Inkatha did not threaten to sweep away the established practices, prerogatives and relationships of traditional culture. On the contrary, it insisted on their intrinsic worth and rewarded them with political influence.

After February 1990 and the unbanning of the ANC, it became more difficult for the IFP to capitalize on the assets and conditions which had built it into a political force with a national presence and international credibility. The transformation of the ANC from a revolutionary insurgent movement to a party of constitutional and fiscal rectitude undercut Buthelezi's moderate appeal to whites. At the same time the sheer force of numbers which the ANC was able to deploy forced whites to recognize it as the major political force in the country. The National Party chose an adversarial partnership with the ANC to drive the negotiation process forward at the expense of an anti-ANC front with Buthelezi. To compound these strategic setbacks, the freeing of political activity legitimized the ANC's challenge to IFP dominance in KwaZulu-Natal. The ending of the state of emergency diluted the IFP's ability to prosecute its rivalry with the

ANC through the security legislation of the KwaZulu government. Perhaps most importantly, the ending of apartheid meant the reintegration of KwaZulu into South Africa and the demise of the one-party statelet which was so important to the IFP.

In the face of these challenges, the IFP adopted several strategies aimed at combating threats to both the ethnic and patronage arms of its mobilizing efforts. It also had to compensate for its increasing marginalization in the negotiation process, which came more and more to be driven by the principle of 'sufficient consensus'. The effective meaning of this was agreement between the ANC and the National Party.[9]

The first strategy was cooperation with the white right and former Bantustan interests in a confederal grouping (called first the Concerned South Africans Group and later the Freedom Alliance) which was intended to combat ANC/NP hegemony. The second was to refuse to recognize the legitimacy of the negotiation process, the transitional authorities and the target date of 27 April 1994 for the election. By this rejectionist stance the IFP, first with the Freedom Alliance and later unilaterally, sought to win concessions which it could not win in the negotiation process itself. A third response to the challenges of the transition period saw Buthelezi and the IFP intensify their identification with Zulu tradition and the monarchy in particular. Issues such as the right to carry 'cultural weapons', the 'ethnic' violence against Zulu migrant workers on the Witwatersrand and above all the question of the status and prerogatives of the Zulu monarch in a new South African dispensation came to be central preoccupations of the party and its leaders.

The overall effect of these strategies was to identify the IFP as a party outside the main process of transition to democracy at national level. From this strategic position, it was potentially a substantial obstacle to that transition, at least as it came to be understood by the NP and the ANC. It became very largely associated with regional (or even subregional)[10] interests and a discourse which conflated and confused federalism, ethnic self-determination and the historic claims of the monarchy. Opponents and observers could not be sure whether the IFP's agenda reflected a genuine confusion of purpose, crude negotiation tactics in which secession was threatened in order to extract democratic federal principles, or a long-term strategy of using federalism as a stalking-horse for independence.

These strategies propelled the IFP into intensifying conflict with the ANC/NP negotiating axis over the prospects of amending the constitution and the conditions under which the IFP would take part in the 27 April 1994 election. The intensification of this conflict coincided with the highest casualty rates yet recorded in political violence in KwaZulu-Natal.[11] This violence, the state of emergency which was declared to deal with it, and the removal of the IFP's allies by the collapse of Bophuthatswana and the disarray of the white right provided the context for the agreement of 19 April which brought the IFP into the election.[12]

Explaining the Violence

With such clear signposts as the UDF/Inkatha conflict and the IFP's rejectionist stance towards the transition, it is not surprising that violence in KwaZulu-Natal is explained predominantly in terms of political rivalry. The links between political conflict and violent death are varied, numerous and visible in this province. Armed crowds deny physical space to meetings of one party or another. Crowds gathering or dispersing for such meetings are attacked by residents of areas they have to traverse. The opening of party branches in 'new' areas is resisted with infantry weapons. Party organizers or other identifiable activists are assassinated by hit squads and private armies are set up for area defence. Forced evictions, sometimes accompanied by assault or murder, are carried out to consolidate territory in terms of political allegiance. Forced recruitment drives or resistance to them end in executions.

Incidents of this nature take place in the context of highly charged adversarial rhetoric from party leaders[13] and popular attitudes of political intolerance.[14] These things reflect a rivalry which has gone through many phases since the UDF began to challenge Inkatha's monopoly of African politics in Natal from the mid-1980s onwards, but whose basic integrity has remained the same. Media accounts, political party rhetoric, the reports of violence monitoring groups[15] and official commissions of inquiry[16] all reflect an acceptance of this rivalry as the basis for political violence in KwaZulu-Natal.

Monitoring groups in particular are essential to the shaping of public discourse on political violence in KwaZulu-Natal. They provide the raw data on which journalists hang stories and politicians rely for ammunition. Academic analyses of the violence also rely heavily on monitoring groups for primary source material. The groups themselves rely on press reports, security force statistics and eyewitness accounts based on a network of informers as their main sources of information. While keeping a tally of casualties is a valuable part of the monitors' work, it is in classifying, categorizing and explaining incidents that the groups have their most important influence. It is in their work that the violence comes to have its public meaning. Incidents, victims and sometimes perpetrators come to acquire their political labels in this way. Situations of conflict in hostels, squatter settlements, townships or tribal areas are ranked as wholly or partly 'political' by inclusion, qualification and/or omission when the monthly reports are made up.

Violence monitoring in South Africa developed in the context of the anti-apartheid struggle, largely to combat official secrecy and disinformation in official statistics such as the police 'unrest reports'. For the most part, the bodies which attempted to make up the deficit of trustworthy information were associated with liberal or liberation movement political groupings.[17] This shared provenance has had two effects. The first is a conceptual orientation towards interpreting the violence in terms of adversarial political groupings and assigning agency to the conscious strategies of political leadership. The second effect is to create an atmosphere in which accusations and counter-accusations of partisanship are common.[18]

A recent study of violence reporting in KwaZulu-Natal clears the monitoring agencies of direct manipulation and disinformation. But it also notes that agencies which are perceived to have roots or affiliations on one side or another of the political divide (effectively, all of them) are incapable of overcoming the problem of obtaining reliable contacts and information from the 'other' side. All of them are resigned to this shortcoming and all are, to this extent at least, 'biased' by omission.[19]

Whatever the merits of each side's case, controversies over alleged bias have introduced an element of propaganda war to the recording of violence. By drawing the lines of party competition through the activities of tallying and interpreting casualties, these disputes then reinforce the political rivalry explanation of the violence.

Works which rely on a combination of investigative journalism, research and observation also subscribe to the view that ANC/IFP rivalry provides the most cogent explanation of the violence.[20] A growing academic literature, however, disputes this interpretation as inadequate or misleading.[21] In some cases, the conventional wisdom is challenged as a by-product of detailed attention to one dimension of conflict, or to a particular micro conflict. Among the former can be numbered studies relating to the role of cultural factors,[22] hostels,[23] gender and generational conflict,[24] warlordism[25] or class conflict[26] in creating and sustaining the conditions for political violence. Studies of micro-conflicts include those of Molweni, Bruntville and Edendale.[27] All of these studies accept the validity of ANC/IFP rivalry, but stress the explanatory importance of other factors which predispose communities to violence, prior to the incursion of political rivalry. Indeed, several of them argue that it is not invariably parties which invade local disputes, but communities which attach themselves to parties in the hope of gaining decisive advantage.

Other challenges to the received consensus about political conflict come from more theoretically conscious attempts to construct revisionist interpretations. The political causes of violence, according to one of these studies, by Morris and Hindson, 'must be more deeply conceptually grounded than simply political rivalry between Inkatha and the ANC'.[28] The authors emphasize 'the formation of competing local centres of power'[29] in black residential areas as the grip of white minority rule slackened from the mid-1980s. Traditional leaders, warlords, politicized youth, criminals and other contenders for resources and influence should be seen as in alliance with the ANC and Inkatha rather than under their control. The impression that emerges from Morris and Hindson's analysis is of the ANC and the IFP involving themselves opportunistically and expediently in a multitude of social conflicts. They are able to practise exploitation and damage limitation where appropriate, but on the whole they are borne along by the force of conflicts in which they are perhaps the principal observable agents (especially from a distance), but by no means the only, or invariably the decisive ones. Another account, by Taylor and Shaw comes to similar conclusions:

> It is clear... that to view the conflict in Natal as an 'Inkatha/ANC war' is too reductionist. Missing from the political conflict view is a deeper contextualisation of how apartheid has played a central role in creating the material conditions and patterns of differentiation which have fostered and structured the conflict.[30]

Taylor and Shaw are concerned first of all to note empirical shortcomings in what they call the 'political conflict' interpretation of the violence. In their summary of these shortcomings they include, 'the fact that it is hard to see how the conflict is in the interests of either the ANC or Inkatha'. They also point to the 'spontaneous and unorganized' form of the violence and the uncertain identity of the participants and victims. Reportedly low levels of awareness of party ideologies on the part of 'comrades' and 'vigilantes' and factional disputes within both the IFP and the ANC are used to strengthen their case.[31]

In all of these issues, a key characteristic of the conflict in KwaZulu-Natal is a hindrance to clarity. That is, despite its clear political overtones, the violence there is relatively 'inarticulate' in that no organized participant has an acknowledged paramilitary strategy. The paradigm of political violence in which there is an openly-acknowledged division of labour between a political party and a military wing, through which acts of violence are publicly linked to specific political objectives for the purposes of propaganda and terrorism, does not apply in KwaZulu-Natal. At its simplest, no group has claimed responsibility for any of the thousands of acts of terror which have occurred there over the last ten years. Despite this, monitoring reports and legal depositions by surviving victims and other eye witnesses frequently claim that perpetrators were known to the victims and are identifiable by party label. In many cases, the violence is inarticulate to the wider public, but by no means anonymous to those most closely affected.

Especially since 1990, the effect of this has been compounded by another characteristic, the absence of the clearly demarcated roles which often give shape to violent political conflicts. Who are the 'authorities'? and who are the 'insurgents'? Which conception of an 'order' (in the sense of a set of values, institutions and material conditions to be defended or challenged) represents the fixed point from which we may plot the orientations of participants? In this sense, the interregnum years between the public acknowledgment of the failure of apartheid and the election which brought a new government to power were very confusing and it was very difficult to assign political meaning to violent conflict. Apartheid's defenders became 'third force' guerrillas. Former insurgents progressively took on de facto responsibility for law and order while some of their comrades remained underground to fight wars of communal defence and party advantage.

In KwaZulu-Natal the situation was particularly confused. The concentration of power represented by the IFP, the Zulu monarchy and the KwaZulu administration especially the KwaZulu Police (KZP) was the formal embodiment of law and order in a regional context. In national politics, however, it came to resemble the nucleus of a dissident, insurgent force. The way in which communities attempted to determine which security forces – the KZP, the South African Police (SAP), the South African Defence Force (SADF) – would be deployed in 'their' areas illustrates the lack of clarity on what constituted 'authority' in the province.

The most enduring symbol of this remains the spectacle of African nationalist and communist members of an unelected junta (the Transitional Executive Council, TEC) ordering a white minority government to deploy settler regiments of the security force reserve, under emergency laws, in the face of an anticipated revolt by Zulu nationalists and monarchists.

In the face of all this, perhaps it is not surprising to read in Shaw and Taylor's article that, 'it is hard to see how the conflict is in the interests of either the ANC or Inkatha'. But it is disappointing that they dispose of the matter in half a sentence, as if it is self-evident that the conflict could not be in the interests of either party. The way the authors raise the question imposes the wrong shape on the issue. It would indeed be difficult to see how the conflict had been in the interests of either Inkatha or the ANC if one or the other (or both) had unleashed a campaign of violence on an ordered and stable society. But their rivalry developed in the context of armed struggle against apartheid, a brutal campaign of counter-insurgency and the constellation of localized conflicts which Morris and Hindson and Shaw and Taylor both describe. Bearing this context in mind, it is difficult to see how the ANC and Inkatha could fail to come to the conclusion that, at the least, defensive, retaliatory and pre-emptive violence was in their interests. To say that conflict is in no-one's interest in a situation which resembles a Hobbesian natural society more than one of legitimate authority in a stable polity is an unhelpful premise for explanation.

Even at the stage of the conflict when Shaw and Taylor were writing, their dismissive approach was difficult to justify. The evidence of monitors' and police reports, even hospital statistics,[32] points to a development from a communal to a paramilitary character and to strategic patterns of a more purposeful and organized nature. The establishment of private party armies, the ANC's Self-Defence Units (SDUs)[33] and the IFP's Self Protection Units (SPUs)[34] strengthens the case for treating the violence within the context of party competition, as do revelations of 'hit-squad' activities, linked especially to Inkatha's cause. Later developments which saw a close coincidence between heightened political conflict and escalating casualty figures in KwaZulu-Natal point in the same direction.

These developments intensified from 1993, by when the election date had been set and the interim constitution had been signed. The transitional institutions (notably the TEC, the Independent Electoral Commission and the ill-fated National Peacekeeping Force) were providing visible evidence of the ANC's increasing access to policy-making and oversight of the state apparatus. At the same time, the IFP's fortunes appeared to be in sharp decline. Its response to the ANC/NP understanding which drove the transition process forward from late 1992 was to distance itself from negotiations and attempt to frustrate them. The rejectionist front which it formed with the white right and bantustan interests worked hard to create an atmosphere in which secession and civil war seemed a likely outcome if their demands were not incorporated in a more inclusive settlement than that shaped by the ANC/NP understanding. While the IFP attempted to negotiate terms for re-entry into the transitional process, the Freedom Alliance was crumbling, owing to the collapse of Bophuthatswana and the disarray of the white right. At the same time, the IFP was performing poorly in opinion polls and the credibility of its leader outside his own party was at a very low ebb.

It was at this point, when conflict between the IFP and the ANC/NP axis was at its height and the IFP's options were narrowing, that the death toll of political violence in KwaZulu-Natal reached new heights. Immediately after the negotiated entry of the IFP to the election was concluded, the number of deaths fell rapidly and steeply.

The Human Rights Committee interpreted these coincidences in bold and direct terms:

> An unprecedented surge of violence in Natal in the run-up to the

elections was the result of a planned, coordinated strategy by anti-election elements in the IFP...In a public statement on the 9 May 1994, the Independent International Observer appointed under the State of Emergency to liaise with the High Command of the SADF and the SAP in Natal/KwaZulu stated that the pre-election surge in violence had been 'political in nature, organized and calibrated'. Reports from many quarters, including church bodies, monitoring groups and human rights organizations, all concurred that the surge in violence was a planned, co-ordinated strategy by anti-election elements within the IFP bent on destabilizing the region.[35]

The HRC's interpretation does not make clear what persons at what level are the targets of these allegations. The lack of detailed sourcing, the element of equivocation in the phrase *anti-election elements*, the free use of the international observers words and the adversarial relationship between the IFP and the HRC have to be taken into account. Nevertheless, it is difficult to see the coincidence between rising and falling death tolls and first a crescendo and then a (temporary) settlement of political conflict as anything but an indication that the political conflict thesis should be taken more seriously than Shaw and Taylor claim.

It might be argued that the pre-election months represented an extraordinary passage of tension, during which the political conflict explanation emerged with a clarity and cogency which it lacked before and subsequently. There is something to be said for this qualification. The HRC's monitoring reports after the election dwell on histories of factional and criminal feuding which, in their informants' estimation, have 'become' political and acquired a dimension of ANC/IFP rivalry.[36] These reports are consistent with the well-established view that local factors play an important part in shaping ANC/IFP conflicts. One aspect of the post-election casualty figures however suggests the durability of the political conflict interpretation. It is the fact that elsewhere in South Africa, the incidence of political violence has declined much more sharply than in KwaZulu-Natal. This is especially true of Gauteng, where in the interregnum years, for long periods, casualties were higher than in KwaZulu-Natal.[37] It is likely that declining casualty levels in Gauteng are partly due to the cessation of Third Force activities. Another factor which should be borne in mind, however, is the way in which the election results confirmed the regional nature of the IFP. If we accept a central role for ANC/IFP rivalry in explaining the violence in both Gauteng and KwaZulu-Natal, it would not be surprising if violence declined much further in the former rather than the latter, given the relative strength of the IFP in the two provinces.

Indeed, one of the general weaknesses of revisionist accounts, which seek to downplay political rivalry at the expense of structural material conditions in explaining the violence, is that they do not adequately account for differences between KwaZulu-Natal and the rest of South Africa. In particular, it is difficult to account for the longevity and intensity of conflict there on the basis of structural material conditions, especially after the election put an end to many of the political uncertainties of the transitional years. After all, the pathological material conditions engendered by forced removals, the collapse of homeland economies, border industrialization and the other matters discussed by revisionist accounts are not unique to KwaZulu-Natal. It may be that some aspect of their conjuncture, or perhaps their collision with traditional society, distinguishes this province from other regions which have been devastated by apartheid, but this crucial issue has not so far been addressed directly and at length.[38] Until it is, it will appear to be the ANC/IFP rivalry which makes KwaZulu-Natal politically unique and singularly violent in comparison to the rest of South Africa.

Reinterpretations of political violence in KwaZulu-Natal which challenge its depiction as an ANC/IFP war have had several salutary effects. They add depth and texture to explanations of conflict by synthesizing and summarizing much primary research which demonstrates how complex the local roots of conflict are, pointing to generational conflict, chieftaincy succession, competition for scarce resources and other elements. They point to the difficulties of assigning responsibility to party strategies where organizational structures are rudimentary and local actors have their own agendas. By correctly stressing the importance of material conditions, they ensure that 'ANC/IFP rivalry' does not become an exculpatory catch-phrase, camouflaging the role played by apartheid in creating a conflict-ridden social context.

While arguing for shifts of explanatory emphasis, the authors of these revisionist accounts warn against 'marginalizing the political' and acknowledge that political rivalry does indeed play a part in the violence. Despite this cautionary note, they do not give due weight to the role of political parties in sustaining the violence through the warlike rhetoric of leaders, by arming and training paramilitary forces and carrying out acts of violence which are clearly neither random nor spontaneous. As has been noted above, the coincidence of political tension and high casualty rates is difficult to explain in terms of pathological social conditions, as are the endemic features of violence in KwaZulu-Natal by comparison with the rest of the country.

By focusing on material conditions and social context, revisionist accounts ensure that apartheid and its creators do not escape a share of the responsibility, but the question of direct agency in the violence remains. It would be ironic if a shift of explanatory emphasis onto sets of impersonal structural conditions were to have the same exculpatory effect as the superficial 'ANC/IFP war' interpretation, allowing individuals and parties who are guilty of sustaining the violence to evade responsibility.

To some extent, the failure to address more directly and vigorously the role of political rivalry in the conflict is explicable in terms of the authors' understandable desire to make their own case and to concentrate on revising what they correctly see as the mistaken emphases of superficial tags like 'black on black violence' and 'ethnic conflict'. It should be enough, perhaps, for them to make a few qualifying remarks signposting the continuing explanatory purchase of political rivalry as a cause of violence, while leaving it to others to integrate it into a more satisfactory interpretative synthesis. If this is to be done, three untested assumptions which colour the revisionist accounts of political rivalry in KwaZulu-Natal have to be addressed.

The first is that the conflict is not in the interests of either the ANC or the IFP. The point has already been made that in a better world, the parties would probably want to prosecute their differences peacefully. But in the less than perfect world of late apartheid and the transitional interregnum, they have felt constrained to pursue certain interests violently. These have included mobilization, territorial and communal defence, the denial of political space to opponents and the opportunity to demonize rivals and designate them as security threats rather than legitimate political actors. The truth probably is that these interests reflect *ad hoc* exploitation of conflict rather than a grand strategic plan to launch it, but if the bald statement that neither side has an interest in the conflict were taken at face value, it would be difficult to see why the violence has lasted for over eight years.

The second assumption is that insofar as violence is political, much of it arises from lack of control by the ANC and IFP over their nominal followers. Both the principal revisionist interpretations and the sources on which they rely give convincing accounts of the difficult internal dynamics of the two parties. None of them, however, attempts to assess how strong the will is to keep the rank and file from violence, preferring the untested assumption that only the wilfulness of subordinates and a lack of organizational depth and reach keep peace from breaking out.

Third, by concentrating so heavily on the socio-economic conditions which provide the context for political conflict and violence, the revisionists underestimate the political differences between the ANC and the IFP. The two are divided by disagreement, not only over how, by whom, and from where South Africa should be governed, but also how 'South Africa' is constituted in the first place. The development of rival agendas – centralizing and modernizing on the ANC's side, parochial and atavistic on that of the IFP – gives a shape and durability to their rivalry and the conflicts of KwaZulu-Natal which set that province off from other parts of the country.

In addition to these considerations, if due weight is to be given to the role of rivalry between political parties in sustaining the violence, one aspect of their relationship which did not apply when the principal revisionist accounts were written has to be considered. That is, the fact that between them the ANC and the IFP have responsibility for state policies in the security and other fields which bear upon the violence in KwaZulu-Natal. Since 27 April 1994, their rivalry has come to encompass not only questions of private armies, hit squads, imperfect control of undisciplined cohorts and so on. Their conflict has become built into official perceptions of the violence and the conduct of state policy towards it.

Violence and the State: Perception and Policy

A key feature of conflict in KwaZulu-Natal since the mid-1980s has been the dynamism of the rivalry between the ANC and the IFP. Among its striking features have been changes in the formal status of the parties and in the balance of power between them. Between 1985 and 1990, Inkatha and the KwaZulu government were part of a status quo which was under attack by armed struggle and insurrection, yet at the same time they portrayed themselves as opposition movements to apartheid. The ANC was a fugitive underground movement, represented on the ground by a surrogate, which was itself subject to severe harassment and repression. Between 1990 and 1994, both were pretenders to power in an interregnum period in which past and future claims to authority co-existed uneasily in a vacuum of legitimate power. In an atmosphere of negotiation, mass action and violence, the continued integrity of the South African state seemed in jeopardy at times. Despite their altered and theoretically equal status during this unstable time, each tended to view the other in its earlier incarnation of apartheid collaborator or revolutionary insurgent. By contrast, since 27 April 1994, each party has had a legitimate claim to authority, based on an electoral mandate, the ANC nationally, the IFP regionally.

The changing status and balance of power between the parties have had an important influence on deciding how the problem of violent conflict in KwaZulu-Natal has been perceived and addressed by the state, through government policy and security force actions. Before 1990, the problem of political violence was seen by the state in the wider framework of insurrection and counter-insurgency which characterized the second half of the 1980s. Covert alliances between the South African security forces, the KwaZulu Police and Inkatha were important parts of a strategy that was overwhelmingly military rather than political. Between 1990 and 1994, no centre of political authority had the legitimacy, the will or the resources to devise a military or political strategy to end the violence, or contain it to a level which would allow space for a political solution. In this policy vacuum, the KwaZulu Police remained a partisan force, allied to one of the pretenders to power. The record of the SAP was patchy. Accusations by monitors and the ANC that individuals and units colluded with the IFP persisted, while it was clear that others embraced the new order with professionalism in the conduct of their duties.[39] The predominant official policy, however, was composed of reactive and piecemeal responses to the violence. No co-ordinated political and security offensive against the violence was possible during the interregnum's years of uncertain political authority.

By providing a popular mandate and appearing to settle the question of legitimacy, the general election of 27 April 1994 should have created the conditions under which the problem of violence in KwaZulu-Natal could be addressed with the full range of state policies and resources. Unfortunately, the mandate delivered by the electorate was divided, in more ways than one. The ANC's 62 per cent of the national vote made it the leading, indeed directing influence in the Government of National Unity, but the IFP's 51 per cent in KwaZulu-Natal allowed it to form a provincial government. Moreover, within KwaZulu-Natal, the IFP's support was concentrated in the areas formerly administered by the KwaZulu homeland government. Thus, the new combined political and administrative unit was divided along lines which separated bantustan and province, rural and urban areas and traditional and modern values. As a result, the things which divided the ANC and the IFP were built into the new institutions of government. These divisions made themselves apparent within provincial and national government and in the relations between the two. One of the most serious effects was to frustrate what should have been one of the priorities of the new administration, a co-ordinated offensive to tackle the root causes of political and other forms of violence in KwaZulu-Natal.

Such an offensive would, ideally, include security, economic, social and political dimensions. Improved security could come from a non-partisan police force, better training, increased manpower and resources, backed by the temporary granting of emergency powers. Increased rates of detection and conviction would give a greater sense of security to front line communities and make inroads into the cycles of deterrent and exemplary violence which arise from the perception that self-help is the only source of security. Putting the onus of controlling the violence on the state, rather than on the role of political organizations in disciplining their members and affiliates, would allow the 'political' nature of the violence to be more accurately charted and clarify the roles of the ANC and the IFP in sustaining the conflict on the ground.

A combined anti-violence strategy would need a socio-economic dimension to improve the material conditions under which competition for resources encourages communal hostilities and creates local power-brokers. The identification of these warlords and warring or divided communities with the ANC or IFP is one of the major features of KwaZulu-Natal's conflicts. If delivery of land, housing, employment and public services could be increased, the alienating effects of struggling for survival in marginal communities would be reduced and the prospects of peace improved. Moreover, increased delivery would make the enjoyment of services appear to depend on common citizenship, rather than partisan affiliation in local power struggles.

The formulation of coordinated policies to combat political violence requires clarity of political purpose and, as far as possible, undivided political will. It also requires a clear demarcation between authority roles and insurgent roles. There is an element of self-definition in this. Those who uphold and those who challenge or subvert a given order in effect have to volunteer to play these parts by pushing their actions beyond some limit of disaffection or repression. A frustrating degree of ambiguity still attaches itself to the contending parties in KwaZulu-Natal, despite the political changes which have been marked by the interim constitution and the election of 27 April 1994.

Much of this can be attributed to the uncertain status of the IFP. By taking part in the election, entering the Government of National Unity and forming a government in KwaZulu-Natal, the IFP has behaved like a 'system' party. But it has made it clear that all these things are conditional. It rejected the process which produced the interim constitution and did not accept the process for finalizing the constitution, preferring bilateral negotiation outside the constitutional assembly, supplemented by international mediation. Boycott of the Constitutional Assembly, repeated threats to leave the National Assembly and Government of National Unity, institutional non-cooperation in joint forums of national and regional government and opposition to security initiatives of the national government, all contribute to the image of a dissident movement rather than a 'loyal opposition'. Added to this is the chronic and calculated measure of ambiguity which attaches itself to both its shifting agenda of federalism and self-determination, and to the warlike rhetoric of IFP leaders.

In effect, for the violence in KwaZulu-Natal to be the subject of a coordinated campaign of state action, one of two perceptions of the nature of the violence would have to prevail. One alternative is for the ANC and the IFP to agree that the violence is a debilitating epidemic which affects them both. This conception would also involve the acceptance that the violence arises out of the pathological legacy of apartheid, combined with the vacuum of authority of the interregnum years, and would be susceptible to the joint self-assertion of the legitimate provincial and national authorities. The other alternative is for the issue of political violence to be addressed by a conscious decision of the ANC to take on the role of a legitimate defender of an established order, morally and legally equipped to deploy emergency measures of counter-insurgency. Alternatively, the IFP could define itself as a liberation movement in the cause of self-determination. Either, or more likely, both acts of self-definition would reconfigure the issue of violence in KwaZulu-Natal in terms of proscription, detention and other emergency measures. This would probably lead to clashes between state and insurgent forces, rather than (as now) inter-communal atrocities carried out by loosely organized private armies, from which the political parties try to distance themselves.

At present, the ANC and the IFP cannot commit themselves to either of these scenarios. Their political divisions are too deep for them to admit a common interest in tackling the violence as if it were the product of impersonal structural forces. But equally, neither relishes the prospect of the brutal trial of strength which would result from giving the conflict the shape of a counter-insurgency war. In the meantime, deaths in political violence in KwaZulu-Natal continue at an average of somewhere between 70 and 80 per month.

This analysis of the situation suggests three possible lines of development. The first is for the rival parties to acquire a shared concern for formulating policies to cope with the violence. The second lies in the opposite direction, that of redefining their political differences in security terms. Third, the situation can remain as it is, with a monthly death toll of between 50 and 100 coming to represent 'an acceptable level of violence' in the presence of political stalemate. Indications as to which of these three is most likely can be sought in an evaluation of how political conflicts and security policies have developed since 1994.

Political Conflict Between the ANC and the IFP since 27 April 1994

The nature of the conflict between the ANC and the IFP is usefully summed up in Chief Buthelezi's description of the ANC as a 'centralizing and modernizing party'. This indicates the constitutional dimension of the parties' differences and draws attention to the contest over the possession of 'tradition', which has become the ground on which they struggle for supremacy in KwaZulu-Natal itself. Although the rivalry between the ANC and the IFP is, of course, seamless, it is worth looking at these dimensions of it separately.

Towards the Final Constitution: Process and Substance

In the months between July 1993, when the IFP left the multilateral constitutional negotiations, and 19 April 1994, when the agreement securing the party's participation in the election was secured, issues of both process and substance divided the ANC and the IFP. The IFP rejected the procedural principle of 'sufficient consensus' as purely a rubber stamp for the ANC's wishes. 'Consensus' had to include the National Party, of course, but in the IFP's eyes, the NP had opted for being a junior partner, abandoning the principled task of being a check to the ANC for the bribe of continued access to government posts and guarantees for key white constituencies in the bureaucracy and the armed forces. Effectively, the IFP wanted as much of the constitution as possible finalized before the election and a veto for itself on key issues, as conditions of participation. These objections to the negotiation process were accompanied by demands that the status and extent of provincial government powers under the new constitution be considerably enhanced. The IFP's stand on regional autonomy – sometimes expressed in terms of democratic federal principles and sometimes in terms of ethnic selfdetermination – was complemented by the parallel demand that the status and prerogatives of the Zulu monarchy be protected under the new dispensation.

The ANC and the NP tried to address these matters of process and content in bilateral and trilateral negotiations which culminated, after an abortive attempt at international mediation, in the 19 April agreement. The text of this stated that, 'The undersigned parties agree to recognize and respect the institutional status and role of the king of the Zulus and the kingdom of KwaZulu' and that, 'Any outstanding issues in respect of the king of the Zulus and the 1993 constitution as amended will be addressed by way of international mediation which will commence as soon as possible after ... the elections.' The agreement addressed the question of the monarchy, but not that of relations between central and provincial government, except through the non-specific label of 'outstanding constitutional issues' and the promise of international mediation.

The question of the status of the 19 April 1994 agreement is the issue around which ANC/IFP differences have revolved. With gathering insistence, especially since the beginning of 1995, the IFP has tried to put pressure on an unwilling ANC to make good its version of the commitments in the document, while the ANC has responded with its own interpretation of the text. The IFP's pressure has taken the form of a temporary walk-out from parliament, a boycott of the proceedings of the Constitutional Assembly, and threats to leave the Government of National Unity and to disrupt the holding of local government elections in KwaZulu-Natal. The IFP claims, in justification of these threats, that terms of reference for the mediation were agreed to in negotiations between January and 19 April 1994 and that the outstanding constitutional issues referred to in the 19

April text are set out in a consolidated document which emanated from these negotiations. Among the issues referred to in this document, 'which will need to be explored through international mediation and renewed negotiation', are:

> The extent of the powers to be given to the provinces, with specific reference to the issue of the central government overrides, exclusivity, residual powers, judicial functions, entrenchment and integrity of provincial autonomy, provincial civil service and police, and jurisdiction over local government.[40]

The ANC denies that the terms of reference are valid for the 19 April agreement and claims that they have to be re-negotiated. It also claims that since the Zulu king has pronounced himself happy with the interim constitution, a key part of the 19 April agreement falls away.[41] Chief Buthelezi argues, counter to this, that 'the monarchy' embraces more than the king's person and the royal family and that '...The future of the chiefs and tribal leaders which are essential "pillars" of the monarchy is all part of the debate which has to be taken to international mediation.'[42]

The ANC has endorsed the principle of international mediation, but its insistence that terms of reference have to be renegotiated and that this should take place only after the resources of the Constitutional Assembly have been exhausted effectively nullifies the principle in any practical expression of its terms. What this means in reality is that the ANC has successfully faced down the IFP over the issue of international mediation. The new constitution was finalized on schedule in May 1996 and the IFP's counter-strategy of passing a provincial constitution which would challenge the national dispensation has misfired, thanks to its slim majority in the provincial assembly and its own inept negotiating tactics.[43]

The Possession of Tradition and the Balance of Power in KwaZulu-Natal

Despite Chief Buthelezi's attempts to depict it as an implacably modernizing force, bent on destroying African traditional culture and authorities, the ANC has recognized the need to integrate tradition into its own version of African popular politics. This has been less a conscious exercise in ideological formulation than a pragmatic response to local electoral and developmental needs, and the promptings of the 'progressive' chiefs' organization, the Congress of Traditional Leaders of South Africa (Contralesa). In KwaZulu-Natal, however, there is the additional inviting prospect of undermining and outflanking the IFP, to add to these general considerations. The ANC's strategy in trying to detach traditional elements in Zulu society from the IFP has been to use reassurance and blandishment, rather than confrontation.

The ANC's acknowledgement of the validity of traditional culture and authority in KwaZulu-Natal received public affirmation at a festival in Durban in October 1993, to which King Goodwill was invited. Although he did not attend, by the end of the year he was making statements which indicated to observers that he might be preparing himself for a more neutral role. He and Buthelezi still appeared close in the tense months of negotiation before the election, but soon after, a rift publicly opened between them. Central to the dispute was the office of 'traditional prime minister' to the Zulu king, which Buthelezi claimed as his own. By mid-1994, King Goodwill was relying on a royal council of advisers and by September, he had made it clear that he no longer regarded Buthelezi as enjoying his confidence. In all of this, the king enjoyed the visible support of the ANC's KwaZulu-Natal regions and the personal attentions of President Mandela. The bitterest blow to Buthelezi came with the announcement that Prince Mcwayizeni Zulu, a member of the ANC's national executive, would henceforth be the king's adviser.

Buthelezi counter-attacked by demonstrating that he and the IFP retained the support of the overwhelming majority of the *amakhosi* (tribal chiefs) who are the backbone of traditional authority in the province. The *amakhosi*, many of whom were members of the KwaZulu homeland parliament, were central to the powerful political alliance which Buthelezi forged out of traditional authorities, homeland institutions and a mass party.[44] Their loyalty would enable him and the IFP to survive the defection of the royal house and still bid to dominate the new provincial system of government.

Buthelezi's chosen instrument for this was the House of Traditional Leaders which the provincial parliament (like all provincial legislatures) was empowered by the constitution to set up as a second chamber. Amid protests from the king and the ANC, who claimed that the monarchy and the few non-IFP chiefs had been sidelined, the KwaZulu-Natal Act on the House of Traditional Leaders was hastily passed.[45] The establishment of the House was considered a coup for Buthelezi on two counts. First, the Act reduces the king to the status of an ordinary member of the *amakhosi* and vests the responsibility for advising and recommending on all matters pertaining to Zulu traditional culture, authority and law in the House rather than in the monarchy. Second, by reserving a seat for the traditional prime minister,[46] the Act ensures a power base in the House for Buthelezi.

Buthelezi's counter-attack through the *amakhosi* had a second front. This was in the negotiations for restructuring local government. The IFP successfully held out for the *amakhosi* to be recognised as having statutory status in rural local government.[47] The inclusion of an unelected element, which was, moreover, overwhelmingly identified with its main opponent, was a bitter pill for the ANC to swallow. In the end, however, it was clear that the chiefs could ensure that the elections simply would not be held in rural areas if they were thwarted. In addition, their positions of authority in rural communities made them essential for schemes of rural development and the delivery of services. In any case, the ANC's wider strategy of working with, rather than against traditional leaders where possible helped rule out confrontation over this issue.

The ANC in its turn has improvised tactics to counter Buthelezi's axis with the *amakhosi*. Using the argument that both the status and remuneration of traditional leaders throughout the country have to be standardized, the cabinet has approved a draft bill which will allow the government to pay traditional leaders, although this matter is designated as a provincial responsibility in the interim constitution. It is not clear whether the effect of this will merely be to allow chiefs the choice of where their stipends are paid from, or to strip provinces of their power to pay chiefs. Even the more limited effect will entail a diminution of provincial governments' powers and patronage which could open the door for the central government to punish dissident chiefs or provinces and incite chiefs whose identification with the IFP is less than wholehearted to distance themselves from the party.[48] These effects, however, are for the future. At present, Buthelezi's close relationship with the *amakhosi* is undamaged. This was demonstrated when President Mandela met with the KwaZulu-Natal *amakhosi* to discuss a projected *Imbizo* (traditional gathering of the Zulu people) with them as part of a peace initiative in March 1996.[49]

Adversarial Images and Political Conflict

The conflicts between the ANC and the IFP over the final constitution and the possession of tradition go much deeper than the differences over policy which characterize party competition in stable democracies. The issue of a federal versus a unitary state is serious enough, but when it is invaded by the question of ethnic self-determination, it takes on an emotive cast, which is not amenable to compromise. The problem of finding a place for traditional authority in a new South Africa is difficult enough, but the question of who possesses the powerful resources of Zulu tradition in KwaZulu-Natal might well decide the political survival of one of the contenders.

The depth of these divisions is reflected and exacerbated by the high levels of political intolerance recorded in attitude surveys and by adversarial images which the parties hold and propagate about each other. To some extent, these run along predictable lines of blaming each other for the violence and denying the validity of each other's constitutional stances. One consistent feature of the ANC's image of its rival deserves particular mention, however. That is the view, held with particular tenacity in the ANC's KwaZulu-Natal regions, that the IFP is not an enduring political force and, rather than having to tolerate continuing rivalry and conflict, the ANC can make the IFP disintegrate. In this view, the IFP was the creation of the apartheid state and once this security shelter and source of patronage was removed with the end of white minority rule, the IFP could not survive. When this did not happen, the focus switched to the monarchy and the argument that the detachment of the royal house would prove fatal to the IFP's ability to reproduce support. Now that this has failed to come about, the logical extension of this mindset is to hope for the dissolution of the IFP through the erosion of the alliance between Buthelezi and the *amakhosi*. Though by no means the only factor which inhibits the growth of 'normal' political competition, this strategic mindset is an aggravating one.

Security Issues and Policies in KwaZulu-Natal since 27 April 1994

Security issues and policies in the province reflect the conflict between the IFP and the ANC. To date they have reproduced the divisions between the parties, rather than offering ways in which the divisions might be bridged by policies which recognize the apartheid provenance of the violence and the material costs to both sides. Control of security is, understandably, regarded as crucial by the protagonists. When the TEC assumed the authority to oversee security forces through its law and order subcommittee in late 1993, a trial of strength immediately began with the KwaZulu Government over whether or not the TEC's jurisdiction applied to the KwaZulu Police. After the new central and provincial governments came to power, the tug-of-war continued.

The interim constitution[50] nominates policing as one of the provinces' areas of legislative competence, subject to the generally limiting provisions regulating relations between central and provincial government[51] and specific provisions contained in Chapter 14. This section provides for a South African Police Service (SAPS), 'which will be structured at both central and provincial levels and shall function under the direction of the national government as well as the various provincial governments'. A national Police Act is envisaged which will provide a framework for responsibilities for ministers of safety and security and police commissioners at the centre and in the provinces. The national commissioner has the power to appoint provincial commissioners, but provincial ministers have the power of veto. Provincial legislatures can pass laws relating to policing, but in addition to the general provisions which allow national legislation to override provincial laws, powers of operational control strengthen the centre's hand. For example, the president is empowered to order the national commissioner to deploy public order units of the police 'in circumstances where the Provincial Commissioner is unable to maintain public order'.[52]

The interim constitution's provisions on policing differ radically from the IFP's most comprehensive statements on the relationship between central and provincial government. In the Constitution of the State of KwaZulu-Natal[53] policing would be under the exclusive jurisdiction of the province (or 'state') and no forces of central government would have, 'the power to enter or be stationed in the state of KwaZulu-Natal without the approval of the state.'[54]

The distance between these different conceptions of policing gives an indication of how difficult it will be to integrate the KwaZulu Police and the SAPS in the province and to develop nonpartisan policies to deal with the violence. The divergent constitutional positions were illustrated in January 1995 when central and provincial governments clashed over the issue of the graduation of 500 KwaZulu Police trainees. The Minister of Safety and Security in the Government of National Unity, Sidney Mufamadi, banned the passing out parade on the grounds that the trainees had been insufficiently screened for criminal records and notifiable diseases.

A newspaper report described the parties' interpretations of the constitution:

> Inkatha parliamentary safety and security spokesman Velaphi Ndlovu told a news conference yesterday that until a new Police Act provided for the integration of SA's 11 police forces, 'Mufamadi has no jurisdiction in KwaZulu-Natal' .... Mufamadi's legal adviser Azhar Cachalia said earlier KwaZulu Natal had not yet assumed powers over policing, which were vested in central government. These would be devolved once the province was ready.[55]

The issue of the recruits' screening involved more important matters than criminal records. Failure by the KwaZulu Police training authorities to fingerprint them meant that they could not be investigated for involvement in 'hit squad' activities. Allegations about the KwaZulu Government and KwaZulu Police use of covert assassination squads in the war against the ANC had been made in claims by the ANC itself, reports of violence monitors, investigative journalism and testimony by defecting policemen to newspapers and in criminal trials. They gained official currency in reports of the Goldstone Commission and the TEC sub-committee on law and order made investigation of hit squads a priority. By late 1993, three separate statutory bodies were investigating hit squads, an SAP team and another of civilian lawyers, both responsible to the TEC and another SAP task force which reported to the Goldstone Commission. By the time the dispute over the trainees came about, the hit squad investigations had been consolidated into the Investigative Task Unit (ITU) which reports to the Ministry of Safety and Security.

The work of the ITU starkly illustrates the politically divided state of policing in KwaZulu-Natal. By mid-1995, the unit had begun to make arrests which pointed to high-level IFP involvement in hit squad activity, but several things militated against the credibility of its operations. These included the ANC connections of its leadership, accusations of irregular methods of investigation and, most importantly, the absence of any evidence that paramilitary assassination groups working for the ANC were the subject of equally vigorous investigation. Although the IFP has made what capital it can out of these issues, the ANC's response has been, on the whole, muted. Denials by the unit's director that the investigations are biased have not yet been backed up by any supplementary information which could clarify the role played by the ITU's work in broader political and security policies for the region. It is not surprising that investigative tasks of this sort should be carried out in an atmosphere of operational secrecy, but, to say the least, the political context of the ITU's mission has been inadequately established.

To some extent, the ITU can be seen as the product of several initiatives, carried forward by determined individuals following discrete lines of enquiry, as much for professional as political reasons. Despite this varied provenance, it is likely that the unit has come to represent something more politically coherent and significant, part of the struggle between the ANC and the IFP for control of the security forces in the province. It is difficult to see how the KwaZulu Police could be integrated into a new, professional and non-partisan police force without its separate ethos and close links with the IFP being broken. It is likely that the ANC has decided that these things cannot be achieved by negotiation and retraining alone, especially in the light of the IFP's views on the power of provinces to control policing. If the work of the ITU gives substance to long-term allegations against the KwaZulu Police, the ANC can hope that this will discredit the force and its political masters to the point where integration, reform and the supremacy of central government will be established on its terms.

The ITU is one indication that the ANC has begun to define its differences with the IFP in security terms.[56] Another is the personal identification of President Mandela with the problem of violence in KwaZulu-Natal. Beginning in April 1995, President Mandela made regular visits to the province on voter registration and electioneering drives, ahead of the (subsequently postponed) local government polls. These visits coincided with a perceptible hardening of his views on security policy, which was at least partly caused by a more intimate acquaintance with conditions on the ground. Threats of financial sanctions against the province, of emergency security measures and even of changes to the constitution all contributed to the impression that President Mandela was prepared to re-define the IFP as a threat to internal security, rather than a legitimate opposition party.[57]

Conclusions

Despite the drop in the number of incidents and casualties since 27 April 1994, KwaZulu-Natal is South Africa's only province in which political violence remains at significant levels. Although it is essential to grasp the importance of structural material conditions in understanding and explaining the violence, the essential characteristic which separates KwaZulu-Natal from the other provinces is the political rivalry between the ANC and the IFP. The focus of this conflict has shifted somewhat since 27 April 1994, from a contest for control of territory and denial of political space to opponents (although these elements remain important) to a war of propaganda and bureaucratic manoeuvre for control of security in the province. Despite increasingly stringent warnings from President Mandela, it is unlikely that in the short term this struggle will result in a full and overt re-definition of the parties' differences in security terms. The operations of the ITU in (thus far) selectively exposing direct IFP involvement in the violence suggest a more indirect approach. In the meantime, the continuing political conflict between the ANC and the IFP obstructs the formulation of a comprehensive strategy to bring the violence to an end.

The progress of the peace talks has been subject to two political developments. The first was the holding of the thrice-postponed local elections in KwaZulu-Natal on 26 June 1996. The need for political stability to ensure that the elections could be held and their results have credibility, was in itself an incentive for both parties to embark on peace talks. The results of the poll confirmed the IFP as the majority party in the province, but only as a result of a massive show of support for it in its rural heartlands. The ANC emerged as the clearly dominant party in the urban areas, partly as a result of the defection of the support the IFP had enjoyed from whites and Indians in the April 1994 general election. The balance of power revealed by this result makes it clear that neither party can hope for the kind of electoral breakthrough which would leave it the undisputed 'ruling party' in the province. Significantly, neither party disputed the validity of the result, a marked contrast with the ANC's strenuous protests in April 1994. These things suggest that both parties ought to think in terms of accommodation and a working relationship, rather than victory obtained through the rifle, the ballot box, or a combination of both.

The second development is the conclusion of the constitution-making process. The draft final constitution was accepted by the Constitutional Assembly and delivered to the Constitutional Court on 8 May 1996. A provincial constitution had previously been passed in March by the KwaZulu-Natal legislature. As was expected, the Court found fault with both constitutions, being particularly severe on the IFP's attempt (even though much diluted by the exigencies of achieving a two-thirds majority in the legislature) to articulate its version of radical provincial autonomy in the KwaZulu-Natal constitution. The court's rejection of both constititions held out the possibility that the IFP might rejoin the constitutional negotiations. But the ANC took its cue from the Constititional Court – which made it clear that only modifications and adjustments were needed to make the national constitution acceptable – and firmly rejected any notion of radical re-negotiation to accommodate the IFP. The draft which went back to the Court in October addresses some of the IFP's concerns about the status of provincial government, but makes little progress towards satisfying its demands for provincial autonomy. The Court held hearings on the revised draft in the first week of November. The constitution was passed into law in December 1996.

For the moment, the outlines[58] of a political settlement remain a matter of conjecture, some of which has been rather far-fetched.[59] The peace process is becalmed, rather than embattled. Both the local elections and the constitution point in the direction of co-existence and settlement, but it remains to be seen whether the parties can make decisive moves to take advantage of the new political conditions.

NOTES

1. The monitoring organization, the Human Rights Committee (formerly the Human Rights Commission) recorded 609 deaths due to political violence in KwaZulu-Natal in the eight months between May and Dec. 1994, an average of 76 fatalities per month. This represented a large drop from the over 1,000 deaths recorded between Jan. and April 1994. The figures from another monitoring group, the Centre for Socio-Legal Studies at the University of Natal, Durban, are consistently higher, with a total for May–Dec. 1994 of 689 and an average of 86. It is not clear why there should be such a discrepancy, although it may be the result of differing conceptions of what constitutes 'political violence'. See e.g. 'Monitors differ on violence' (*The Saturday Paper*, Durban, 16 Sept. 1995). This reports one monitor's tally of 168 politically related deaths for Aug., as against the HRC's total of 83, less than half. For other examples of discrepancies between monitors' reports and for the significance of this for interpreting the violence, see M. de Haas, 'Political Violence' in E. Louw (ed.) *South African Human Rights Yearbook 1994*, Centre for Socio-legal Studies, Durban, 1995. There is another question of perspective; deaths in 'political' violence account for only a small proportion of violent deaths in the province. During 1995, there were 5,146 recorded murders in KwaZulu-Natal, more than any other province, of which only about 10 per cent were 'political'. See 'When it comes to murder, KZN tops it', *Mercury* (Durban) 19 March 1996.
2. A newspaper report in Aug. 1990 specified 4,200 deaths since the beginning of 1987, based

on a digest of tallies from several monitoring groups. See 'The killings in Natal, chilling statistics', *Daily News* (Durban), 20 Aug. 1990. An earlier report mentioned a figure of 3,500 deaths between Jan. 1987 and April 1990. See 'Into the valley of death', *Observer*, 8 April 1990.

3. Inkatha was founded in 1975 as a Zulu cultural liberation movement. It was relaunched as a multiracial political party, the Inkatha Freedom Party, in Aug. 1990.

4. The state of emergency which had been in force throughout the country from 1986 was lifted everywhere but Natal in June 1990. It was lifted in Natal in Oct. The State President, F.W. de Klerk, on the urging of the Transitional Executive Council, imposed a new state of emergency in KwaZulu-Natal on 31 March 1994. It was lifted again on 31 Aug. 1994. See Human Rights Committee (Natal), *The KwaZulu-Natal State of Emergency* (mimeo), Sept. 1994; Human Rights Committee of South Africa *Human Rights Review* 1994 (Johannesburg 1994). See also Eduardo Marino, *KwaZulu-Natal Emergency: Statements and Observations from the International Observer to the Emergency* (mimeo, n.d.)

5. Formerly Pretoria/Witwatersrand/Vereeniging, the new province created out of the most populous parts of the pre-1990 Transvaal province, and renamed in 1994. Violence monitors and journalists often referred in their reports to the Witwatersrand as the main theatre of the violence between 1990 and 1994.

6. These calculations were done using the Centre for Socio-legal Studies' figures.

7. Figures for 1995 are similar to the post-election months of 1994. According to the Human Rights Commission, 331 people died in political violence between Jan. and April, a monthly average of 82. Further reductions brought the average down to around 70, with low figures of 57 in Aug. and 37 in Nov. A series of massacres on the South Coast, inland from Port Shepstone, in late Dec., reversed this trend. The figures for early 1996 were Jan., 26, Feb., 30, March, 46. See 'Warnings of bloody poll in KwaZulu', *Sunday Times* 7 April 1996.

8. On questions of political mythology and the Zulu past, see G. Mare, *Brothers Born of Warrior Blood* (Johannesburg: Ravan Press 1992); C. Hamilton, 'An Appetite for the Past: the Re-creation of Shaka and the Crisis in Popular Historical Consciousness', *South African Historical Jnl* 22 (1990) pp.141–57; J. Wright, 'Political Mythology and the Making of Natal's Mfecane', *Canadian Jnl of African Studies* 23 (1989) pp.271–2.

9. On the IFP's objections to the 'sufficient consensus' principle, see D. Atkinson, 'Brokering a Miracle: The Multiparty Negotiating Forum' in S. Friedman and idem (eds.) *The Small Miracle: South Africa's Negotiated Settlement* (Johannesburg: Ravan Press 1994) pp.13–43, at pp.29–33.

10. Although the IFP claims to be the leading party in KwaZulu-Natal, its support is concentrated very heavily in the rural areas. This fact was somewhat obscured by its narrow aggregate win (whose legitimacy was in any case contested by the ANC) in the proportional representation elections of April 1994, but starkly revealed by the thrice-postponed local elections which were held in June 1996. The substantial element of geographical (ward) representation emphasised the ANC's overwhelming victory in the cities and the IFP's confinement to areas in which traditional leaders are a force to be reckoned with.

11. The Human Rights Committee's figures for the first four months of 1994 are: Jan., 172; Feb., 180; March, 311; April, 338; total 1,001. The Centre for Socio-legal Studies' figure was 21 less for the period, 980.

12. For fuller coverage of the issues in this section, see A.M. Johnston, 'The Political World of KwaZulu-Natal' in R.W. Johnson and L. Schlemmer (eds.) *Launching Democracy: the First Open Election, April 1944* (New Haven, CT: Yale UP 1995).

13. The rhetoric of the highest leaders swings from exhortations to peace to President Mandela's threat to 'crush dissidents' and Chief Buthelezi's call to 'rise and resist' central government. Lower down the hierarchy, leaders are often more direct and unambiguous in their threats.

14. An authoritative pre-election study of political attitudes found that in KwaZulu-Natal, 'By international standards, tolerance was shockingly low in all communities'. Across a range of issues, '…among Africans…on no issue did those favouring tolerance reach even 40%' R.W. Johnson *et al. Launching Democracy: Seventh Report* (Durban: Inst. For Multi-Party Democracy 1994) p.16. Political intolerance is a nation-wide phenomenon (see for instance the evidence for the Eastern Cape and Transkei in J. Coetzee and G. Wood, 'How the Vote

Will Go: A Survey of African Potential Voters in the Eastern Cape', *Politikon* 20/2 (Dec. 1993) pp.25–45), but a national survey found the problem more severe in KwaZulu-Natal than in other provinces. For instance, 25 per cent of Africans believed that their area was under the control of political groups 'who will make sure that people will vote for a particular party whether they like it or not.' R.W. Johnson and L. Schlemmer, *Launching Democracy: Fifth Report* (Durban: Inst. for Multi-Party Democracy 1994).

15. For instance, the Human Rights Committee's annual overview of political violence for 1994 concludes that, 'The majority of the deaths occurred as a result of fighting between ANC and IFP supporters. Subsequent to the elections, a growing trend of internal power struggles within both the ANC and IFP also led to loss of life.' Accepting the political interpretation however, as the Centre for Adult Education at the U. of Natal, Pietermaritzburg points out, 'does not mean rejecting the obvious multi-causal influences on the conflict'.

16. '...it remains clear that a primary trigger of current violence and intimidation remains the rivalry between, and the fight for territory and the control thereof by the Inkatha Freedom party and the African National Congress.' Commission of Inquiry Regarding the Prevention of Public Violence and Intimidation (the Goldstone Commission) *Third Interim Report* (21 Dec. 1992) pp.2–3. See also, p.8 on the need for free political activity in all areas.

17. Among the groups which fall into these categories are the Human Rights Committee, the South African Inst. of Race Relations (hereafter SAIRR), the Democratic Party and the Black Sash. Of them, the Human Rights Committee is the most influential recorder of the violence in KwaZulu-Natal. Several past and present members of its governing body have close links to the ANC. The IFP has developed its own violence monitoring capacities as a reaction to what it sees as a predominantly pro-ANC bias among monitoring groups. Two university-linked groups, which to some extent 'monitor the monitors', have also been influential. These are the Centre for Adult Education at the U. of Natal, Pietermaritzburg and the Centre for Socio-legal Studies at the U. of Natal, Durban. *Indicator South Africa*, also at the U. of Natal, Durban, has published much research on the violence and produces a regular supplement – the 'Conflict Monitor' which offers statistical interpretation of trends in the data collected by monitoring groups.

18. See e.g. A. Jeffery, *Spotlight on Disinformation About Violence in South Africa* (Johannesburg: SAIRR Oct. 1992), which accuses Amnesty International, the International Commission of Jurists and the Human Rights Commission of inaccurate and one-sided reporting of the violence. Jeffery's work was vigorously contested in turn, in the first place from within the SAIRR itself. See G. Ellis, 'Third Force: The Weight of Evidence', *SAIRR Western Cape Region Research Committee* (Oct. 1992). It was also criticized in the Star newspaper by D. Davies and G. Marcus, 9 Oct.1992. Elsewhere, J. Aitchison of the Centre for Adult Education at the U. of Natal, Pietermaritzburg called *Spotlight on Disinformation* 'highly contentious and tendentious'. See the Centre's *Submission to the Commission of Inquiry into Public Violence and Intimidation* Dec. 1992 (mimeo). Ms Jeffrey replied to her critics in 'The Criticism is Unfounded' Race Relations News (Johannesburg: December 1992). Ms Jeffrey's work, and to some extent that of SAIRR director John Kane-Berman (*Political Violence in South Africa*, Johannesburg, SAIRR 1993) draws attention, among other things, to alleged underreporting of security force and IFP casualties.

19. A. Louw, 'Reporting Violent Conflict in KwaZulu-Natal: an assessment of selected sources for conflict research', MA thesis, Dept of Politics, U. of Natal, Durban.

20. A good example of this genre is Matthew Kentridge, *An Unofficial War: Inside the Conflict in Pietermaritzburg* (Cape Town: David Philip 1990).

21. Helpful discussions of rival explanations of the violence can be found in S. Bekker and A.Louw (eds.) *Capturing the Event: Conflict Trends in the Natal Region 1986–92* (Durban: Indicator SA Issue Focus 1992) and J. Aitchison, *Interpreting the Violence: The Struggle to Understand the Natal Conflict* (U. of Natal, Pietermaritzburg: Centre for Adult Education 1992) mimeo. Both note the predominance of the 'political rivalry' explanation, but while Bekker and Louw are strictly non-committal, Aitchison inclines towards acceptance of it as well.

22. See for instance J. Argyle, 'Faction Fights, Feuds, Ethnicity and Political Conflict in Natal', paper presented at a conference on 'Ethnicity, Society and Conflict in Natal' (U. of Natal,

Pietermaritzburg, Sept. 1992). Another source sees the violence as self-sustaining, although it does not put the same explanatory weight on traditional cultures as Argyle's paper. S. Collins, 'Things Fall Apart: The Culture of Violence Becomes Entrenched' in A. Minnaar, *Patterns of Violence: An Overview of Conflict in Natal During the 1980s and 1990s* (Pretoria: Human Sciences Research Council 1992) pp.95–106.

23. P. Zulu, 'Durban Hostels and Political Violence: Case Studies in KwaMashu and Umlazi', *Transformation* (Durban) 21 (1993) pp.1–23.

24. C. Campbell, 'Learning to Kill? Masculinity, the Family and Violence in Natal', *Jnl of Southern African Studies* 18/3 (Sept. 1992) pp.614–28. This article combines arguments about gender and generational conflict. See also, in the same issue, A. Sitas, 'The Making of the "Comrades" Movement in Natal, 1985–91' (pp.629–42), which deals with the 'youth culture' aspects of political violence.

25. See A. Minnaar, 'Undisputed Kings: Warlordism in Natal' in idem (ed.) *Patterns of Violence* (note 22) pp.61–93.

26. N. Gwala, 'Political Violence and the Struggle for Control in Pietermaritzburg', *Jnl of Southern African Studies* 15/3 (April 1989) pp.506–24.

27. On Molweni, see S. Stavrou and A. Crouch, 'Molweni: Violence on the Periphery', *Indicator SA* 6/3 (Winter 1989) pp.46-50. On Edendale, see S. Stavrou, 'Underdevelopment: Natal's Formula for Conflict', *Indicator SA* 7/3 (Autumn 1990) pp.52–6. On Bruntville, see A. Minnaar, 'Locked in a Cycle of Violence: The Anatomy of Conflict in Bruntville 1990–92' in idem, *Patterns of Violence* (note 22) pp.143–62.

28. M. Morris and D. Hindson, 'South Africa: Political Violence and Reconstruction', *Review of African Political Economy* 53 (1992) pp.43–59, at p.49. See also, by the same authors, 'The Disintegration of Apartheid: From Violence to Reconstruction' in Glenn Moss and Ingrid Obery (eds.) *South African Review* 6 (Johannesburg: Ravan Press 1992) pp.152–70. For criticism, see, R. Ajulu, 'Political Violence in South Africa: A Rejoinder to Morris and Hindson', *Review of African Political Economy 55*, (1992) pp.67–83 and M.E. Bennun, 'Understanding the Nightmare: Politics and Violence in South Africa', in *Negotiating Justice: A New Constitution for South Africa* (Exeter UP 1995), pp.26–61. Both favour a conspiratorial explanation for the violence which places the blame on 'the apartheid state'.

29. Hindson and Morris (note 28) pp.49–55.

30. R. Taylor and M. Shaw, 'Interpreting the Conflict in Natal', *Africa Perspective* 2/1 (Dec. 1993) pp.1–14, at p.13.

31. Taylor and Shaw, p.2.

32. See for instance 'Law of the gun', *Natal Mercury,* 15 May 1993, in which the head of Durban's King Edward VIII Hospital surgical intensive care unit reports a dramatic rise in the proportion of gunshot to stab wounds.

33. See the resolution of the ANC National Executive Committee, 20 Sept. 1990, in which SDU's were officially sanctioned by the organization.

34. IFP SPUs were based on personnel who had received military training by South African security forces in 1986 as part of covert assistance to Inkatha. An ambitious scheme to train thousands of rank and file members began in 1993 and was investigated by the TEC law and order sub-committee in early 1994.

35. Human Rights Committee, *Natal's Total Onslaught* (Johannesburg, Sept. 1994), mimeo.

36. For example, the Human Rights Committee's Jan. 1995 report includes the following account: 'In the first attack on 18 January, five ANC supporters were killed by alleged IFP supporters from the Greytown area *in a politicized faction fight*' (emphasis added). Another example is a case study of a violent area on the South Coast where a chiefship succession dispute, traceable back to 1984, divided a community into two factions. These rivals are now identifiable with the IFP and ANC, and the possession of chieftaincy is now being disputed through the medium of party conflict. See N. Claude, 'The Kwamadlala Dispute: Conflict on the Ground', *KwaZulu-Natal Briefing* (Durban) 2 (May 1992) pp.10–11.

37. In the six months prior to the election (Nov. 1993–April 1994), there were 689 deaths from political violence in Gauteng (average 115). In the remaining 8 months of 1994, there were only 260, an average of 32.

38. But see H. Adam and K. Moodley 'Political Violence, "Tribalism" and Inkatha', *Jnl of*

Modern African Studies 30/3 (1992) pp.485–510, esp. at p.504, where the authors briefly note that, 'The late conquest of Natal meant that the traditional economy remains more intact than elsewhere' and that urban and rural life collide more there than in other provinces.

39. For examples of the mixed record of the police in the new order in KwaZulu-Natal, see de Haas, 'Political Violence' (note 1) pp.239–40.

40. This is the first paragraph of a seven part section of the consolidated terms of reference, which goes on to list numerous other issues for mediation and negotiation. The 'override powers' referred to in the quotation are contained in Art. 126 of the interim constitution, the section on which the IFP's most strenuous objections are centred. See S. Mzimela, 'Our democratic options', *Sunday Times* (Johannesburg) 26 Feb. 1995. Mr. Mzimela is Minister of Correctional Services in the Government of National Unity and chief IFP negotiator on the Constitutional Committee. See also 'Inkatha puts case for international mediation' *Business Day* (Johannesburg) 23 Feb. 1995.

41. 'King rejects outside help', *Natal Mercury,* 6 Feb. 1995.

42. 'IFP holds its ground on mediation', ibid. 7 March 1995.

43. The interim constitution empowered provinces to pass their own constitutions if they wished, provided they were not incompatible with the national constitution. On 15 March 1996 a constitution was passed by the KwaZulu-Natal provincial assembly, but it was a far cry from the vigorous statement of provincial autonomy which the IFP had proposed in earlier drafts. See 'KwaZulu-Natal's New Constitution', *KwaZulu-Natal Briefing* 1 (March 1996) pp.1–11. The Constitutional Court has ruled that the Provincial Constitution is invalid on the grounds that it is inconsistent with the National Constitution. Individual judges expressed themselves very strongly on what they saw as the provincial constitution's threat to the integrity of the country as a whole.

44. For a critical view of the part played by traditional leaders in KwaZulu's system of homeland rule see G. Mare and G. Hamilton, *An Appetite for Power: Buthelezi's Inkatha and South Africa* (Johannesburg: Ravan Press 1987). See also P.M. Zulu, 'The Rural Crisis: Authority Structures and their role in Development' in H. Giliomee and L. Schlemmer, *Up Against the Fences: Poverty, Passes and Privilege in South Africa* (Cape Town: David Philip 1985).

45. Parliament of KwaZulu-Natal, Act No.7 of 1994; Assented to by the premier, 11 Nov. 1994.

46. The gist of the dispute between the monarchy and Chief Buthelezi over this office is that the monarchy claims there is no such thing as a 'traditional prime minister' and that the king may chose whomever he pleases. According to the king and the royal council, the office is merely a fiction invented by Buthelezi to exploit the monarchy for party political purposes. Chief Buthelezi claims that the office is independent of the king's wishes and is based on custom, including a hereditary element. By defining the traditional prime minister as 'in accordance with Zulu custom and tradition' (Section 1), of which the House itself is acknowledged as custodian (Section 4), the Act purports to give a legal and constitutional basis for Buthelezi's claim.

47. They are allowed to constitute up to 20 per cent of local authorities in tribal areas.

48. For discussion, see 'What Mandela is doing in Natal', *Sunday Times* (Johannesburg) 11 June 1995 and 'A R100m buy-off brings chiefs under ANC wing', ibid. 18 June 1995. As of mid-1996, the constitutional wrangle over chiefs' payment is still before the Constitutional Court.

49. For a discussion see 'Whither the Imbizo?' *KwaZulu-Natal Briefing* 1 (March 1996) pp.4–5. For a discussion of the problem of traditional authority in KwaZulu-Natal, see 'The Clash that Had to Come: African Nationalism and the 'Problem of Traditional Authority', ibid. pp.11–15.

50. *Constitution of the Republic of South Africa* (Act 200, 1993) Ch.14.

51. Art. 126 of the interim constitution sets out wide-ranging grounds on which national legislation may override that of provinces in the event of inconsistency between the two. Sect. 2 (c) which invokes the imperative of setting 'minimum standards across the nation for the rendering of public services' and 2 (d), which invokes national security, are particularly relevant to the question of control of policing.

52. *Constitution of the Republic of South Africa*, Ch.14, Sect. 1 (k).

53. This document was adopted by the KwaZulu Legislative Assembly on 1 Dec. 1992. All but

convinced IFP supporters interpreted it as a statement of confederal, if not secessionist intent. Despite the chronic ambiguity of the IFP's position on provincial autonomy, there is a good case for regarding the 1992 document as the IFP leadership's preferred option, from which they moved only reluctantly and tactically. For instance, documents leaked to the press in mid-1995 suggest that the IFP's positions on several constitutional issues remained close to the 1992 Constitution. See 'IFP constitution provides for sovereign KwaZulu-Natal', *Sunday Tribune*, 11 June 1995. For a critical interpretation of the 1992 document, see D. van Wyk 'Federalism and Governance', paper presented to a seminar on 'The Federal Option: Choices for KwaZulu-Natal' (Durban 15 July 1993). Dawid van Wyk is professor of constitutional law at the U. of South Africa.

54. The Constitution of the State of KwaZulu-Natal, Sect. 67 (b), p.14. The IFP's ambitions for autonomous and extensive policing powers and for militia forces in the province were watered down somewhat in the negotiations which led to the passing of the provincial constitution. Nevertheless, such provisions have still elicited unfavourable comment from judges of the Constitutional Court in the course of the ANC's challenge to the constitution.

55. 'Inkatha throws down the gauntlet to government', *Business Day*, 26 Jan. 1995.

56. By mid-1996, the ITU principle had been extended by the deployment of four special teams to investigate political massacres. Numerous arrests, especially of IFP supporters (and some policemen) on the South Coast, testify to the success of the principle. The IFP bitterly opposes its 'bias', although there have been a few arrests of ANC supporters.

57. For a discussion of the political context of security policies and the opportunities and limits of intensified security initiatives, see A.M. Johnston, 'Security Dilemmas: Confronting the Violence in KwaZulu-Natal', *KwaZulu-Natal Briefing* 2 (May 1996) pp.17–20.

58. For an assessment see A.M. Johnston, 'The KwaZulu-Natal Local Elections and the Prospects of Political re-alignment', *KwaZulu-Natal Briefing* 3 (Aug. 1996).

59. For instance the *Sunday Times* (Johannesburg) predicted a *rapprochement* so radical that it would lead to an early merger between the two parties in the province; 'Miracle deal: party heavyweights back unity plan', 7 July 1996.

Riding the Tiger:
Urban Warfare on the East Rand

JUDITH HUDSON

In the 1990s the black townships of the East Rand have become synonymous with violent conflict. This essay examines this violence and attempts to draw out some trends and themes which have emerged during its course. It examines the efficacy of various measures to intervene in the conflict, such as the National Peace Accord, an the deployment of security forces – the Internal Stability Unit (ISU), the South African Defence Force (SADF), and the disastrous National Peacekeeping Force (NPKF). It is argued that the high levels of crime and violence in the region are exacerbated by social inequalities, poverty and joblessness. These factors become mutually reinforcing with the result that the area's ability to shake off its violent past and begin the task of economic regeneration is compromised. For this reason, a two-prong strategy which combines security and development is necessary.

That everyone has the right to life, liberty and security of person has not always been evident in the black townships on the East Rand in South Africa. In the 1990s these townships descended into semi-civil war that has left scars on hundreds of thousands of black people living there. The history of this urban area is one of conflict, violence and blood. Indeed, in the public imagination the East Rand has become synonymous with violence.

This is not surprising. Analysts have pinpointed the start of what has been termed the 'Reef township war' as July 1990, when violence that had been raging in the Natal province (approximately 600 kilometres away) seemed to spread like an infection to the then Pretoria/Witwatersrand/Vereeniging (PWV) area. Headlines of newspapers announced: 'Transvaal may become new killing fields', 'Violence spreads like wildfire'; one headline stated simply, 'WAR'. This 'Reef war' continued unabated until April 1994 and was fought to a large extent on the East Rand, the approximately 3,000 square kilometres on the eastern side of the Witwatersrand. It was ostensibly driven by hostilities between the Inkatha Freedom Party (IFP)- and African National Congress (ANC)-aligned combatants. Of the 136 massacres which occurred in the then PWV area for the period 1990 to 1993, 35 took place within the Katorus (Katlehong, Thokoza, Vosloorus) area, which includes the Phola Park informal settlement, on the east Rand. In these 35 massacres 311 people were killed.[1] (A massacre is defined here as the killing of five or more people in a single attack). Until June 1993, the East Rand accounted for about 45 per cent of all Witwatersrand fatalities. In the six months that followed, 80 per cent of those who died on the Reef did so in a battle over a few square kilometres of contested terrain in Katlehong and Thokoza. Well over 1,000 houses were severely damaged, and at least another thousand families were driven from their homes.[2] In 1993, 1,058 of South Africa's 20,000 murders were committed in Katlehong and 593 in Thokoza, most of these war-related. At one stage Katorus accounted for about half of all the violent incidents reported across South Africa.

This essay will focus on political violence in townships on the East Rand, particularly the Katorus area, in the 1990s. It attempts to draw out some trends and themes in the conflict, not just as an academic exercise but in the belief that it is necessary to know all there is to know about the conflict if we are to successfully bring it to an end. It examines the efficacy of various measures to intervene in the conflict, such as the National Peace Accord, and the deployment of security forces – the Internal Stability Unit (ISU), the South African Defence Force (SADF), and the disastrous National Peacekeeping Force (NPKF). It is argued that the high levels of crime and violence in the region are exacerbated by social inequalities, poverty and joblessness. These factors become mutually reinforcing with the result that the area's ability to shake off its violent past and begin the task of economic regeneration is compromised. A strategy which combines security and development is therefore necessary.

Counting the Costs

In the four years from 1990 to 1994 approximately 3,000 people were killed in townships on the East Rand. The disruption to people's lives caused by violence was severe.

Prior to the violence, hostel residents and their township counterparts apparently mixed quite freely. Said one hostel resident, 'We have lived together with township residents for a long time ... There is no problem between us. I have many friends and relatives in the township. If my wife visits me [from Natal] I go to the township to ask for a temporary accommodation whilst [she] is around.'[3] However, this changed as the conflict escalated. Even people with relatives occupying hostels were forced to flee their homes, as they were suspected to be collaborating with hostel residents. By the beginning of 1991 several of the IFP-controlled hostels were housing entire families and were no longer simply single-sex hostels, becoming known as 'refugee hostels'. The hostels became in the words of one commentator 'isolated communities cut off and alienated from the surrounding township.'[4] Older Zulu men living in the hostels spoke of their victimization at the hands of young 'comrades', of rumours that flew

MAP 1
THE KATORUS AREA

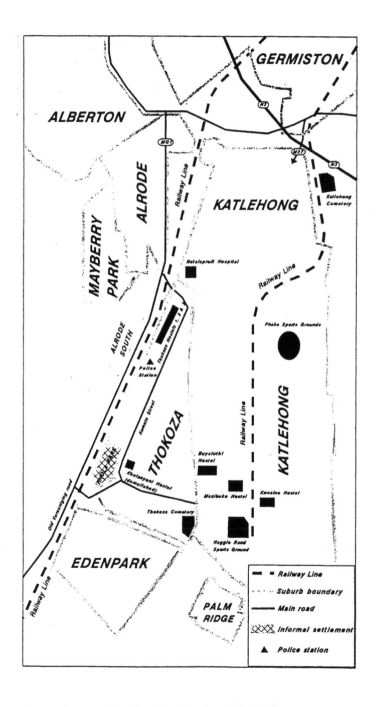

through the hostel that the 'comrades are coming' and of the 'arrogance' of township youth and their lack of respect for older people. In the eyes of their township counterparts, the hostel residents were 'boorish aliens' who competed for their jobs – as *'mogus'* or *'amagoduka'* (fools or wanderers).

Travelling by taxi became dangerous. Taxi organizations came to be aligned with certain political organizations. McCaul notes that the taxi industry was already characterized by the prevalence of a 'gang mentality', partly the result of drivers being prime targets for muggings and the fact that they group together for protection, which often led to violence. Deregulation of the industry led to market saturation and threatened profitability, so stirring up violent feuding.[5] When violence increased, taxis serving IFP-controlled hostels could only pick up passengers and use streets through areas controlled by the IFP. Similarly taxi associations serving ANC areas could only stop in ANC controlled areas. Taxis on the 'wrong' roads would come under fire from the opposing side.[6] In Alberton separate taxi ranks operate for hostel and township residents. In May 1991 gunmen fired on a taxi rank in Katlehong killing six people and wounding 23 others. One of the victims was wearing ANC colours.

People are dying in East Rand townships because each side wants to make the townships no-go areas for the other. There are ANC areas and IFP areas and as in gang warfare, the object is to protect your turf and try to capture others. This leads to the unofficial demarcation of territory and sections of townships as either ANC or IFP; what this means in effect is that all opposition had been killed, silenced and removed and a false hegemony established.

It is however unlikely that we will ever know the full extent of the violence and hardship that has affected this area. For a start, accurate violence statistics do not exist. Many incidents of violence go unreported and when they are, this is not necessarily done accurately, objectively or with adequate verification. More to the point, the cost in human terms is not amenable to statistical analysis.

With the general elections on 27 April 1994 came a decline in political violence on the East Rand. This was partly due to high levels of security force deployment, which the ANC had called for, and the large number of local and international monitors. The area is experiencing relative peace and stability. Past patterns, however, suggest that when deaths fall it is very often only a reprieve and they soon begin to rise again. The large amount of weaponry on the East Rand means that violence could flare up very quickly.

Violent crime is, however, increasing in the area. As Schlemmer observes, 'where one type of violence is prevalent, other types of violence are likely to occur as well.'[7] In the first three months of 1995, 675 hijackings took place (with Katlehong, Thokoza and Tembisa the worst spots for hijacking on the Witwatersrand) and the hijacking of goods vehicles is reported daily from industrial zones adjacent to the East Rand townships.[8] It is important to note that in the 1990s it has become increasingly difficult to separate criminal and political violence. Activists of all political persuasions nurtured in a climate of political intolerance and driven by zealotry often behaved like common criminals.

The Effects of Industrialization and Urbanization

Violence on the East Rand took place within the context of a declining sub-region. The East Rand area is the heart of South Africa's manufacturing economy, with up to 51 per cent of its Gross Geographic Product (GGP) coming from manufacturing alone.[9] The area succeeded in making the transition from a mining region in the 1960s to an industrial region by the 1980s.[10] This transition was the result not only of the growth of industrial activity, but also of the decline in mining and agricultural sectors. It is now the largest single territorial concentration of manufacturing in the country. In 1988, the East Rand had 3,341 manufacturing establishments, 240,340 employees, and a gross output of R22.2 billion.[11] The output was nearly 19 per cent of the national manufacturing output of R118.2 billion, and just above 40 per cent of the then PWV region output of R54.8 billion.[12] Manufacturing has then become 'the industrial focus of the PWV region.'[13] This sector remains fairly diverse in character. While basic industries like iron and steel production dominate other sub-sectors are involved in the production of vehicle components, machinery, chemicals, food and synthetic products.

The manufacturing sector's performance on the East Rand, however, has been in decline: manufacturing performance in 1988 was lower than that in 1978.[14] As Shaw notes, 'While balanced by growth in other areas – notably in the service and transportation sectors – this has not halted the general downturn and turnover in the sub-region has been declining in real terms.' Although this downturn is consistent with the rest of the PWV region, the decline was sharper on the East Rand with real turnover in 1992/3 being 17.7 per cent below the 1989/90 level.[15] More recently, this decline may be tapering off.

The largest concentration of settlements is in the Katorus areas. This geographic core of townships is surrounded by the white towns of Germiston, Bedfordview, Boksburg and Alberton. The economic differentials between black and white areas are notable. The average income of whites is nearly six times that of the East Rand's approximately 2 million Africans. A recent market research profile describes the area's roughly 600,000 whites as: primarily Afrikaans-speaking; containing a high proportion of adults over the age of 35; highly educated; typically employed full-time;

mostly married, with both husband and wife working; shopping at the area's hyper- or supermarkets; and, finally, as enthusiastic home-owners with a great interest in activities like home-improvement, painting, and gardening. About 60 per cent of households earn more than R4,000 a month; the income profile on the Near East Rand is both relatively higher than that of the Far East Rand and the country as a whole.[16]

By contrast, just over 96 per cent of Africans earn less than R4,000 (compared to 40 per cent) of whites. The income of many employed Africans is below subsistence levels, with 35 per cent of households earning less than R500 per month, and 82 per cent less than R1,400 per month.[17] Close to a third of Africans are shack dwellers. Unemployment is running at around 40 per cent of the adult African population. Thokoza's population rose from 2,500 in 1965 to 228,000 in 1990, with a density per stand of above 20 people, this to a large extent the result of the presence of 65,000 backyard shacks (as compared to 17,650 formal housing units). East Rand townships also feature many hostel residents – Katorus alone has about 50,000 people in 29 hostels which contributes to the East Rand's high proportion of Zulu speakers.

In 1995 it was estimated that the East Rand contained at least 30 per cent of a smaller Gauteng's 6.9 million population. If this growth trend continues, the East Rand's population will at least have doubled from 1.5 million in 1985 to 3 million in 2010 – 'the fastest growth rate in Gauteng, reflecting both the natural increase and the area's status as a magnet for immigrants from all over South Africa.'[18]

As stated in *Post-Apartheid Population and Income Trends* published by the Centre for Development and Enterprise, 'Poverty in [South Africa's] urban areas should not be ignored. Urban poverty will increase, and if left unattended could become explosive.'[19] This would appear to be the case on the East Rand. A rapidly growing and poorly-skilled population faces a shortage of formal and informal jobs and a shrinking of a metals production and processing economic base. This situation is exacerbated by heavily overcrowded and dense townships.

Capturing the Conflict

It is not possible to provide a blow-by-blow account of the conflict that has characterized the area.[20] It is however, possible to make a few observations on some trends which have surfaced during its course. It must be emphasized that generalizations about the origins and causes of politically motivated violence are difficult to make. The battlelines in the conflict are incredibly complicated. There are also some misconceptions that further muddy the water.

The first of these relates to when the 'Reef war' started. A 'diary of events' complied by the South African Institute of Race Relations showed a steady increase in tension and conflict in the area from the beginning of 1990. What this means is that violence in the PWV area did not 'suddenly explode' or 'come out of the blue', nor should it have 'surprised' many commentators when it increased dramatically in the second half of 1990. As early as February/March 1990, for example, violence in a dispute between two taxi associations over a 'defence of routes' jealously regarded as belonging to one group of operators resulted in a conflict which spread from Katlehong to other parts of the East Rand and claimed the lives of 50 people and left 350 injured. This taxi feud spread to the hostels when a hostel was petrol-bombed, leading to a thousand hostel residents going 'on the rampage', and spilled over into the schools as six pupils and teachers were killed and more than 80 injured. The ripple fed on the 'outsider' status of the hostel residents, and was perpetuated by their reaction.[21] Prior to this in the 1980s various states of emergency had been imposed to curb violence in the area. This violence should not be ignored.

A striking trend to emerge in the conflict is its erratic nature. Indeed, the peaks and valleys that characterize it stand in contradistinction with the more sustained nature of the conflict in KwaZulu/Natal. Related to this is that the 'peaks' of violence on the Reef tended to be 'matched' by a trough in the Natal midlands, which seemed to indicate a connection between the two conflicts. It has been suggested that the movement of migrant workers from Natal to the PWV area and vice versa might contribute to this 'see-saw' trend.

In 1991 violence on the East Rand seemed to change its pattern. Mourners at funeral vigils, train passengers or those at taxi ranks, patrons of shebeens and other 'soft targets' became the victims. Large-scale, open conflicts between hostel residents and their township counterparts were replaced by professionally executed attacks against key individuals, by drive-by shootings, isolated revenge attacks and assassination.

On 8 September 1991, just six days before the signing of the National Peace Accord, gunmen opened fire on a group of Inkatha supporters who were marching to a rally, killing 23 people. The wife of an IFP official, Ms Gertrude Mzizi, who was driving behind the Inkatha supporters, said she saw a man 'in a long black jacket come out of a house holding an AK47 rifle, blowing a whistle. As he blew the whistle, other men came from other houses and they also had rifles... Then they started shooting.' She said the occupants of the house were dedicated ANC supporters. The death toll for this attack was officially put at 42, with more than 50 injured, as retaliatory attacks swept Katlehong, Tembisa and Johannesburg. In evidence gathered by a sub-committee of the Commission of Inquiry Regarding the Prevention of Public Violence and Intimidation, chaired by Justice Richard Goldstone (and commonly known as the Goldstone Commission), it was found that these attacks were premeditated, planned and carried out by residents of the Phola Park informal settlement and members of the Phola Park Self-defence Unit.[22]

This situation was further exacerbated by the assassination of the general secretary of the Civic Associations of Southern Transvaal, Sam Ntuli, a few days later. His funeral was marked by at least 19 deaths, despite a large police presence. The first attack was on taxi drivers by mourners, followed by retaliatory attacks by members of the Katlehong People's Taxi Association – widely considered to be overwhelmingly IFP supporters – and lastly by hostel dwellers on funeral goers marching to and fro past the Thokoza hostel taunting hostel residents.

Why these killings in Thokoza were significant is because they represented a planned ambushing of residents from the hostel on the way to the rally, and illustrated the increased proliferation of AK47s in the possession of many of the participants. The increasing use of firepower in political violence was fast becoming a cause for concern. Conflict on the East Rand was originally fought with sticks, spears, knives, homemade guns (or *quashas* – called that because of the sound they made when fired), and automatic weapons. By 1993 more people were being killed than wounded in violent incidents.

The Problems of Policing

Policing the conflict on the East Rand, and indeed elsewhere in South Africa, has been the source of much controversy. Poor relations between the police and the community stemmed from apartheid days when policing townships was intended to eliminate opposition to the Nationalist government, rather than crime prevention or peacekeeping purposes. So, when conflict escalated on the East Rand the police were seen as part of the problem by many township residents, not the solution. Moreover, security forces were also accused of collusion with IFP-supporting hostel residents when the latter attacked townships, which furthered reduced confidence in them.

High levels of violence in this area can partly be attributed to ineffective security force intervention. It sounds counter-intuitive to state that South Africa – 'the apartheid police state' – is under-policed. But South Africa has one policeman for every 358 people, one of the lowest ratios in the developed world. In the country's urban areas 'the thin blue line' is too narrow, demoralized and under-resourced to perform adequately. Violent behaviour has often been allowed to go unchecked through lack of resources to deal with it. This in turn has given criminals enormous confidence in their ability to escape arrest or defeat prosecution. Police stations in townships are also understaffed and lack resources. The East Rand is no exception. For example, the police station in Thokoza, which comprises a quarter of a million people, has only four patrol vehicles. This is compounded by the further shortage of resources such as telephone services.

Effective policing is made more difficult by the parlous condition of infrastructure services in the area. In the words of one commentator, 'Crime prevention is difficult when roads are inaccessible, houses are not numbered and streets do not have names or lights.'[23]

The increasing 'wild west' atmosphere and the seeming inability of police patrols to curb the violence led many township residents to resort to a variety of means such as setting up self-defence and self-protection units (SDUs and SPUs respectively) and organizing street patrols to protect communities. Justice of a rough and ready kind was achieved personally and inevitably violently – direct action to obtain revenge seemed like a better option for many people. Whites in nearby suburbs responded by arming themselves, erecting high walls with razor wire trimming and electronic gates, and turned more and more to private security firms to guard their privileged position. In the words of a South African weekly, 'The proliferation of self-defence and self-protection units in townships, vigilantes and neighbourhood watches in suburbs and private security companies in wealthy residential areas indicates that South Africans have given up on the police as a protective force.'[24] This trend towards the 'privatization' of policing/security functions is potentially alarming since it is very difficult to regulate and monitor.

Interpreting the Conflict

Above the violence on the ground was an altogether different kind of conflict, conducted at a safe distance from the actual conflict. As events unfolded, they demanded some kind of explanation and political commentators, journalists, monitoring agencies and academics set themselves this task. This led to a fierce debate about the causes of violence.

Some suggested that the conflict was ethnically driven between Zulus and Xhosas who were apparently battling out tribally based animosities that date back centuries. This view was undermined by the increasing political overtones that emerged in the conflict. Others viewed it as mainly a power struggle between the ANC and the IFP. But the lines of political activity are extremely complicated. The equation can be reduced to ANC and IFP as the two main variables for the purposes of generalization, but provided the limits in doing so are properly understood. The battlelines are not clear-cut and there are also intra-organizational conflicts. Moreover, much of the violence has assumed a spontaneous form in which it has often been far more difficult to clearly identify sides, aggressors and targets that is commonly assumed. Initiators of violence and the affiliations of their victims often remained unknown. Whatever its origins, the ANC/IFP conflict has no doubt been exploited by straight criminal elements.

Conspiracy theorists harboured strong suspicions that the security forces, or perhaps renegade freelancers attached to the far-right paramilitary groups, operated secret 'hit-squads' and constituted a 'third force' which stirred up violence. Indeed, the term 'third force' has been used to explain all, or a large part of, political violence. There is, however, some debate as to what this 'third force' is – it could refer to deliberate efforts by unknown *ad hoc* groups or a premanent structure to fuel the violence. For our purposes, 'third force' activities generally refer to actions by the government and security forces to stir up conflict in the townships. Snapshots of this tendency can be found in:

– the revelations concerning the 'Inkathagate' scandal, as it came to be known, in which it was revealed that the Nationalist government funded two Inkatha rallies and the IFP-linked trade union, the United Workers' Union of South Africa;

– the Goldstone Commission report in November 1992, which revealed the existence of top-secret military intelligence called the Directorate of Covert Collections specialising in 'dirty tricks' against political opponents. Its aim was to smear the ANC by linking its military wing, Umkhonto We Sizwe (MK), to criminal acts and crime syndicates. What was interesting about this revelation is that the plan was hatched 18 months after the lifting of the ban on the ANC.

The problem with this thesis is that any offensive actions by the ANC, in particular undisciplined actions, are ignored. In addition to this, it is difficult to explain the often spontaneous character of the violence with reference to state policies. This theory underplays the 'human factor' in the violence – the phenomenon of score-settling and the cycle of attack and counter-attack which emerged during the conflict.

Others saw the violence as a criminal response to socio-economic deprivation. There is little doubt that poverty and joblessness coupled with an angry and volatile youth impacted on the violence. However, this thesis cannot explain why the PWV area, with twice the average per capita Gross Domestic Product, accounted for half the violence countrywide. Nor can it explain why the Eastern Cape (characterized by extreme poverty) has remained relatively calm. Moreover, poor people are depicted as incapable of understanding their predicament and dealing with it. This needs to be explained.

Clearly, there is no shortage of theories. Through repetition and widespread publicity these theories have achieved the status of conventional wisdom. This is unhelpful since the problem with the grand theories to explain the violence – which may be useful to explain an aspect of the violence – is that the incidents of violence themselves often spill out of and sometimes demolish the conceptual frameworks used to explain them. Violence often seems to take on a life of its own, spill over from one area to another and acquire a dynamic independent of any original causal factor. In this way the effects of earlier factors become new causes. In the process issues blur and intertwine. For example, the Katlehong taxi war quoted earlier, which stemmed from a dispute over the plying of routes, generated a ripple that spread to a hostel and disrupted the school calendar.

While attempting to understand and interpret the volatile mix that makes up the conflict on the East Rand is a necessary exercise, attempting to bring it under control, at least, became a more pressing priority.

Intervening in the Conflict

One attempt to intervene in the situation was the National Peace Accord, brokered by important members of the church and business communities, and signed by a cross-section of political groups in September 1991. The Accord set out a vision both for peace and a new democracy. It included codes of conduct for the political parties, police and army; set the ground rules for free political activity; and laid down the brief for a commission of inquiry (to be chaired by a Supreme Court judge) to investigate cases of public violence and relevant laws and regulations along with ombudsmen for complaints about police behaviour. The Accord also included provisions for the establishment of peace committees at national, regional and local levels which would monitor and facilitate public political activity (marches, rallies and so on), intervene in crises and resolve disputes in cases of violence and potential violence, and also become involved in socio-economic reconstruction and development. The overriding aim of the peace committees was to establish communication between the leaders of parties in conflict and 'put out fires'. It is testimony to the high levels of violence in the area that these types of structures laid down by the Accord were based on the experience of those attempting to bring peace through the establishment of mediation structures in the Katorus area in 1990.

The National Peace Accord's drafters supported the view that the roots of the violence lay in the dire poverty of conflict ridden areas and local and regional peace bodies set up under the Accord were meant to aid development and economic empowerment.[25] The chairman of the National

Peace Committee, John Hall, argued, '[Peace structures] should be peace *and* development committees, with greater emphasis on development... the over-arching goal is development, job creation and [the] recovery of [local] mini economies.'[26] However, most local peace committees [LPCs] were overwhelmed by the immediacy of violent conflict with the result that long-term development was put on the backburner. As Shaw observes, 'The dilemma which faced the peace structures was that tackling the root causes of violence may have been impossible as long as violence persisted.'[27] This was particularly the case in the Katorus area. It was simply not possible to implement development in violence-torn areas. Commenting further on the LPCs, one report stated, 'while not lacking commitment, [LPCs] were short on resources – many simply lacked the capacity to call political supporters of one or the other side to order. Importantly, many of the people who sat in on Peace Committee meetings were not those who were directly engaged in the violence.'[28]

The extent and scope of the conflict in the Katorus area necessitated first the intervention of the SADF in an effort to stabilize the situation, followed by the deployment of the underprepared NPKF in April 1994, and then the redeployment of the SADF and the return of peace to the area. The ISU – a paramilitary policing agency – was deployed in East Rand townships from the beginning of the conflict, but was removed because residents of Katorus felt that it used excessive force in searches for arms and in making arrests, and was partial. There were also other allegations against it including kidnapping, murder, assault and indiscriminate shooting. In effect, the ISU could not effectively police the area and was replaced by the SADF in February 1994.

From the start the SADF was welcomed by the ANC, which had vilified the ISU and was thus compelled to support the alternative. Welcoming rallies were held at which ANC leaders called for the community to co-operate with the army. According to Minnaar and Shaw, 'township rumour has it that both sides in the conflict respected SADF troops because of their willingness to press home attacks when fired on, their impartiality and their disciplined operation.'[29] In all, three battalions were deployed in the Katorus area which effectively saturated it with army personnel. Moreover, the SADF rapidly established communication channels with community and other leaders in Katorus, which increased its efficacy.

While the SADF deployment in Katorus was relatively successful in containing violence, it must be borne in mind that its deployment was the result of an agreement between Nelson Mandela and the then President F.W. de Klerk. This agreement was designed to be more 'broad-based than the simple deployment of troops' and had as its aim the generation of development projects – with the help of the SADF, the Peace Secretariat and local business interests – on the East Rand. As Shaw points out, 'the development side of the project appears to be slow moving.'[30]

The SADF was withdrawn and replaced by the NPKF, essentially a political creation incorporating all the armed formations in South Africa, with a substantial component coming from MK, to ensure legitimacy. The NPKF was the product of national negotiations and was to be deployed in areas of large-scale conflict. The IFP's withdrawal from the negotiation process, however, meant that there was no Inkatha representation in the NPKF. This non-participation by the IFP was to prove central to the failure of the NPKF to deal with the violence on the East Rand. Many Inkatha-supporting hostel residents on the East Rand viewed it as an extension of MK. Moreover, the NPKF was underprepared, ill-equipped and effectively unable to curb the conflict in the area.[31] SADF troops were welcomed back into the townships on the East Rand.

From Economic Decline to Economic Regeneration

One of the consequences of the SADF's redeployment was that development initiatives once again became a key focus in efforts to restore peace. This was made more urgent considering that many areas were devastated by violence and in need of reconstruction, not to mention the poor condition of infrastructure services, such as electricity, water, roads and so on.

The establishment of legitimate local government following the local government elections in November 1995, it is hoped, will facilitate more co-ordinated local development.[32] These local government structures are suitably positioned to begin the process of upgrading the townships and are seen by many as the key fulcrum for development initiatives. Now that the region is relatively peaceful more concerted development action is made more possible. The strength of the local authorities, both financially and politically, is crucial to the success of development initiatives. But there is a need for caution: weak institutional capacity of new local government authorities means that the establishment of sustainable development projects may take a while. One is struck by the frailty of a new local government system that will have to find its place in a complicated environment with many pressures confronting it.

Moreover, development should not be seen as the panacea for the ills of the body social. In a study of development initiatives in Phola Park, Julian Baskin describes how violence had resulted in a 'militaristic' type of leadership in the form of the local self-defence unit. When it became clear that these individuals lacked the skills, both organizational and conceptual, to serve on the development committee they were gradually replaced. The result was a violent backlash against the development committee, the development process coming to an abrupt halt, and the deaths of four people.[33] Thus there is a need for caution. Development disrupts the balance between and within communities, it is a highly politicized activity which has the potential to be divisive. Conflict over resources is common on the Reef, and the allocation of resources is a highly politicized activity in South Africa. Those with a stake in what development efforts seek to change may resist development initiatives with potentially explosive consequences. There is still the possibility that violence in this area may flare up, tensions caused by development could be the spark.

Indeed, there are no quick solutions to this conflict. Having legitimate local government structures in place is indeed very important, but several challenges still confront the area. Perhaps the most important of these is economic growth and the generation of employment to provide for an increasing population. The top priority of development in this area must surely be the creation of wealth and jobs as fast and in as great a number as possible. The effect unemployment has on people's ability to pay for services, its effect on community cohesion and the viability of development strategies must be taken into consideration in turning around the region's economic malaise. This will be a difficult task since business enterprises no longer consider the East Rand generally to be a safe place to invest and the area suffers from what has been termed 'image problems'. It is thus critical that civic leaders create a vision of the East Rand's future with which all sections of the community can identify and support. Following from this, clear and achievable priorities for action must be identified and the roles of different players – local authorities, private sector, non-governmental organizations and so on – spelt out.

Finally and perhaps most importantly, successful development in this area will require effective adherence to the law and the certainty of punishment if this law is transgressed. In effect security and development become different sides of the same coin. All requests for private sector investment will come to nought unless investors know that 'the rules of the investment game' will apply and transgressions will be severely dealt with. Without this, it is unlikely that any strategy for the future will work.

NOTES

1. Anthony Minnaar, Trevor Keith and Sam Pretorius, 'Hostels and violent conflict on the Reef', in A. Minnaar (ed.) *Communities in Isolation: Perspectives on hostels in South Africa* (Pretoria: Human Sciences Research Council 1994) p.63.
2. Independent Board of Inquiry, *Before we were good friends: An account and analysis of displacement in the East Rand Townships of Thokoza and Katlehong.* (Johannesburg: Independent Board of Inquiry and Peace Action 1994) p.15
3. Quoted in Lauren Segal 'The Human Face of Violence: Hostel Dwellers Speak', Seminar

Paper No.6, Project for the Study of Violence (U. of Witwatersrand Sept. 1991).

4. Anthony Minnaar and Mark Shaw, 'Violence on the East Rand 1990–1994', in Jackie Cilliers, *The National Peacekeeping Force, Violence on the East Rand and Public Perceptions of the NPKF in Katorus* (Johannesburg: Inst. for Defence Policy [hereafter IDP] 1994) p.30.

5. See Colleen McCaul, *No Easy Ride: The Rise and Future of the Black Taxi Industry.* (Johannesburg: South African Inst. of Race Relations [hereafter SAIRR] 1990).

6. For a fuller treatment of taxi-related violence see Anthony Minnaar and Sam Pretorius, *A Year of Living Dangerously: Hitmen, Corruption, Competition, Conflict and Violence in the Taxi Industry during 1994* (Johannesburg: Centre for Socio-Political Analysis, Human Sciences Research Council 1995).

7. Lawrence Schlemmer, *Black township residents amidst protest, negotiation and violence: an empirical study.* (Johannesburg: Centre for Policy Studies 1991) p.3

8. Montshiwa Moroke, 'The dockets of death', *The Star,* 2 Sept. 1994; Jocelyn Maker, 'Enough is enough, say folk in SA's hijacking capital', *Sunday Times,* 20 Feb. 1994.

9. ORMET Report No. 35/92, *Economic and Financial Status of the East Rand,* p.4. [ORMET was formerly the Metropolitan Transportation Planning Institution for the East Rand].

10. East Rand Metropolitan Transport Area, *Financial Management – Economic and Financial Status of the East Rand,* Report No.35/92, April 1992

11. Census of Manufacturing 1988, Principal Statistics on a Regional Basis (Report No. 30-01-02).

12. Central Statistical Services *Report* No. 30-01-02 (Pretoria: Central Statistical Services 1988).

13. East Rand Regional Services Council, Regional Planning, *Proceedings of the Second Workshop on a Management Framework for Urban Growth,* Germiston, 25 June 1994.

14. Alan Mabin and Roland Hunter, *Final Draft – Report of the Review of Conditions and Trends Affecting Development in the PWV,* PWV Forum, 28 Oct. 1993, pp.91–4.

15. Ibid.

16. BMI Building Research Strategy Consulting Unit, *Current and Future Building Activity on the PWV: Focus on the East Rand* (Johannesburg: BMT Building Research Strategy Consulting Unit 1994) p.60.

17. Ibid. p.19.

18. Gauteng encompasses the former Pretoria/Witwatersrand/Vereeniging area, and is one of South Africa's nine provinces.

19. *See forthcoming CDE Research* by Ann Bernstein and Dr Robin Bloch, *Facing a Metropolitan Future on the East Rand* (Johannesburg: Centre for Development and Enterprise 1997).

20. Quoted in *The Citizen,* 13 Sept. 1995.

21. Those interested in this see Judith Hudson, *Violence in the Pretoria/Witwatersrand/Vereeniging area 1990–1992: A Diary of Events* (Johannesburg: SAIRR 1993) This study is an attempt to allow the story of violence to 'tell itself' and thus allow the complexity of dynamics at play to emerge. It provides the backdrop against which the many and various attempts to explain and interpret the violence can be measured.

22. Judith Hudson, *More to violence than meets the eye* (Johannesburg: SAIRR 1993) pp.13–14.

23. Commission of Inquiry Regarding the Prevention of Public Violence and Intimidation *Report of the committee appointed to investigate the violence in Thokoza* (Pretoria: Goldstone Commission 1992) pp.9–13.

23. Paul Thulare, 'Policing and Security on the East Rand – Katorus Area', Jackie Cilliers (ed.) *African Security Review 5/2* (Johannesburg: IDP 1996) p.51.

25. *Financial Mail,* 2 Dec. 1994.

26. Mark Shaw *Crying Peace Where There is None? The Functioning and Future of Local Peace Committees of the National Peace Accord* (Johannesburg: Centre for Policy Studies 1993) p.9.

27. Ibid.

28. Ibid. p.42.

29. Minnaar and Shaw (note 4) p.37.

30. Ibid. p.39.

31. For a fuller treatment of the reasons for the failure of this force see Jackie Cilliers, 'The

History of the National Peacekeeping Force', in *The National Peacekeeping Force, Violence on the East Rand and Public Perceptions of the NPKF in Katorus*. (Johannesburg: IDP 1994).

32. The results for the East Rand were interesting: all six wards in Vosloorus were taken by civic leaders running as independent candidates against ANC candidates. But, in Phola Park an ANC candidate from outside the community beat a local ANC man and a supposedly popular local civic leaders. Chipkin comments, 'The disparity suggests a divergence of interests among communities ... the more settled Vosloorus residents were primarily concerned with local issues, while poorer Phola Park sought security in the broader party's interests.' (*Financial Mail*, 10 Nov. 1995).

33. Julian Baskin 'Communities, Conflict and Negotiated Development', Seminar No. 4. Centre for the Study of Violence and Reconciliation, U. of the Witwatersrand, 1993.

The Evolving Security Architecture in (Southern) Africa

JAKKIE CILLIERS

This study deals first with recent developments at the Organization of African Unity (OAU), in particular discussing developments regarding preventive diplomacy, the greater use of observer missions and general attempts to build capacity towards conflict avoidance and mediation within that organization. This section is followed by an analysis of the Southern African Development Community (SADC), in particular the recently-established Organ on Politics, Security and Stability and the Inter State Defence and Security Committee. The aims, functions and purpose of each organizations are presented together with some comments on the potential contribution that these organizations can make to peace and security in the sub-region. The final section deals with the potential involvement of South Africa in peacekeeping operations.

The post-Cold War era has collapsed most of the political space that the Third World occupied during the East/West struggle. For the most part the former Third World is no longer of much strategic interest for the developed countries, neither as a location for military bases nor as the source of prizes in the ideological competition. The demise of the Socialist World has thus not resulted in a promotion for the developing world, but in its demotion into peripheral status. Cutting evidence of African marginalization is evident from the comment of the US Institute for National Strategic Studies in their *Strategic Assessment 1995:* 'The US has essentially no serious military/geostrategic interests in Africa anymore, other than the inescapable fact that its vastness poses an obstacle to deployment to the Middle East and South Asia, whether by sea or air.'[1]

The vast majority of conflicts in southern Africa have nominally been intra-state, yet without exception neigbouring countries have played a role in supporting one or other faction. Complex as they are, the situation is further aggravated by distrust, religious fanaticism and ethnicism. Old animosities are kept alive and the development of a culture of tolerance remains evasive. In Africa and southern Africa in particular, the legacy of apartheid, colonial exploitation and policies of the ruling elite contributed to refugee problems, economic migration, smuggling, drug-trafficking, poaching and piracy. Ethnic divisions have forced countries into a downward spiral of civil wars, lawlessness, anarchy and misery. The extent of the decline brought about by the struggle for independence, the resistance to such struggles, and by corrupt and inept despots, can hardly be overestimated. The collapse of state institutions and the disruption in the functions of governments severely complicate any attempt to intervene and assist these countries – either by the more affluent, developed countries, or by Africans themselves.

In exploring security, co-operation and interdependence, the debate on collective and co-operative security has covered a wide range of policy issues. These include so-called 'new-thinking on security', the nature of the threats facing Africa, conflict mediation and arbitration, confidence building measures, disarmament, food and health security, etc. A second issue has been the level at which linkage should occur, namely, at the level of the OAU (Africa), SADC (sub-regional) or bilaterally, or possibly the requirement for entirely new bodies and structures. Other issues were those regarding the establishment of regional or sub-regional peacekeeping forces and even defence and non-aggression pacts. At every stage the danger of political agreements being undermined by the limited administrative, technical and military ability of African states to convert idealistic goals into content, has introduced caution into expectations and progress.

Progress towards a shared democratic value system among the various constituent states of the region, and sustainable and rapid economic growth are clearly the building blocks for greater regional, national and individual security in southern Africa. However, the prospects for a greater degree of regional economic integration are not favourable. This is principally due to the fact that most African economies are similarly structured, they produce, consume, export and import essentially the same things. Instead of complementing each other, African countries are competing, especially in exports of primary commodities that are sent to similar markets, generally in Western Europe. They also compete in importing the same products from the same source – again mostly Western Europe. In a comprehensive historical study that was released during April 1995, of attempts at regional integration, irrespective of whether they succeeded or failed and involving all five continents, the World Bank found that the 20 countries in sub-Saharan Africa had the lowest level of complementarity of all those studied. 'This', the bank concluded, 'strongly suggests that the structure of African countries' exports and imports differs so widely that regional trade integration efforts hold little promise for accelerating industrialization and growth.'[2] In fact, only 2.7 per cent of the region's total trade is among members.

Whilst co-operation is easily achievable among partners sharing a common system of values and the same level of development, this is not readily so when significant disparities are evident amongst the participating countries, as in southern Africa. South Africa's economy is nearly four times as big as that of all the other 11 SADC members combined. South Africans are 35 times richer than Mozambicans, the poorest SADC country although development indicators indicate that black South Africans are, in fact, often not much better off than many of their neighbours. This absence of parity could lead to the establishment of a hierarchy and domination amongst co-operating partners. Economic leverage tends to determine decision making and ability to execute a mandate. In the long run, this could undermine effective regional co-operative structures. However, the successful examples of preventive diplomacy and peacemaking in restoring democracy to Lesotho and breaking the impasse which stalled the implementation of the Lusaka Agreement in Angola have enthused doubters and sceptics alike. It has also become clear that many African states are looking to South Africa to exert much stronger leadership than it has done thus far.

This essay examines regional security arrangements, within the broader framework of developments at the level of the Organization of African Unity (OAU). The bulk of the discussion focuses on the evolution of sub-regional co-operative structures in southern Africa, with specific reference to the SADC and its component elements. The concluding comments relate to the prospects for peacekeeping at the regional and sub-regional level.

The Organization of African Unity

The United Nations (UN) Charter anticipated the involvement of 'regional arrangements or agencies' for maintaining international peace and security along with the UN. Article 53 of the UN Charter even refers to enforcement action by regional bodies, but requires that '... no enforcement action shall be taken under regional arrangement or by regional agencies without the authorization of the Security Council ...' Until recently the involvement of regional organizations in conflict was severely constrained by the political realities of the Cold War. This may be changing. Not only is the United Nations overburdened with the demands made upon it to maintain peace and security in the world, but public opinion in the larger developed countries appears increasingly reticent to support intervention in conflicts in the developing world. The richer countries increasingly question the balance between their financial obligations and the tangible benefits that they receive from the UN in this and other areas. Hence the recent trend towards strengthening the capacities and effectiveness of regional and sub-regional organizations.

Since the establishment of the OAU some 32 years ago, a system of *ad hoc* arrangements has been used to deal with inter-state conflict, while intra-state conflict was largely left to each member state to handle in whatever manner it best saw fit. Only in the 1990s would the OAU move towards a permanent structure to formalize and intensify its ability to assist in building peace in Africa. The end of the Cold War and liberation of South Africa would serve to galvanize the OAU's efforts in this regard.

The OAU Charter of 1964 made provision for a Commission of Mediation, Conciliation and Arbitration to encourage OAU members to settle their disputes peacefully, but the Commission remained unused as the OAU, caught up in the decolonialization efforts of the time, and torn between the East-West conflict, sought merely to maintain the inviolability of its inter-state boundaries at all costs and ignored the gross violation of human rights which characterized many African governments. At various times proposals were made for an African Security Council and for Africa to follow the model of the former CSCE through the establishment of a Conference on Peace, Security, Stability, Development and Co-operation in Africa. Little came of these initiatives.

Following the collapse of the Berlin Wall OAU leaders officially pledged to work towards the peaceful and speedy resolution of conflicts in 1990. For the first time, the 1991 OAU Summit of African Heads of State and Government acknowledged in its final Communiqué that '... there is a link between security, stability, development and co-operation in Africa' and that the problems of security and stability in many African countries had impaired the capacity of the OAU to achieve co-operation.[3]

A Division of Conflict Management was established in March 1992 and given a small budget. In July 1992 the OAU Assembly Heads of State and Government in Dakar agreed 'in principle' to establish a mechanism for conflict prevention, management and resolution and then in June 1993 with the OAU Summit in Cairo the mechanism was formally adopted in a Declaration by the Heads of State and Government.

The Central Mechanism for Conflict Prevention, Management and Resolution was established by the OAU on 30 June 1993 in Addis Ababa. Dr Salim Ahmed Salim, Secretary-General of the OAU later stated that: 'The establishment of the Mechanism was an act of historical significance and self-empowerment. What Africa said to the world is that yes, we may continue to need outside help in dealing with our problems, but we will be centrally involved and provide leadership in any efforts at conflict resolution.... we can no longer fold our hands and wait for the foreigners to come and resolve our problems.'[4] The Central Organ of the Mechanism for Conflict Prevention, Management and Resolution assumes the overall direction and co-ordination of the activities of the Mechanism between Ordinary Sessions of the Assembly of the Heads of State and Government. The Central Organ functions at the level of the Heads of State and Ministers as well as that of Ambassadors accredited to the OAU or dully authorized representatives.[5] The Ambassadors meet once a month in ordinary session and can also meet in extra-ordinary session. The Ministers meet twice a year in ordinary session and can also meet in extra-ordinary session. The Heads of State meet once a year.

The Declaration of the Assembly of Heads of State and Government on the establishment of the Mechanism committed the OAU to co-operate closely with the UN in respect of peacemaking and peacekeeping. Moreover, the Mechanism is also committed to close co-operation with regional organizations such as SADC. The establishment of the Mechanism was an important step, although its actions has not been a spectacular success thus far.[6] Possibly the area which has seen the most activity is in observing elections, a practice which has become particularly prevalent since 1990. By mid-1995 the OAU had observed 39 elections or referenda in 25 member countries.[7] According to a senior official within the Conflict Management Centre of the OAU, William Nhara:

> Conflict resolution has also been handled effectively by the OAU through the exercise of preventive diplomacy in many forms, including the use of the good offices of the Secretary-General, Eminent Persons, Special Envoys and Representatives of the Secretary-General. In addition, there has been direct contact between the OAU and governments of countries concerned, as well as missions from the General Secretariat to countries in question. Field trips recently undertaken to the Congo, Gabon, Sierra Leone, Somalia, Rwanda, Burundi, Sudan, Nigeria, Cameroon and Lesotho have aimed at facilitating the process of mediation between the conflicting parties, or assessing the conflict situation on the ground, with a view to reporting to the Secretary-General and/or the Central Organ for further action. Within the area of conflict resolution, the OAU has been at the centre stage in the use of mediation as a tool for resolving actual conflicts in countries such as South Africa, Mozambique, the Congo, Liberia, Burundi and Rwanda.[8]

While these claims are, admittedly, flattering to the importance of the role of the OAU, they do indicate an increased activity and role for that organization which eclipses its previously virtually dormant existence. Much more recently, at its annual summit in Yaoundé in July 1996, the OAU has backed a regional assistance plan intended to end the bloodbath in Burundi where an estimated 150,000 people had died in the preceding three years. The Burundi plan was agreed to by a regional summit at Arusha, Tanzania, in June 1996, and foresaw the use of Tanzanian, Ugandan and Ethiopian troops in Burundi. The same summit also decided to push for a

UN war crimes tribunal to try warlords in Liberia's six-year-old civil war.[9] However, when the Burundian warlords began to raise questions around sovereignty, the OAU retreated from its previous position. Clearly, even by 1996, its capacity does not yet match its pronouncements.

Preventive diplomacy and its attendant functions fall directly within the jurisdiction of the Secretary-General of the OAU and the Central Organ. The OAU has an ambitious programme in mind. It intends to:

- establish an Early Warning Network to '... *cover the entire continent.*' (a first Africa-wide seminar on the subject was held in Addis Ababa on this subject during January 1996 and a strategy group appointed to assist the OAU with the establishment of the network[10]);

- establish and enhance the capacity of the OAU Conflict Management Centre through the secondment of personnel from Member Countries (to which some African countries, notably South Africa, have already responded);

- establish a database covering all 53 Member States, detailing each country's general profile, its conflict profile, as well as profiles of individuals who can be engaged as Special Envoys or Special Representatives for conflict prevention duties (some of these envoys are already in the field in Burundi. Recently the OAU asked member states for a list of the names of eminent persons who could be considered for posts as special envoy or special representative.);

- have '... Member States earmark forces in their respective armies and security structures for possible utilization in peace observation and peacemaking operations first and foremost by the United Nations and in exceptional situations by the OAU' (during May 1996 the OAU held a meeting of the Chiefs of Staff of the Central Organ, on this subject – see below);

- '... establish a proper machinery and unit to manage peacekeeping operations.' (with the financial assistance of the USA and other countries the construction of the Conflict Management Centre at the OAU is now complete, barring some furnishing);

- '... examining possibilities of establishing a proper military Co-ordinating Unit at the [OAU] Secretariat and Funding.' (at present two military officers already serve within the Conflict Management Centre).

The OAU has also decided to establish a capacity for a 100-person preventive observer mission which could be kept on stand-by. OAU member states would then be approached to identify personnel who might participate on a stand-by basis.

Although the OAU decided that peacekeeping should not constitute a priority activity of the organization and that conflict prevention and peacemaking were the most important and cost effective areas for OAU activity, immense pressure is building up for the OAU to extend its activities to these areas, both from member countries, and perhaps more importantly, from donors.[11] By September 1995 the Assistant Secretary-General of the OAU would state:

> Our experience of the last year and a half with the [Central] Mechanism clearly reveals two shortcomings: The first shortcoming is our inadequacy to fully operationalize the Mechanism in the area of preventing incipient conflicts from erupting into full-blown conflicts mainly due to the lack of speedy exchange of information of conflict situations within Member States. The second problem that the General Secretariat has faced in operationalizing the Mechanism, lies in the area of peacekeeping. ... our experience demonstrates the increasing reluctance on the side of the United Nations, especially the major powers, to get more involved in peace-keeping operations directly. The General Secretariat continues to believe that time has come for Africa to be prepared to take some degree of responsibility for peace-keeping.'[12]

Partly to address these deficiencies, the OAU has established an observer mission at the UN in New York and is giving thought to an enhanced UN liaison system in Addis Ababa, staff exchanges and the electronic exchange of information. Good intentions aside, early implementation of some of these ideas are constrained by the shortage of personnel and inadequate capacity within the OAU's secretariat.

At bilateral and multilateral levels, donor countries are active in building African capacity towards conflict prevention and peacekeeping in Africa. The British government has, for example, convened a series of seminars to investigate doctrine, training, logistics, an early warning system, preventive diplomacy, etc. The French have proposed an African Intervention Force during the Biarritz Summit of 1994. Recently the United States proposed an Africa Rapid Reaction Force, primarily to prepare to meet the emerging crisis in Burundi. Finally, the US government (and to a lesser extent the British Government) has funded the Central Organ of the OAU to the tune of several million dollars, while some Scandinavian countries are also active at a policy level.

In response the OAU believes that it '... must provide the necessary leadership needed to co-ordinate the various initiatives from Africa's external partners. It must also prepare itself to undertake peacekeeping responsibilities.'[13]

In view of the perilous state of the OAU's finances, debate regarding the funding of such ventures is a key consideration, although a special fund, the OAU Peace Fund, was created in the wake of the adoption of the OAU Mechanism for Conflict Prevention, Management and Resolution in Cairo in June 1993. The purpose of the Fund is '... to provide exclusive, OAU support to operational activities relating to conflict management and resolution.'[14] The fund receives an annual donation of at least US $1 million from the OAU as well as donations from other countries.

In June 1995, as a result of these and other discussions, the OAU summit endorsed the establishment, in Addis Ababa, of an Early Warning Network. This will be based on a co-ordinating facility located in the Conflict Management Centre. The subsequent seminar on early warning systems which was hosted in Addis Ababa during January 1996 recommended the establishment of the Early Warning system to, among others:[15]

- '... function under the exclusive control of the OAU ...'

- that it should also ' ... monitor ... socio-economic indicators ...'

- '... not only [be involved in].. the gathering, analysis and dissemination of information, and informed decision making, but also and more critically ... [to] provide the framework for actual and timely implementation of appropriate diplomatic and preventive action ...'

- ' ... identify focal points [for the provision of information] on the level of member states, regional organizations and other interested parties.'

- that it should support ' ... respect of human rights, popular participation, freedom of expression, transparency and accountability.'

- '... that the OAU should give consideration to an open-ended consultative forum of NGOs to meet regularly in Addis Ababa and provide their insight to the OAU Secretariat.'

- ' ... that the OAU should obtain an inventory of relevant projects [databases] and explore how links with such databases could enhance the operational capacity of the Mechanism.'

- '... that the OAU considers publishing an annual survey of conflict on the continent.'

- ' ... that a follow-up mechanism be established in the form of a strategy group to assist the OAU with strategic planning regarding the establishment of the envisaged Early Warning system.'

Once there is early warning of a potential crisis, and given the will to act, theoretically a wide variety of tools exists for such action, whether it be undertaken by the UN, the OAU, SADC or by one or more countries acting in collusion. These include fact-finding missions, small preventive or observer missions (such as those of the UN and OAU in Burundi), and the use of a special envoy or a similar eminent person.

An additional development has been the recommendation by the 62nd Ordinary Session of the OAU Council of Ministers to hold a meeting of the Chiefs of Staff of the members of the Central Organ to deal with the technical issues related to peacekeeping. The objectives of this meeting were:[16]

- exchange views and information on the technical issues relating to peacekeeping operations, including doctrine, planning, command and control, preparedness and training as well as procedures;

- to come up with concrete and practical recommendations to guide the OAU Secretariat on matters pertaining to peacekeeping such as structure, stand-by contingents, training, logistic bases, external assistance, relationship between the UN, OAU and sub-regional groupings, procedures.

The subsequent *Recommendations from the First Meeting of the Chiefs of Staff of the Member States of the Central Organ of the OAU Mechanism for Conflict Prevention, Management and Resolution*, which was held in Addis Ababa from 3 to 5 June 1996, states:

1. The meeting recalled the principle that the primary responsibility of the OAU should lie with the anticipation and prevention of conflict in accordance with the relevant provision of the 1993 Cairo Declaration. It also recognized that the primary responsibility for the maintenance of international peace and security, particularly in the area of peacekeeping, rests with the United Nations Security Council. At the same time, the meeting recognized that certain exceptional circumstances can arise which may lead to the deployment of limited peacekeeping or observation missions by the OAU.

2. In order to equip the OAU to better undertake peace support missions, the meeting saw the need to strengthen the existing military unit of the General Secretariat subject to further study.

3. For purposes of strengthening the co-ordination between the OAU and the UN in peace related issues, the meeting recommended that the relationship between the two Organizations should be formalized. It was also recommended that the OAU should continue to co-ordinate closely with sub-regional Organizations in its peace support operations, taking advantage of existing arrangements within sub-regions.

4. The meeting accepted the principle of stand-by arrangements and earmarked contingents on a voluntary basis. Such earmarked contingents could serve either under the aegis of the United Nations or the OAU or under sub-regional arrangements. In this regard, the meeting recognized the need for proper preparation and the standardization of training.

5. In order to provide further clarity and to come out with practical and realistic recommendations on the technical issues raised in the working document, and the meeting's report, especially those relating to logistics, it as recommended that a working group of military experts from Member States of the Central Organ be set up.

6. The meeting recommended that there should be meetings of the Chiefs of Staff of Member States of the Central Organ as and when the need arises.

7. The meeting recognized the need for further clarity with regard to the guidelines which apply to possible OAU peacekeeping operations. The meeting therefore calls upon the OAU Secretary-General to take the necessary action so that a clear position in this regard is formulated at the highest level.'

There has, therefore, been a flurry of initiatives at the level of the OAU to enhance capacity at that level, although the extent to which the OAU is able to intervene and effectively co-ordinate operations, remains dubious to many countries and analysts. For various reasons it is, therefore, perhaps at the sub-regional level, then, that preventive diplomacy, conflict resolution, mediation and peacekeeping in Africa by Africans may come to the fore.

The Southern African Development Community

Currently there are five main sub-regions in Africa, with each hosting a sub-regional organization: the Inter-Governmental Authority on Drought and Development (IGADD) in the east; the Economic Community of West African States (ECOWAS); the Maghreb Union in the north; the Southern African Development Community (SADC); and the Economic Community of Central African States (ECCAS). While the main focus of existing African sub-regional groupings is economic development, intra-regional rivalries and squabbles between the member states have impeded integration and development. In addition, the rising tide of domestic tension and conflict has damaged their economic performance. Through the 'spillover' effect, intra-state conflicts have affected even those neighbouring states that were once stable. Speaking at a conference on peacekeeping in

Africa, William Nhara stated that: 'There is, ..., a pressing need to restructure and strengthen these sub-regional organizations so that they can become an integral part of the partnership, with the UN as a world body and the OAU as a regional organization, to foster peace and security on the African continent.'[17] Of the various organizations, it is to the Southern African Development Community (SADC) that much of Africa is looking as an example to follow.

South Africa's joining of the SADC in 1994 and Mauritius' in 1995, brought the number of member states of this sub-regional organization up to 12. The other members are Angola, Botswana, Lesotho, Malawi, Mozambique, Namibia, Swaziland, Tanzania and Zimbabwe. Among these members are some of the poorest nations in the world with a declining share in the global economic product – a paltry 0.58 per cent in 1993, or 0.13 per cent without South Africa's input.[18] Despite its size within SADC, in the global context, however, South Africa is a dwarf. Its GNP is only one third that of the Netherlands and 6 per cent that of Germany.[19]

The Southern African Development Community (SADC) was established in 1980 as the Southern African Development Co-ordination Conference (SADCC).[20] For the first 12 years of its existence the SADCC operated without a legal framework, treaty or protocol. Conscious of the poor record of regional economic integration schemes in Africa and elsewhere in developing countries, the founders opted for a loose organization to promote co-operation and co-ordination rather than formal integration. Their aim was to reduce members' external economic dependence, mainly – but not exclusively – on apartheid South Africa, and to promote development. SADCC's original strategy was to concentrate on promoting co-operation in the field of infrastructure. In practice its primary activities were aimed at the co-ordination of members' development initiatives an assisting in raising donor funds for these projects. The focus of the organization, therefore, has been on issues of economic co-operation and development.

SADC has had only limited success. Trade with South Africa increased, even during the time when SADCC actively sought to limit this growing dependency, and so has dependence on donors. According to the *Africa Institute*, SADC projects depended on donor finance for 90 per cent of total costs during 1995. Donors are openly critical of the members' failure to mobilize their own resources and to maintain completed projects. The efficiency of the organization's internal structures is also criticized. Even SADC was to admit in 1992 that the '... the progress towards reduction of the region's economic dependence, and towards economic integration, has been modest.'[21] Yet, despite the criticism, SADC has been a qualified success in one important respect. 'Of all the contributions made by SADC to regional development, the greatest has been the forging of a regional identity and a sense of common destiny among the countries and peoples of Southern Africa.'[22]

Only in 1989, at the SADCC Heads of State meeting in Harare, was a decision taken to formalize the organization and to give it a legal status to replace the existing Memorandum of Agreement. Four years of consultation followed before the Declaration and Treaty of the SADC was eventually signed by Heads of State and Government in Windhoek in 1992. The Treaty and expressed confidence that recent developments such as the independence of Namibia and the transition in South Africa '... will take the region out of an era of conflict and confrontation, to one of co-operation; in a climate of peace, security and stability. These are prerequisites for development ...'.[23] With the change of name the emphasis of the SADC changed from 'development co-ordination' to 'development integration'. In essence the true vision of the SADC is that of full economic integration of the Southern Africa region and trade liberalization. Yet, Pamela Dube is perceptive: 'While the old SADCC always portrayed itself as an economic body, the organization had more political and ideological inclinations than economic concerns. Its policies always portrayed political beliefs, particularly of the founding farther. Still, like other international bodies such as the Organization of African Unity, SADC failed in many instances to condemn its own members.'[24] Although SADC defines itself as a development agreement, at the same time it sees itself as a sub-regional political organization under the OAU, that is, essentially a political organization. As a result there is considerable ambiguity and confusion on the real nature of SADC with the organization often entering areas far removed from that of development co-ordination and facilitation.

One possible explanation for this situation is that the SADC Treaty remains weak in terms of the central focus of the organization. In Article 4 of its Treaty, member states adopted the following *principles* without any discussion of elucidation of the implications of each principle:

* sovereign equality of all Member States;

* solidarity, peace and security;

* human rights, democracy, and the rule of law;

* equity, balance and mutual benefit; and

* peaceful settlement of disputes.[25]

The SADC Treaty, in Article 5, further lists eight *objectives*, including to '... promote and defend peace and security'. In order to achieve its objectives, the SADC Treaty finally lists ten *activities* to achieve its objectives, yet none refer to defence or security co-operation, the closest being a commitment to 'promote the co-ordination and harmonization of the international relations of Member States' and 'develop such other activities as Member States may decide in furtherance of the objectives of this Treaty'.[26]

The Windhoek Declaration of 1992 which established the SADC called, among others for '... a framework of co-operation which provides for ... strengthening regional solidarity, peace and security, in order for the people of the region to live and work together in peace and harmony. ... The region needs, therefore, to establish a framework and mechanisms to strengthen regional solidarity, and provide for mutual peace and security.'[27]

The SADC has already established two Commissions and 19 sectors and sub-sectors to guide and co-ordinate regional development policies and programmes in specific functional areas. The sectors are allocated to individual member States to co-ordinate and provide regional leadership. Sectoral activities are supervised by Sectoral Committees of Ministers. A major advantage of this approach has been that it has helped to keep costs (and bureaucracy) to a minimum.

This being said, in reality the capacity of many countries to co-ordinate activities in their allocated sector is limited – and progress in that particular sector consequently slow. In a case where the local civil service suffers a lack of resources in the fulfillment of its daily, ongoing tasks, SADC responsibilities are an 'over-and-above' function that often gets left to the last. Some type of formalization and expansion of the existing SADC bureaucracy in Gaberone is, therefore, inevitable, with the most likely avenue a movement towards a greater reliance on commissions, of which there are already two – one on Transport and Communications and one on Agricultural Research (SACCAR). In this process the small size of the secretariat in Gaberone is a severe handicap.

Most observers do not realise how small an organization the SADC secretariat in Gaberone is. Countries contribute to SADC not on the basis of their total GDP or even GDP per capita, but on an equal basis. The result being that South Africa (the largest country) and Swaziland (the smallest country) each contribute less than $1 million annually. In fact, SADC has only 10 professional staff members and about 20 administrative persons at its head office. To the 30 persons in Gaberone could be added the 15 persons who work in the food and agricultural and transport commissions. The work load of this small staff is very heavy. SADC has over 400 projects running which require a total of US$80 billion in funding. Of this funding 50 per cent was secured by 1994 of which no more than about 15 per cent comes from member countries themselves, the remainder being provided by donors.[28] With so many projects covering a very diverse field, the requirement for an integrated regional development plan (i.e. the top down framework) is obvious. Yet the vast majority of the projects appear to be discrete (i.e. bottom up), largely because they are driven by individual countries and not by the region (i.e. SADC or through multilateral agreements) and as a result of the absence of a coherent regional framework. SADC has only recently tried to introduce such an integrated policy framework at a time when many of the projects are already in place. Part of the regional policy framework will come from the adoption of a series of 'protocols'. Article 22(1) of the SADC Treaty provides for member States to conclude protocols to 'spell out the objectives and scope of, and institutional mechanisms for co-operation and integration'. These protocols are to be negotiated by the member states and, after approval by the Summit (namely, the Heads of State), become an integral part of the SADC Treaty. During their August 1995 meeting, SADC signed the first such binding agreement, the Protocol on Shared Water Course Systems on sharing the scarce water resources available in the region.[29]

At the SADC Heads of State and Government Summit in Lesotho during August 1996, four additional protocols were signed. These were on: Combating Illicit Drug Trafficking; Energy; Transport, Communication and Meteorology; and Trade.[30] The draft protocol on the Free Movement of SADC Persons that would have served at the Lesotho Summit met with resistance from the regional Ministers responsible for Home Affairs and was therefore not tabled. The feeling is that the inequalities in the region will result in the mass movement of peoples if restrictions are lifted too soon. The most basic statistics bear this out – the South African GNP is more than three times that of the other 11 members of SADC put together, three times larger than that of Nigeria and 20 times that of Zimbabwe.[31] As a result, the draft protocol was referred back to the drawing board to be structured according to the current realities in the region. Angola did not sign the protocols on Trade and Transport, Communications and Meteorology to '… allow internal processes to be completed.'[32]

Despite its weaknesses, the SADC has a very ambitious agenda, if the plans of its Executive Secretary Kaire Mbuende, are anything to go by.[33] The Community is, for example, drafting a treaty that would eliminate internal trade barriers and export subsidies within the region by the year 2000.[34] A further treaty on the free movement of people should follow. Both agreements would present South Africa and some of the other member countries with a major headache. Although intra-regional trade is growing: South Africa's exports to its own continent (70 per cent of which goes to the SADC region) jumped by over a quarter from 1993 to 1994, although imports remain at very low levels. Any talk of sharing a single currency will be difficult without much more intra-regional trade, despite the fact that the currencies of Namibia, Swaziland and Lesotho are all pegged, at par, to the

South African Rand. No wonder that South Africa, which has been put in charge of the SADC sector on finance, has not even begun to look at the matter of spreading that monetary area further. With an estimated five million illegal immigrants already in the country, the South African government is also afraid that the complete freedom of movement pursued by the SADC would mean that millions more people will move down South, legally and illegally.[35] None of these concerns question the logic of regional integration and co-operation, but do suggest that South Africa would probably err on the side of caution in the pursuit of regional integration in certain respects and would prefer an open ended and phased process without a pre-determined time-table.[36]

Following the resolutions and recommendations of the SADC *Workshop on Democracy, Peace and Security*, which was held in Windhoek from 11 to 16 July 1994, SADC appeared set to enter into the fields of security co-ordination, conflict mediation and even military co-operation on a grand scale. This move was strengthened by the decision of the Front-line States, on 30 July 1994, to dissolve and *'become the political and security wing of SADC'*. Most importantly one of the Windhoek working groups on Conflict Resolution, recommended that '... Conflict Resolution and Political Co-operation become a "Sector", the responsibility for which would be allocated to a SADC member state.' and that a Protocol on Peace, Security and Conflict Resolution be drawn up. This recommendation was eventually confirmed at the Heads of State meeting in South Africa during August 1995, but only after many of the other recommendations of the Windhoek conference had either been watered down, or been abandoned. Among a multitude of recommendations the Windhoek Working Group on Disarmament and Demilitarization called for the 'development of regional mechanisms for peacekeeping and peace enforcement activities' and 'equipping and training of national forces for peace keeping roles'.

The Windhoek proposals were subsequently referred to the next meeting of the Council of Ministers in Botswana during which many of the intrusive and potentially prescriptive recommendations which could infringe upon the sovereignty of member countries were abandoned. At this meeting it was decided to establish a wing for conflict mediation and prevention, as opposed to a sector. This was followed by yet further dissension and discussion in Lilongwe, Malawi, in February 1995.

At Lilongwe the SADC Secretariat tabled a Non-Paper which proposed the creation of a regional peacekeeping capacity within the national armies of the region, but this received a cold response from South Africa and the proposal was apparently not resuscitated at the Heads of State meeting in August 1995.

Proposal for an Association of Southern African States

In pursuit of the decision to establish a wing for conflict mediation and prevention, a meeting of the SADC Foreign Ministers in Harare on 3 March 1995 recommended the establishment of an Association of Southern African States (ASAS) as the political arm of SADC under Chapter 7, Article 21(3)(g) of the SADC Treaty. ASAS would, according to these recommendations, replace the now defunct Front-line States co-operative framework and become the primary mechanism for dealing with conflict prevention, management and resolution in southern Africa.[37] The meeting proposed that two specialized sectors be organized within ASAS, namely a political sector and a military security sector. ASAS would be guided by the principles set out in the July 1994 Windhoek document, which included the following:[38]

• the sovereign equality of all member states;

• respect for the sovereignty and territorial integrity of each state and for its inalienable right to independent existence;

• peaceful settlement of disputes through negotiation, mediation or arbitration; and

• military intervention of whatever nature to be decided upon only after all possible remedies have been exhausted, in accordance with the Charters of the OAU and the UN.

The Ministers further proposed that the terms of reference of ASAS should include the following objectives:[39]

• to protect people of the region against instability arising from the internal breakdown of law and order, inter-state conflict and from external aggression;

• to co-operate fully in regional security and defence, through conflict prevention, management and resolution;

• to give maximum support to the organs and institutions of SADC;

• to mediate in inter-state and intra-state disputes and conflicts;

• to co-ordinate and harmonize, as far as possible, policy on international issues;

• to promote and enhance the development of democratic institutions and practices within each Member State, and to encourage Member States to observe universal human rights as provided for in the Charters and Conventions of the OAU and the UN;

- to promote peace and stability; and

- to promote peacemaking and peacekeeping in order to achieve
  sustainable peace and security.

ASAS would be independent from the SADC Secretariat, and report
directly to the SADC Summit, namely, the Heads of State. The ASAS
proposal was, therefore, a deliberate attempt to preserve the key features of
the previous Front-line States arrangement, namely an informal and flexible
modus operandi with unimpeded access to the SADC Heads of State, while
keeping bureaucracy to a minimum. Speaking in parliament on the Foreign
Affairs budget vote on 18 May 1995, South African Minister of Foreign
Affairs Alfred Nzo commented that '.. the Foreign Ministers of SADC have
proposed that the former Front-line States be turned into a new political and
security arm of the SADC.'[40]

But this was not to be. The first problem which subsequently surfaced
was the fact that the various Ministers of Defence, Police and the intelligence
communities had not been consulted in the formulation of these
recommendations. Nor, for that matter, had some of the Ministers
responsible for SADC liaison within all the member countries. As a result, at
the August 1995 Summit Meeting in Johannesburg, a final decision on the
structure which had, by now, become known as ASAS was delayed for an
additional 12 months.

The first sign that the ASAS proposal was going to run into problems at
the Johannesburg summit came from Nzo, who told a press briefing that the
foreign ministers of the SADC would have to again look at the name ASAS
and decide whether it would be an association or a sector. To many
commentators the decision to delay the creation of ASAS was rooted in a
disgruntled President Robert Mugabe who felt that Zimbabwe had a right to
a commanding position in any new grouping, similar to the role it had
played in the Front-line States and was piqued at the increased dominance
of South Africa. Zimbabwe, had, among others, apparently insisted that the
permanent chairmanship of ASAS be given to the longest-serving SADC
head of state (i.e. Mugabe), but it was Namibia's proposal that a two-yearly
revolving chairmanship would be more appropriate which won the day.[41]
But a two-year revolving chairmanship appears to err on the side of
excessive caution, for it would imply that it would be a quarter of a century
before any single country would again chair the sector. The final
Communiqué issued in Johannesburg therefore deliberately omitted any
mention of the name ASAS, but simply stated that:

> The Summit reviewed its decision of Gaborone in August 1994, to
> establish the sector on Political Co-operation, Democracy, Peace and

Security. The Summit considered and granted the request of the Foreign Ministers of SADC, that the allocation of the sector, to any Member State be deferred and that they be given more time for consultations among themselves and with Ministers responsible for Defence and Security and SADC Matters, on the structures, terms of reference, and operational procedures, for the sector.[42]

In preparation for the next Heads of State meeting in 1996 (scheduled to be held in Maseru), the various ministers of defence, foreign affairs, police, etc. were expected to produce specific proposals in this regard. To this end the SADC Ministers for Foreign Affairs, Defence and Security met in Gaberone on 18 January 1996 with the task to '... make recommendations on how best to merge the decisions of the SADC Council to establish a Sector for Politics, Diplomacy, Defence and Security with the proposal of Foreign Ministers of the Front-line States to establish an Association of Southern African States (ASAS).'[43] The subsequent press statement recorded the recommendation to the SADC Summit in favour of '... the establishment of a SADC Organ for Politics, Defence and Security which would allow more flexibility and timely response, at the highest level, to sensitive and potentially explosive situations. Modalities of how the proposed SADC Organ could be structured and operationalized would be determined by Summit.'[44] A Sector had now become an organ in an obvious copy of the rather strange terminology adopted by the OAU.

The SADC Organ for Politics, Defence and Security

Senior SADC officials are frank in stating that '...without stability, investment and development will not follow'. This recognition of the interrelationship between economic growth, stability and democracy heralds an important mind-shift within the region. Similar to developments at the level of the OAU, sovereignty is no longer a holy cow in Southern Africa and, albeit grudgingly, governments accept that the manner in which they conduct their internal affairs are open to legitimate scrutiny. The move to include a focus on conflict mediation, preventive diplomacy and peacekeeping in SADC with the establishment of the Organ for Politics, Defence and Security is, therefore, born from a process and perspective of development.

Right from the start, the SADC wisely decided to separate political and security considerations from 'SADC proper' (i.e. economic development) through the creation of a separate structure which should arguably also not be co-located with the SADC Secretariat in Botswana. Through the establishment of the Organ, SADC has moved away from an *ad hoc* approach to addressing common foreign and security issues.

The Organ will abide by the same principles as that of SADC, including the sovereign equality of all member states, the peaceful settlement of disputes, and the observance of human rights, democracy and the rule of law.[45] Its objectives include:[46]

- safeguarding the region against instability from within or outside its borders;

- promoting political co-operation and common political values and institutions (this commits SADC to the promotion of democracy and an observance of human rights);

- developing a common foreign policy and a joint international lobby on issues of common interest (the SADC Treaty itself commits that organization to 'promote the co-ordination and harmonization of the international relations of Member States');

- security and defence co-operation through conflict prevention, management and resolution;

- mediation of disputes and conflicts;

- preventive diplomacy and mechanisms, with punitive measures as a last resort (in other words the possibility of enforcement actions as a last resort is explicitly recognized);

- sustainable peace and security through peace-making and peace-keeping (this and the preceding objectives effectively place the Organ in line with the Charter of the UN);

- development of a collective security capacity and a Mutual Defence Pact, and regional peacekeeping capacity (an unprecedented and, in fact, unrealistic goal for the foreseeable future);

- co-ordination of participation of members in international and regional peacekeeping operations (opening the door to an arrangement similar to the Nordic division of labour in peacekeeping); and

- to address extra-regional conflicts which impact on peace and security in Southern Africa (confirming that SADC does not have an inward orientation, but acknowledges the realities of its position in the region).

The Organ will operate at summit level, as well as ministerial and technical levels. It will also function separately from other SADC structures. Exactly how this is to work in practice is still unclear, but what is evident is that the chairpersonship of the SADC (presently President Mandela) and of the Organ (presently President Mugabe) will ensure a differentiation between the two institutions at the level of the Heads of State and Government. At present the annual SADC Heads of State and Government summit meeting has already instituted a practice (reflected in the subsequent press releases) of commenting upon sources of concern within each of the SADC countries. It is not clear if this practice will continue or if the agenda items related to peace, stability and democracy will be moved to a second annual Summit meeting. Logically the two events (the SADC and the Organ Heads of State and Government Summit meetings) will probably be combined or the Heads of State and Government will only convene in terms of the Organ when necessary.

Arguably the loss of the traditional SADC 'sector' approach within the Organ was unfortunate. Sticking to a sectoral approach would have allowed the Organ to operate at a more technical level right from the start (i.e. at that of bureaucrats and not politicians). Allocating the Organ to a single country would have been very difficult due to the highly sensitive and political nature of the issues that the Organ deals with, such as early warning of potential conflict and crises within the various SADC countries. Given the rotating nature of the chairpersonship (presently with President Mugabe of Zimbabwe), there is presently some debate if the Organ will require a permanent secretariat – without which it may struggle to operate effectively and keep abreast of events. This is particularly necessary should the Organ wish to proceed with the establishment of an early warning system similar to that being established at the OAU. Possibly the Organ may, in time, come to replicate the way in which the Central Organ works at the OAU, namely, where the regular, and by far the majority of business, is conducted at Ambassadorial level and the need to consult at the levels of Ministers and Heads of State is very limited. The problem with this vision is that it implies both permanent officials and infrastructure for the Organ.

One of the proposed institutions which will be absorbed into the Organ is the existing Inter-State Defence and Security Committee (ISDSC – see below) with its impressive system of committees on defence, police and intelligence matters and numerous sub-committees. For the time being the ISDSC brings some structure to the Organ and does so at no central expense to SADC since the various governments pay for their involvement within the ISDSC from their own budgets. Should it become clear that a permanent secretariat is required, the Organ will be faced with the following choices:

- To establish a small, multinational permanent secretariat at a permanent location. The country who chairs the Organ then takes the responsibility to provide the liaison function to the permanent secretariat.

- The alternative is the establishment of a multinational secretariat which relocates to the country which chairs the Organ – clearly impractical.

Finally, SADC may yet accept that the country that chairs the Organ provide all staff for the duration of the chairpersonship with some mechanisms to ensure a degree of continuity with the rotation of the chair.

In fact, it may make sense to ensure that the Organ is not co-located with the existing SADC Secretariat in Botswana – in effect physically separating the development and peace/stability functions so that the two do not interfere with one another. Such a clear distinction should provide the Organ with a greater ability to operate in a flexible and informal manner and could occur from separate offices in a country such as Zimbabwe.

However, the pre-eminence of the military, police and intelligence departments within ISDSC which is chaired by the Ministers of Defence of the various SADC countries on a rotational basis is a real problem. The establishment of the Organ and its focus on preventive action clearly places the responsibility for interaction and liaison with the Organ squarely within the domain of the Department of Foreign Affairs. The formalization of the Organ will, therefore, clearly impact upon the way in which the ISDSC operates at present, including the level (Ministerial) and department of the chairperson (presently Defence). Within its structures the ISDSC also includes a standing sub-committee on maritime affairs and one on aviation, both of which include non-military agencies and concerns. As a result the establishment of the Organ will also impact upon the manner in which the ISDSC has operated and in which it was structured in the past.

Furthermore, since the elections in South Africa the ISDSC has been looking at issues such as vehicle theft and cross border crime (apart from discussing the exchange of military personnel, collaboration in training, etc.). As such, it would follow that the implementation of the recently signed protocol on Combating Illicit Drug Trafficking would become a responsibility of the Organ and not of SADC in Gaberone. This further raises the issue of who looks after implementation and monitors progress without a permanent structure.

The highly sensitive issue relating to the establishment of an early warning system for conflict prevention within the ISDSC is also now up for discussion. Should this still remain the implicit task of the intelligence communities as seems to be the ISDSC approach, or would it not make sense to also move this to the diplomats, but obviously supported by the various intelligence agencies?

Another issue now becoming urgent is that of the national focal points for SADC within the various member countries. Previously this was generally through the departments of trade and industry of each government, although not necessarily so. In the case of South Africa, Tanzania, Zambia, Zimbabwe and Mauritius, the total SADC involvement is the responsibility of their foreign ministries. With the Organ committed to peace, preventive diplomacy and security issues, liaison is increasingly through other departments such as defence, police and foreign affairs. Therefore SADC would have to either continue with the practices of accepting that all liaison occurs through a single department such as trade and industry (which would be hugely impractical when dealing with a crisis requiring rapid reaction) move to a system where the various government departments increasingly work together on a direct basis with the co-ordination of national policies occurring within each country on an inter-departmental basis, or accept that liaison with SADC occurs through one department on the development side and through another (Foreign Affairs) in the case of the Organ. At present South Africa already has a ministerial committee on SADC which co-ordinates all South African interaction with SADC on an interdepartmental level.

All of this being said, it is clear that the establishment of the Organ for Politics, Defence and Security heralds a new dimension for SADC and its member countries. It is the start of a long road which must be travelled as a first step towards acceptance of an integrated vision of comprehensive and co-operative security built on interdependence. Although there is little clarity on the plans for the formalization of the Organ, the existing Inter-State Defence and Security Committee, previously part of the Frontline groupings, does provide the Organ with a nascent co-ordinating and planning structure.

The Inter-State Defence and Security Committee

The Inter-State Defence and Security Committee (ISDSC) is the most important sub-structure of the SADC Organ. In brief, it is a forum at which Ministers responsible for Defence, Home Affairs/Public Security as well as State Security of Southern African States meet to discuss issues relating to their individual and collective defence and security issues.

The ISDSC does not have an Executive Secretary nor a permanent secretariat. The Chief of the Zambia Air Force has listed the objectives of the ISDSC as follows.

- Prevention of aggression from within the region and from outside the region.

- Prevention of *coups d'états.*

- Management and resolution of conflicts.

- The promotion of regional stability.

- The promotion of regional peace.

- Promotion and enhancement of regional development.[47]

On the basis of its agenda, the primary functions of the three ISDSC sub-committees may be summarized as follows:[48]

Defence:

- To review and share experiences on the military security situation prevailing in respective member states.

- To explore areas of further multilateral military co-operation and practical means for the realization of that objective.

- To exchange views and propose mechanisms for the prevention, management and resolution of conflicts in the southern African sub-region in particular, and Africa in general.

- Public Security.

- To co-ordinate public security activities in the sub-region.

- To exchange experience and information between member states on public security issues such as motor vehicle thefts, drug trafficking, counterfeit currency, illegal immigrants, forged travel documents as well as smuggling of fire arms.

- To explore areas and means of enhancing co-operation among police agencies in the sub-region.

State Security:

- To review the security situation in the sub-region and to analyse issues affecting respective member states. The issues include political instability, armed conflict, influx of refugees, religious extremism and organized crime.

- To recommend appropriate measures to deal with potential threats to the stability of the sub-region.

- To look into ways and means of consolidating and expanding co-operation between member states on matters relating to state security.

In the past the ISDSC played a key role in conjunction with the liberation movements in co-ordinating strategy and activities against colonialism and apartheid in Southern Africa. Its mandate, however, has always been, and appears to remain, confined to making recommendations for the consideration of the Heads of State and Government of member states.

The sub-structure of the Military Sub-committee of the ISDSC consists of a functional sub-sub-committee (which included operations, intelligence, personnel development and logistics), a professional sub-sub committee (which included the chaplains, lawyers and medical associations), a sports committee and the standing maritime and aviation sub-sub-committees. The Defence Sub-Committee also decided to support the East and Southern African Liaison Office of the International Military Sports Council (Conseil International du Sort Militaire – CISM) in their efforts to build confidence and friendship through sport. In practice each country would nominate one or two persons to attend each of the committees.

The proposed functions of the Military Operations and Intelligence components are as follows:

- To promote a common understanding among the member states of each of the state's operating and planning procedures.

- Determine to what extent command and staff procedures, tactics and equipment are compatible and in what fields standardization should be sought.

- Do contingency planning for the establishment of an operational centre in the case of disaster relief operations being launched.

- To co-ordinate the conduct of intelligence and counter-intelligence on military and military related activities from outside the region which may threaten the sovereignty and stability of one or more of the states in the region.

- To co-ordinate the conduct and integration of intelligence and counter-intelligence on military related factors and developments influencing/ affecting security stability within the region.

- To support strategic planning within the Region.

- To facilitate and support combined operations.

- To co-ordinate military intelligence and counter-intelligence in the functional fields to be identified.

- To participate in an ASAS or any other Early Warning Mechanism: which may be established.[49]

The extent of potential co-operation on maritime affairs was significantly extended with Mauritius, the only island member of SADC, joining the Community in 1995. This being said, the Arusha meeting had already recommended that Madagascar, Kenya, Zaire, Congo and Gabon be invited to join the Standing Committee on Maritime Co-operation, although these countries were not SADC members.

Attendance of the maritime and aviation meetings will occur at the level of the naval and air force chiefs respectively. The proposed purpose of the Maritime Committee is to promote co-operation with a view of developing professional capabilities and a common doctrine and standing operating procedures to achieve inter-operability. This was to be achieved by having certain common training, combined exercises and operations, an exchange of students, etc. An obvious priority would be to establish an effective command, control, communications and intelligence infrastructure for maritime co-ordination. The agenda of the Standing Committee could also induce assistance with the protection of marine resources (notably fishing); the protection of the marine environment and the ecology pollution control (including oil spills, transportation of hazardous cargo); disaster relief; the combating of piracy, drug and arms trafficking, and illegal immigration, safety of life at sea (through search and rescue operations and monitoring of sub-standard vessels); hydrography and navigation aids and the support of scientific research. This implies that civilian components such as the Departments of Transport, Environment, Safety and Security would have to be involved.[50]

The decision to opt for a single professional sub-sub-committee replaced the earlier idea to establish separate Military Medical Doctors Association, Military Lawyers Association and a Military Chaplains forum to discuss the training, development and management of a military chaplains' organization within the armed forces.[51]

The ISDSC has adopted as a principle, unrestricted bilateral defence co-operation between member states as well as between member states outside of the region. The ISDSC will, therefore, promote multilateral co-operation and provide the intelligence support for preventive diplomacy initiatives in the case of pending or actual hostilities. It must also be able to plan combined operations, such as staff procedures, drills, tactics and telecommunications equipment. Increasingly it would now appear as if the ISDSC would become the formal mechanism for multilateral military, police and intelligence co-ordination within the SADC Organ.

It is to be expected that discussions on the establishment of a regional non-aggression pact will proceed shortly, but that any movement on a mutual defence pact (or treaty organization), as proposed at the Windhoek conference in July 1994, will not occur that readily. While a non-aggression pact is a virtual requirement to help ensure a stable region and to build confidence among SADC member states, the implications of a defence pact are far-reaching and complex.

As yet, there is no agreement on the establishment of a regional 'early-warning system' within the ISDSC or at the level of SADC that would enable timely preventive diplomacy and thereby avoid the requirement for additional military or other measures. Although this aspect has been under discussion for some time, the only consensus appears to be that any such mechanism should not be a permanent structure (part of the ISDSC, for example) and that this role could be fulfilled through co-operation among members based on information provided by non-state actors, such as NGOs and academic institutions. In southern Africa, South Africa is the only country with a diversity of research institutions and would tend to dominate such a system. In this context, the establishment of a regional security 'think-tank', as has been considered by various organizations, may be appropriate. However, its establishment has been hampered thus far by institutional rivalry.

Increased military co-operation in the region could diminish reliance on external assistance and provide additional stability in a volatile area. In this regard, eight measures are already either in place or being planned to increase transparency, inter-operability and professional standards:

- the mutual secondment of soldiers, including regional training co-operation;
- equipping and assisting African forces in, for example, landmine clearance;
- goodwill visits and informal liaison;
- conducting combined exercises;
- a non-threatening force design;
- the development of common doctrine and procedures;
- participation in multilateral co-ordination structures; and
- co-operation in terms of logistics.

The fact that South Africa is taking the ISDSC quite seriously is evident from the fact that a ministerial co-ordination mechanism has been set up to co-ordinate the input of all the relevant South African ministries dealing with the ISDSC, namely intelligence, defence, safety and security, and justice.

Conclusion: Prospects for Sub-Regional Peacekeeping Initiatives

Any military attempts at ensuring a settlement, intervening in a dispute, or deploying armed forces for humanitarian assistance in Africa, are bound to be either of a very limited nature, or would require substantial resources. Peacemaking and peacekeeping involve constant danger and are more complex and expensive than the classic monitoring of ceasefires, the control of buffer zones or even preventive deployment. This implies that outside intervention, as in the case in Somalia and Rwanda, must extend beyond military and humanitarian tasks and might include the re-establishment of effective government and the promotion of national reconciliation. Should the 'intervening powers' be from the region, the potential difference between the needs of the population who require assistance and the national interest of those countries intervening will inevitably further complicate the situation. But more importantly, there must be serious doubts about the persistence and ability of either Africa or the international community to effect these type of measures.

In the interim there are at least six ways in which member countries, the OAU and sub-regional organizations can improve their preparedness for eventual participation in peace support operations in Africa. These include:[52]

- Improving the level of preparedness of troops, that is, better trained, equipped and battle ready troops to enable participation.

- Encouragement of standardization of equipment, doctrine and standing operating procedures among African countries. Such standardization would greatly enhance inter-operability and co-operation.

- Encouragement of countries to participate in the UN stand-by arrangements whereby governments indicate in advance to the UN the types of personnel and equipment they are, in principle, willing to make available for UN peacekeeping operations. By July 1995 only 5 out of the 41 countries participating in UN stand-by arrangements were from Africa.

- Partnership arrangements between African and donor countries whereby the former provide troops and the latter assist in the provision of heavy equipment for peacekeeping.

- The pre-positioning of non-lethal equipment such as tents and communication equipment at advance logistic centres in select locations throughout the continent.

- Dedicated peacekeeping training assistance by and to African countries, as well as conferences and seminars on the subject.

One reason for the increased enthusiasm of the OAU to involve itself in peacekeeping activities, is the pressure from foreign donor governments who have been attempting to encourage African countries to accept a greater degree of responsibility for peacekeeping in Africa. There are also some powerful reasons and motives for the creation of an African and

Southern African capacity for greater involvement in regional peacekeeping endeavours. Regional security arrangements could play an important role in stabilizing the continent, although such arrangements are only part of the recipe that will eventually enable sustainable development and stability. Sub-regional organizations, such as SADC, have the potential to act as building blocks in a system of preventive action, as well as early warning. Increased military co-operation in the region could diminish reliance on external assistance and provide additional stability in a volatile area.

However, the enthusiasm of SADC member states to create a regional standby capacity of peacekeepers depends largely on South Africa demonstrating the necessary will to become involved in peace operations, even though it has not yet provided troops for such operations. In contrast, Zambia, Botswana, Zimbabwe, Malawi and Tanzania have all previously contributed to peacekeeping operations. As the most powerful state in Southern Africa, South Africa has a strong international voice and will exert a decisive influence on the destiny of the region. Economic domination aside, South Africa has armed forces which number nearly twice as many as any other in the region, and, if one were to remove war-ravaged Angola from the equation, spends 15 times more on defence than the next closest SADC contender, Zimbabwe.

Repeated calls have been made by the OAU and by leaders, such as the President of Botswana and the Executive Secretary of the SADC, for the establishment of either an African or a Southern African peacekeeping force. Given the obvious burden that this would place on South Africa, the South African government, thus far, has treated these suggestions with a great degree of caution and scepticism. Emotionally, South Africa leans towards focusing its efforts on Africa, despite the obvious risks that such involvement hold. Africa clearly cannot sustain an autonomous peacekeeping force of any significant capacity without substantial international assistance. With the exception of South Africa, no country within SADC can independently mount a complex peace operation into a direct neighbouring country – and even South Africa's capacity has been demonstrably cut in recent years. As a whole, the vast majority of African states lack the resources and experience to conduct peace operations independently of the international donor community. In fact, the real question is to what extent the international community is prepared to support, fund and assist peacekeeping in Africa by Africans in material terms.

Against this background, it comes as little surprise that the South African White Paper on Defence is wary of being too ambitious in its approach, stating that '... the creation of a standing peacekeeping force in the region is neither desirable nor practically feasible. It is far more likely that the SADC countries will engage in *ad hoc* peace support operations if the need arises ... It may by worthwhile to establish a small peace support operations centre, under the auspices of regional defence structures, to develop and co-ordinate planning, training, logistics, communications and field liaison teams for multinational forces.'[53]

The bottom line is that neither Africa nor Southern Africa can 'go it alone' in providing the stability which is essential for development. The region does not have the means, in terms of doctrine, training, trained manpower, finances, and resources. Tentative democracies and *de facto* one-party states will find it difficult to transfer the values of respect for human rights and impartiality to the armed forces of neighbouring countries, when they have been unable to inculcate the same within their own borders.

Should the international community attempt to delegate the international role of the UN in peacekeeping to either the OAU or a regional organization such as SADC in the foreseeable future, the result is entirely predictable. The consequences of such abrogation of responsibility have been aptly illustrated by recent events in Liberia, where peacekeeping, peace enforcement, military intervention and banditry have become synonymous with one another. Despite the infusion of capacity and resources which South Africa has brought to the region, peacekeeping in Africa by Africans, can only work if it occurs in close collaboration and collusion with the UN and the international community. This will remain the case for years to come.

African armed forces, therefore, should prepare and co-operate with the international community. In effect, the only feasible scenario for keeping the peace in Africa, is the creation of an internationally-sponsored UN rapid reaction force in Africa for Africa. Such a force should consist of designated units which are placed on standby, and trained in their respective countries by the UN, for common deployment by the UN, in collaboration with organizations such as SADC or the OAU.

The lack of an effective and timely international response to the ongoing crises in the Great Lakes region during the latter half of 1996 demonstrates the urgent need for increased involvement in peacekeeping by African countries under the auspices of the UN, or even on the initiative of an organization such as the OAU or the SADC. Southern Africa must consider its responsibilities in this regard and put its own house in order. If the region is to accept its responsibilities, it is essential that discussion, negotiation, commitment and co-operation should occur at the level of the UN, OAU, SADC and individual countries, before the next major crisis erupts. If decision-making bodies are necessary, if joint military ties must be established, if combined exercises must take place, then now is the time to start.

The substantive challenge facing all African countries, however, is not peacekeeping or the ability to conduct humanitarian assistance operations. It is the challenge of designing mechanisms and practices that will effectively contain the destabilizing role of the security forces in their efforts to oust democratically elected governments, entrenching civil and legislative control over these forces, and inculcating a culture of accountability, transparency and professionalism. This challenge is of much greater importance to the region than peacekeeping, but will predictably receive much less attention.

NOTES

1. Inst. for National Strategic Studies, *Strategic Assessment 1995*, US Security Challenges in Transition (Washington DC 1995) p.101.
2. R. Umoren, 'World Bank Pessimistic about Region's Economic Integration', *Economic Bulletin*, IPS (April 1995) p.14.
3. A. Haggag, 'OAU Mechanism for Conflict Prevention, Management and Resolution in Africa', paper presented at the meeting of the Inter-State Defence and Security Comiittee in Cape Town, 7 Sept. 1995, pp.4–5.
4. S.A. Salim, 'The Front-line States: A New Alliance for Peace and Development in Southern Africa', Keynote address to the Meeting of the Ministers of Defence and Security of the Front-line States, Arusha, Tanzania, 10 Nov. 1994. Repr. in *Backgrounder*, No. 17, U. of the Western Cape, Cape Town, 1994, p.8.
5. The composition of the Central Organ by late 1995 was as follows: Ethiopia (chair), Tunisia (outgoing), Cameroon (incoming), Namibia, Mauritania, Algeria, Djibouti, Swaziland, Mali, Burundi, Egypt, Kenya, Senegal, Lesotho, Gabon, Nigeria. *Resolving Conflicts*, OAU Conflict Management Bulletin 1/1 (Dec. 1995/Jan. 1996) p.6.
6. W. Nhara, 'The OAU and the Potential Role of Regional and Sub-Regional Organizations', paper delivered at an IDP/SAIIA conference, *South Africa and Peace-keeping in Africa*, Johannesburg, 13–14 July 1995, p.5.
7. Ibid. p.5.
8. Ibid. pp.5–6.
9. Reuters, 'OAU members get together on Burundi peace', *The Star*, Johannesburg, 11 July 1996.
10. *Summary Record of the Seminar for the Establishment, within the OAU, of an Early Warning System on Conflict Situations in Africa*, Institute for Defence Policy [hereafter IDP], Paper No.1, Feb. 1996, p.7.
11. See e.g. I. Johnstone and T. Nkiwana, *The Organization of African Unity and Conflict Management in Africa*, Report of a Joint OAU/IPA Consultation, Addis Ababa, Ethiopia, 19–21 May 1993, undated, p.4.
12. Haggag (note 3) p.8.
13. Ibid. p.20.
14. Ibid. p.8.
15. See note 10.
16. OAU (note 5).
17. See e.g. the remarks by Nhara (note 6) p.3.
18. J. Herbst, 'Africa and the International Economy', paper presented at a conference on *South Africa in the Global Economy*, South African Inst. for Int. Affairs, Johannesburg, 11–12 July 1996, p.21.
19. R. Cornwell, 'Lost Prophets', in *Africa Insight* 26/2 (1996) p.90.
20. Through the 'Declaration: Southern Africa: Towards Economic Liberation', adopted in

Lusaka, Zambia, on 1 April 1980. The concept of regional economic co-operation was first discussed at a meeting of the Front-line States foreign ministers in May 1979 in Gaberone. The meeting led to an international conference in Arusha Tanzania two months later which brought together all independent countries, with the exception of the then Rhodesia, South West Africa and South Africa – and international donor agencies. The Arusha conference in turn led to the Lusaka Summit held in the Zambian capital in April 1980. After adopting the declaration, which was to become known as 'Southern Africa: Towards Economic Liberation', Sir Seretse Khama was elected the first chairman of the SADCC. P. Dube, 'Historic SADC summit in SA', *Sowetan*, 25 Aug. 1995

21. Ibid. p.4.
22. Ibid. p.3.
23. Declaration by the Heads of State or Government of Southern African States, 'Towards the Southern African Development Community', Declaration Treaty and Protocol of Southern African Development Community, Windhoek 17 Aug. 1992, p.2.
24. Dube (note 20).
25. *Treaty Declaration and Protocol of the Southern African Development Community*, ibid., p.5.
26. Ibid. pp.7–8.
27. Ibid. pp.5 and 10.
28. Interview with Dr Charles Hove, Chief Economist, SADC, Gaberone, 30 July 1996.
29. Only nine of the SADC member countries sighned the protocol. Angola and Zambia did not sign and asked for time to conduct internal consultations. From a report by Virginia Muwanigwa it would now appear as if Zambia wants a trade-off between the water protocol and a bilateral preferential trade agreement with South Africa, similar to the agreement recently signed between South Africa and Zimbabwe.
30. Communiqué, SADC Summit, Maseru, Lesotho, 24 Aug. 1996.
31. Cornwall (note 19).
32. Communiqué (note 30).
33. Mbuende, Namibia's former assistant minister of agriculture, took over the reins of SADC in January 1994 after the unceremonious departure of Zimbabwe's Dr Simba Makoni. P. Dube, 'Making economies grow', in *Sowetan*, Johannesburg, 25 Aug. 1995.
34. As a first step SADC embarked on an impact study in 1996 to assess the effect of dropping tariffs. This study would also form the basis for a mechanism to be used to compensate counties which stood to be harmed from the loss of import tariff revenue. The trade and industry sector was also involved in removing non-tariff barriers to trade through the harmonization of standards in the region. A key part of this process was the establishment of national standards authorities. Only five SADC countries have these institutions. J. Dludlu, 'SADC plans free trade area', in *Business Day*, Johannesburg, 24 Aug. 1995.
35. Anon 'Catching the golden goose may be easier said than done', *The Star*, Johannesburg, 5 Sept. 1995.
36. DFA, The Southern African Development Community ..., ibid. p.1.
37. The Front-line states organization was set up in 1970 by the already independent southern African states, notably Zambia and Tanzania, to lobby for the liberation of Zimbabwe, Namibia and South Africa.
38. From A. Pahad, 'South Africa and Preventive Diplomacy', in J. Cilliers and G. Mills (eds.) *Peacekeeping in Africa* (Halfway House: IDP 1995) pp.156–7.
39. Ibid. p.157.
40. Remarks by Minister Alfred Nzo, Foreign Affairs budget vote, National Assembly, Cape Town, 18 May 1995, p.6.
41. S. Brummer, 'Mugabe is a spanner in the works', in *Mail & Guardian*, Johannesburg, 25–31 Aug. 1995.
42. *SADC Summit Communiqué*, 28 Aug. 1995, Johannesburg, p.3.
43. Press release, *SADC Ministers meet in Gaberone*, issued by the SADC Secretariate, 19 Jan. 1996.
44. Ibid.
45. Communiqué on the establishment of the Organ for Politics, Defence and Security, Gaberone, Jan. 1996.

46. Ibid.
47. See R.S. Shikapwashya, 'Presentation on the Aim, Roles, Functions and Organization of the Standing Aviation Committee of the Inter-State Defence and Security Committee for the Southern African region', paper presented at the Sir Pierre van Rhyneveld Air Power Conference, Pretoria, 3 Oct. 1995, p.14.
48. The kind assistance of Maj. Gen. D. Hamman (Ret.) is acknowledged.
49. D. Hamman, 'Paper on the Inter-State Defence and Security Committee: Defence Sub-Committee', presented at a IDP roundtable seminar on South African and Global Peace Support Initiatives, Cape Town, 17–18 May 1995, p.5.
50. Ibid. pp.5–6.
51. Ibid. p.2.
52. Based on H.K. Anyidoho, 'Prospects for Co-operation in Peacekeeping in Africa', paper presented at an IDP/SAIIA conference, 'South Africa and Peace-keeping in Africa', Johannesburg, 13–14 July 1995, pp.5–7.
53. South African White Paper on Defence, Pretoria, May 1996, p.24.

South Africa: Crime in Transition

MARK SHAW

Ending crime has become the leading challenge of South Africa's democratic government. While the growth of criminality in the society began in the early 1980s it peaked – in common with other societies attempting to move from authoritarian rule to democratic governance – during the years of political transition. But, South Africa's system of criminal justice is ill-prepared to face the challenges of growing crime. Policing remains centralized, unresponsive to local needs and requires the upgrading of detection services. urgent reform is also required in the areas of prosecution, sentencing and incarceration. The National Crime Prevention Strategy, the key response of the new government to growing levels of crime, while an important initiative, remains too centralized and reliant on Pretoria-led rather than local initiatives. On the ground, critizens are responding in their own way: for the wealthy (and generally white) this means greater use of the burgeoning private security industry, for less fortunate communities it increasingly raises the possibility of taking the law into community hands through vigilante action.

Political and social transformation have affected South Africa profoundly. New and non-racial forms of democratic government have been established at national, provincial and now local level, and reconstruction and development has (slowly) begun. But the process has been far from painless: while political violence – excluding parts of KwaZulu-Natal – has ended, the transition to democracy has been characterized by rising levels of crime.

There is a clear and crucial link between South Africa's transition and the growth in crime which has accompanied it. But, it would be dangerously simplistic to argue that crime is purely a consequence of the transition: indeed, there is strong evidence to suggest that its roots lie in the apartheid system which the transition sought to negotiate an end to. But there is little doubt that the increase in criminality from 1990 – and in the decade before – cannot be divorced from the political, social and economic changes which ended apartheid.

Increases in crime from 1990 are consistent with the experiences of other countries undergoing transition to democracy: as change proceeds, society and its instruments of social control – formal and informal – are reshaped. The result is that new areas for the development of crime, which are bolstered by the legacies of the past, open up.

Inevitably, newspaper headlines, police reports and the experiences of citizens have brought the issue of crime on to the public agenda. To many, the problem has assumed crisis dimensions as the country is swamped by a 'crime wave'. And crime is seen by both political elites and the media as a threat to the stability of the new democracy and a deterrent to investment. 'Crime', the populist Premier of Gauteng, Tokyo Sexwale, has declared, 'is the soft underbelly of the Reconstruction and Development Programme'.[1] Crime is therefore implicitly and explicitly seen as a central test of the capacity of the government to rule and the new democracy to consolidate.

The transition has not brought with it a system of criminal justice which is immediately in a position to respond to these challenges. The institutions of criminal justice remain weighed down under public perceptions that they are tools to enforce the rule of the minority over the majority rather than instruments to deliver protection to all. Also, the state security apparatus, while monstrously efficient in defending white rule through so-called 'insertion' or 'fire force' policing (sending in outside military or police units to quell disorder), is too under-resourced and under-skilled to take on conventional policing functions. And the new government – given the desire to control the pace of transformation and ensure that policing functions remain firmly in its control – has sought to retain policing as a central function, despite growing evidence that a centralized approach to crime control and prevention fails to take into account local problems. Pretoria-centric controls undermine the establishment of clear accountability links between local communities and the police, reinforcing perceptions that the South African Police Service (SAPS) remains unaccountable and unresponsive to citizen needs.

Of course, citizens have not necessarily always reacted to growing levels of crime by demanding that politicians do something about it: rising crime has effectively prompted South Africans to create substitute policing institutions, a trend which has strengthened through 1996. The private security industry continues to grow while vigilante groups have consolidated their position. The dangers of the growth of alternative forms of policing are obvious: they represent initiatives outside of and uncontrolled by state authority able (and often willing) to replace the formal public policing apparatus.

The challenges that await the new order should not be underestimated – nor are they easily resolved. Indeed the new government is faced with a dilemma. A failure to act reinforces public perceptions that government is weak, whilst over-reaction – with characteristic 'fire force' policing – leaves the impression that not much has changed. And, there is also little comparative evidence to draw on: most countries emerging from transition (many with less of a socio-economic divide than South Africa) have not yet been able to reduce their crime rates significantly. There is thus much to learn from the country's experience – but to date, the lessons are few.

A Criminal Society

Crime and politics in South Africa have been closely intertwined: in the era of race domination, apartheid offences were classified as crime, while those people engaged in the 'the struggle', particularly from the mid-1980s onwards, justified forms of violence as legitimate weapons against the system. Instability prompted a growing number of South Africans to acquire weapons: the use of guns to settle personal and family disputes became more common. On to this complex mix was grafted violence in KwaZulu-Natal from the mid-1980s, and on the Reef from 1990. Actions which were strictly violent crimes were seen by their perpetrators as a legitimate defence against political 'enemies': the result was a society in which the use of violence to achieve political and personal aims became endemic.

Measuring crime during apartheid's last decade reveals contradictory trends: at the height of political conflict during the 1980s, increases in some crimes appeared to have bottomed out. Political liberalization brought a crime explosion, so apparently following other societies (like states in Eastern Europe and those emerging from the former Soviet Union) undergoing sustained periods of democratic transition: as social controls are loosened, spaces open which allow growth in criminal activity. And, in developing countries attempting to make the transition, fewer resources mean that the cost of a growth in crime is far higher (even if rates of increase are comparatively smaller).[2]

But, at the outset, any understanding of criminality in South Africa is complicated by the fact that it is difficult to measure effectively the extent of lawlessness, or its costs. Recording crime relies on a two stage process: victims or bystanders need to report the crime to the police, who then need to record it. In fact, only a portion of some offences make it that far. In South Africa the collection of statistics has been complicated by the historic divide between people and police and the vagaries of apartheid record keeping. South African Police figures, for example, historically excluded those of the bantustans – statistics show all recorded crime in KwaZulu-Natal, for example, as occurring in the 'white' Natal section. This implies that the 'dark figure' of unrecorded crime in the country is substantial.

Barring the carrying out of a comprehensive victimization survey in South Africa, official crime statistics are the only ones available. If they are to be useful, they should not be analyzed for minutiae and rejected out of hand, but probed for broad trends. There is a common perception, for example, that crime in South Africa only began to increase from 1990 onwards in conjunction with political transition. In fact most serious crime, notably murder, robbery and housebreaking, began to increase from the mid-1980s onwards.

So it must be emphasized that South Africa's crime problem is not recent: the society, given levels of inequality and political conflict, has always been 'crimo-generic'. The decade 1980 to 1990, in which the apartheid state was most strongly challenged, showed significant increases in crime. According to police figures, serious offences rose by 22 per cent, and less serious ones by 17 per cent; murders increased by 32 per cent, rape by 24 percent, and burglary by 31 per cent.[3]

The increase in levels of crime peaked in 1990, the year in which the political transition began. Recorded levels of almost all crime showed absolute increases for the period 1990 to 1994. While the murder rate declined by 7 per cent, in line with declining levels of political violence (from 16,042 fatalities in 1990 to 14,920 in 1994) other crimes increased phenomenally during this period: assault increased by 18 per cent, rape by 42 per cent, robbery by 40 per cent, vehicle theft by 34 per cent, and burglary by 20 per cent. There was also an increase in crime of the affluent: although no accurate figures are available, commercial crimes increased significantly during this period. Trends throughout the country were not uniform, with the greatest increases occurring in the urban complexes around Johannesburg, Durban and Cape Town.

The problems related to the recording of crime suggest that government will need to continue to manage perceptions of increasing levels of crime for the next decade. If police reform succeeds and over time wealth is distributed more evenly throughout the society recorded levels of crime will continue to rise. This will apply particularly to property crime: a growth in the insurance industry, the numbers of cars on the road, the number of telephones and the approachability of the police (through, for example, a single emergency phone-reporting system) will allow higher levels of reporting. These recorded increases will need to be managed by government – something which the Ministry of Safety and Security has conceded that it is not particularly good at doing.

This outcome though will apply mainly to less serious crimes. Given the greater likelihood of reporting, figures for crimes such as murder may be more accurate. South Africa leads a comparative measure of citizens killed in crime related instances in a range of countries. The figure for the first six months of 1996 of 30 citizens killed per 100,000 head of population is nearly four times that of the United States. And hospital records (which are often more accurate than crime statistics) show that every day 2,500 South Africans required treatment as a result of stabbings, beatings and shootings. Indeed, reporting figures for the first part of 1996 continue to show dramatic increases in levels of reporting for assaults, domestic violence and rape.[4]

The growth in organized crime in the new democratic order has also been dramatic. There are now said to be 481 criminal organizations in the country (although police definitions of these remain unclear) who engage in a wide range of activities ranging from weapons, drug and vehicle smuggling. Countering organized crime now is a priority. Comparative evidence from other states in transition suggests that unless organized crime operations are countered quickly after their formation they have the potential to harden, penetrate the state and form parallel and competing centres of power. The rise of criminal enterprises in parts of Eastern Europe, the former Soviet Union and West Africa illustrate these developments.[5]

The impact of crime on the country, however, is not uniform and increases in crime appear to affect different parts of South African society in different ways. This implies that since not all South Africans are exposed to equal dangers, different strategies should be used in different areas to curb crime. Thus while crime in general has increased over the past decade, this does not necessarily apply to all crime, nor do all areas of the country suffer equally. Broadly an examination of statistics over time, shows that the Northern province displays high levels of crime against property, but a comparatively low figure for crimes of violence. KwaZulu-Natal shows high levels for property and violence related offences. The Northern and Western Cape show high assault figures, yet comparatively smaller readings for theft and housebreaking. The Free State consistently shows the lowest reported rate for all categories of crime.

These provincial variations suggest that national crime figures may be deceptive, since levels of victimization and forms of criminality vary between provinces. For instance, while vehicle hijacking is feared nationally, almost all cases occur in Gauteng. This conclusion is reinforced by local police station figures which show that categories of crime vary considerably between station areas. A detailed examination of crime totals for various magisterial districts in Gauteng show that districts with very high crime rates and those with very low crime rates are often situated close together.[6]

These conclusions are hardly surprising: it is an established truth in policing that the causes and consequences of crime are often locally specific and as such require locally driven answers. While this principle is generally recognized in South Africa, given the political imperatives of a country in transition, it has not necessarily been subscribed to by policy makers. The result is a messy breakdown of police functions and levels of accountability which serve to hinder police effectiveness.

Most serious is the fact that there is currently no connection between elected local government and police agencies. Community Police Forums (CPFs), designed to give local communities a say in policing priorities, have been written into the constitution. But the introduction of CPFs has not been unproblematic. At the outset, such structures, given their volunteer nature, are seldom representative. In addition, since CPFs can do little to influence the operational priorities of the police – depending of course on the personalities involved – they are often little more than toy telephones.

In any event, local station commissioners report straight through the police command structure to the National Commissioner in Pretoria and so have little incentive to respond to community needs. Promotions and transfers depend on the hierarchy in Pretoria and not on the community's voice on the ground. The problem of accountability is compounded at provincial level. Provincial Members of Executive Councils for Safety and Security are tasked under the new constitution with monitoring and oversight functions over the police – in effect they have little say (beyond political influence) over operational policing issues in their provinces.

The result is often (although not always) that local policing priorities are subsumed under a complex bureaucratic structure directed from Pretoria. The centralization of police functions is based on a political imperative to maintain the coercive apparatus of the state controlled from the centre. To break up the police agency, the argument goes, may invite exploitation and abuse from the provinces and further down the spectrum at local level. Also, there is some doubt about the capacity of many localized structures and station commanders to take full responsibility for policing in their area. And, proponents of centralized policing argue, to devolve policing functions would mean good services in some areas and poor ones in others. These arguments are spurious: given adequate degrees of regulation and the maintaining of certain key police functions – like public order and organized crime investigations – at national level would prevent abuse occurring. The key to better policing is to allow communities to take responsibility for safety and security rather than assuming that they are incapable.

Colonialism with its specific brand of policing required a centralized police agency, as did apartheid with its desire to control and suppress opposition. Ironically, the post-apartheid government in seeking to establish order in the society and transform the policing functions of the state, argues for the need to retain centralised control of the police function. The result is increasing levels of disorder in many local communities and little democratic linkage to ensure accountable forms of policing at local level.

Criminal Justice in Crisis

Beyond its policing function, South Africa's system of criminal justice is in crisis. If its ability to prevent, process and deter crime is any measure of its effectiveness than reforming the system is now not only a necessity but a national priority. Unfortunately the system is not easily fixed; it is not characterized by a single problem which can be resolved speedily but is characterized by multiple blockages, many of which cause delays in other parts of the criminal justice pipeline. The system, stretching across the Departments of Safety and Security, Justice and Correctional Services, has never been a unified one. The links between the various departments are weak and the involvement of departments such as Welfare, Education and Health – who have a key role to play in the prevention of crime – is minimal.'

Broadly, if it functioned effectively, the system should consist of both proactive and reactive components. Proactive crime prevention strategies are key to the longer term reduction of crime in South Africa. But they themselves are limited without effective institutions to process (and rehabilitate) offenders once crime has been committed. While the development of proactive solutions to crime should be a priority, the focus – at least in the short to medium term – should rest on transforming the reactive components of the criminal justice system. Within this context, however, there is significant scope for the development of proactive strategies – rehabilitation of offenders being the most obvious.

Inevitably reform efforts after 1994 concentrated almost exclusively on the front end of the criminal justice system – essentially the visible component of policing. Community policing has been the watch word of police efforts to sell themselves as more acceptable to the majority of the South African public – in truth that focus has been as important a tool for transforming citizens' views of the police as it has been to the change in ethos among police officers themselves. The transformation of the most publicly visible component of the criminal justice system is still far from complete. But equally serious problems characterize the system further along: these are primarily in the areas of the detection of crime, the prosecution of offenders and in the system of incarceration.

What has virtually been ignored by the policy makers in the new order has been the issue of detecting crime. The consequences have been severe. In 1995 only a quarter of all robberies were resolved, one fifth of all house breakings, one tenth of all vehicle thefts and about 50 per cent of all murders.[8] Hardly surprisingly South Africa's detectives have always been a threatened breed; under apartheid the quick road to promotion for bright and ambitious officers was through the security branch; in the new order the fast track is uniform or visible policing. This has been exacerbated in the past year by the large numbers of experienced detectives leaving the services for the more handsome pickings of the private sector and by the difficulty of recruiting more detectives.

Currently there are few incentives for detective work: uniformed officers work four days on and fours days off, good detectives often work seven days a week with no overtime, under poor and dangerous conditions with little support. Most detectives, often with no training (only about 26 per cent have been on a detective course), carry upwards of 50 dockets. There is no mentoring or assistance programme to speak of and the vast majority of new detectives are thrown in at the deep end. There is also a high degree of inexperience: only 13 per cent of all detectives (and these mainly in specialized units) have over six years experience.

The position has been aggravated over time by police structural changes. Given that station level detectives were seen as ineffective, specialized units were created. The next result over time has been the removal from stations of experienced officers and loss of morale among ordinary street level detectives. In a recent development, the SAPS has mooted a detective academy to begin to train detectives and pass skills from specialized units to station-level officers.

The Department of Justice is also not blameless. Most public prosecutors have little experience and magistrates courts are often badly managed. Constant postponements frustrate witnesses who often fail to appear when cases are finally heard. Most critical though is the inter-face between detectives and public prosecutors. Greater co-operation and co-ordination between justice and police officials at this point in the system would ensure a higher rate of prosecutions. At the moment, prosecutors and investigating officers in the lower courts often only meet each other for the first time when the detective is in the witness box.

While both departments protest that the systems are in place to ensure effective functioning, what appears to be a common problem is a lack of skilled (and motivated) middle management. Old order civil servants are disillusioned and new or recently promoted officials have little experience and (often deliberately) receive no support .

South Africa's prisons are also in dire need of reform. Ironically, the prisons have been fuller in the past – in the mid-1980s more than four in every 1,000 citizens were in jail – but apparently better managed. Staff shortages, prisoner and warder unrest and increasing corruption (the majority of escapes are apparently a result of bribing prison officials and the Department of Correctional Services is known by its employees as the Department of Corruptional Services) are bringing the crisis to a head.

South African prison conditions are near Victorian. The announcement that Correctional Services would begin issuing condoms – hoping at least to protect unwilling prisoners forced into sexual intercourse from Aids – has brought the issue into sharp relief. Most prisons are dank and dark, maintenance budgets are limited, and internally some jail areas are virtually controlled not by warders but by the prisoners themselves.

To be fair, the problem is not all of Correctional Services making – about one quarter of all South Africa's 130,000 inmates are still awaiting trail. In effect, Correctional Services must cater for those whose passage through the criminal justice system is blocked at the point where crime is investigated and processed through the courts. Given that those prisoners awaiting trail are not yet sentenced and are merely held by Correctional Services pending the outcome of their court cases, the effect is that they are not considered as fully-fledged convicts and not subject to (albeit) limited privileges such as prison clothes and recreational services.

The clearest indication that the system is failing lies simply in the fact that more than half of those who have been imprisoned will again commit crime on their release. Rehabilitation in South Africa's prisons (admittedly like most other countries in the world) is a farce. The likelihood of improvements in future are slim given that any new budgetary allocations will be for yet more prisons and staff to guard them. Public opinion is also geared more to the ending of crime than the rehabilitation of prisoners (although the two are closely linked) and convicts are widely viewed as deserving of the conditions under which they live. Business Against Crime, a prominent private sector initiative aimed at ending lawlessness, for example, while supplying resources to the front end of the criminal justice pipeline where criminals are caught has displayed little interest in its back waters where crime is often learned. SAPS officers refer to prisons as 'the universities'.

At least part of the problem lies in the rigidity of the South African penal system: alternative forms of sentencing are, virtually unavailable and where they are magistrates (influenced by public perceptions that the system is criminal friendly) seem unwilling to use them. In Europe and North America parole and correctional supervision are increasingly seen as modern alternatives to shutting people away. In some US states up to 80 per cent of all convicted prisoners are on probation or parole – in South Africa the comparative figure is 20 per cent. And parole in South Africa prisons is determined by the Department of Correctional Services itself – an open invitation for bribery and an easy (but inappropriate) mechanism to release pressure on the prison system.[9]

In effect the Department virtually has the power to alter sentences established by an independent judiciary. What is urgently needed is an investigation into community forms of sentencing for some categories of offenders. This would mean the appointment of a greater number of supervisors (as opposed to prison wardens). There are currently only 1,100 supervisors for a total of 33,340 convicted offenders (including those who have been granted parole) serving their sentences outside the prisons. And, the enlisting of business and government support to ensure alternative forms of sentencing to prison is also required.

Corruption throughout the Criminal Justice System is said to be pervasive; although few figures are available the current prosecution rate can only be the tip of the iceberg. Corruption – bred by declining morale, poor controls, management and training within the system itself – is a symptom rather than a cause. And it should not be viewed as an issue outside of and unrelated to the poor functioning and management of the criminal justice system. But, its consequences for public perceptions of the institutions of criminal justice are severe.

There is a dilemma here. Any large crackdown on corruption is bound to undermine already flagging public confidence in the criminal justice system. But denial of the extent of the problem will continue to undermine public confidence in the institutions of criminal justice. This will be particularly so, if, over the longer term, it becomes the common knowledge and experience of ordinary citizens that the system's representatives – in the form of the police, court and correctional officials – are open to corruption. This dilemma is one of the most significant challenges awaiting policy makers in the next five years. The only alternative, unattractive in the short term, is some high profile prosecutions.

Government Initiatives

The growing weakness of the criminal justice system has not escaped government. The recently released National Crime Prevention Strategy has as its central task the bringing together of departments involved in crime control and prevention and the co-ordination of their activities. This suggests a more unified approach to the problems of the criminal justice system. But the greatest strength of the crime prevention strategy – its inclusive and comprehensive nature – also holds the potential to be its greatest weakness. The very complexity and wide ranging nature of the strategy suggests that co-ordination and leadership will be critical to success.

While the strategy provides a vision for a society which has begun to confront the problem of criminality eating at its core, what still has to be demonstrated now is an ability to manage the process of reform of the criminal justice system. That strategy will be central to any crime prevention effort. The strategy – an 88-page document in small, single-space type – aims to draw together key role players in government in an attempt to provide the basis for the restructuring of the criminal justice system, and in the longer term, more effective crime prevention programmes.[10]

The development of the strategy involved six core government departments: Correctional Services, Defence, Intelligence, Justice, Safety and Security and Welfare. This is in itself an important development – a holistic (as opposed to sectoral) approach to crime prevention which has been sorely lacking. What is also clear from the document is the reorientation of the intelligence community which now, and increasingly it seems, will assume a crime combating role in relation to specific types of crime.

At a different level the strategy indicates another significant shift in the discourse of safety and security in South Africa: from 'community policing' (which is barely mentioned in the document) to 'crime prevention' and the building of 'partnerships' both between government agencies and with outside organizations in business and civil society in an effort to stem the tide of crime.

The document provides a detailed analysis of the reason for the growth of crime in the country – seen (correctly) as a complex intermeshing of a diversity of factors – and outlines steps under way in various government departments to counter crime. Outside of the repair of the criminal justice process, three key issues – environmental design, education and transnational crime – are identified as being critical areas for intervention to reduce crime. In addition, the strategy lays down 18 nationally driven programmes to be implemented. These are diverse, ranging from improving information systems (poor information transfer is at the heart of the system's problems), victim empowerment and support and mechanisms to counter organized crime.

What seems notably absent from the list of new programmes are specific preventative strategies related to drug use, the proliferation of small arms and the gang problem in certain parts of the country. While all are covered either directly or indirectly within various sections of the document, it would have been worth consolidating current initiatives and developing specific strategies to form two or three additional (and high profile) prevention programmes. These areas are of increasing concern given that they hold the potential to spawn wider forms of criminality.

The issue of increasing drug usage, for instance, is a critical one. Government response to the drug problem has historically been fragmented and poorly funded with no co-ordination between reactive and proactive programmes. What needs to be explored is the establishment of a law enforcement body separate from the current police and intelligence structures which would provide leadership in areas of both prevention and enforcement.

On a different level, it is a pity that the strategy does not contain a more detailed section on initiatives by local government. International experience suggests that the key to crime prevention lies at the city level. The strategy could have advanced the process and debate at local level substantially had the issue of crime prevention at a metropolitan level, for example, been emphasized. A useful mechanism in other countries has been the establishment of city forums to compare experiences and determine joint guidelines for crime prevention.

Nor have South African city authorities been idle. Many are beginning to work on crime prevention plans and the establishment of further local authority police agencies. But central government has dragged its heels on these developments; no framework yet exists for local government policing or crime prevention strategies, and, if current developments are anything to go by, local governments will run ahead of the national authorities in this sphere. Many, including crime-ridden Johannesburg, are in the process of formulating plans for city police services designed to supplement the SAPS.

What the National Crime Prevention Strategy does correctly suggest, however, is that local-level initiatives should be able to take account of local level conditions and circumstances in tailoring individual programmes. But not clear are the consequences should local authorities stray outside the broad boundaries delineated by the strategy. The document could have suggested guidelines to contain, or where necessary, focus any such initiatives.

The key to the success of the strategy is co-ordination; otherwise it simply becomes a reflection of a wide variety of programmes which may eventually, in any event, have occurred in one form or the other. A related problem with such a large and complex initiative is that at a national level it is virtually immune to measurement; there is a danger that success will simply be equated with a flurry of activity (in this case, committee meetings) rather than any real decreases in crime. Given the number of players involved, the complexity of the strategy should not be underestimated. Apart from, and in conjunction with, the 18 programmes initiated through the strategy, there will be various initiatives in line function departments and the seeking of partnerships with outsiders.

While the document makes allowance for monitoring at departmental and programme level, it is not clear the extent to which the whole enterprise will be subject to review. While it would be inappropriate, given the difficulty of interpreting crime statistics, to suggest that the crime rates should be cut by a given percentage by the year 2,000 programme deliverables need to be more clearly outlined. So, it is of concern that the strategy – despite the fact that it is a framework for implementation – contains virtually no time frames (although in some cases it appears that these are still to be determined) for the completion of the various programmes.

And management is by committee: an interministerial committee will supplement the Cabinet committee on security and intelligence and will be made up of the Ministers of Safety and Security, Correctional Services, Defence, Justice, Correctional Services, Welfare and Intelligence. The committee will meet only quarterly, or be convened on an *ad hoc* basis should it be required. Underneath the ministerial committee will be a committee of directors-general which will also be chaired by the lead department which is Safety and Security.

With no deadlines to work to, the committees, which have apparently already met, have made little progress. A publicly released set of objectives and deadlines would have provided some accessible points of measurement to judge any progress. Without these the danger is that the plan will be perceived as simply another paper strategy creating expectations which the government will not be able to meet.

Indeed, this has already occurred. High-profile media coverage of specific instances of criminal activity has turned the spotlight once again on the issue of crime. Government responses that these are just individual instances (or a media plot) fundamentally misunderstand the role of the press. Unless government law enforcement agencies are seen to work on the ground – in the short term – where most citizens experience crime, no amount of strategies formulated in Pretoria will bring relief. In fact, quite the opposite: if every fresh outburst of crime is met only with words and no visible implementation, public cynicism will grow. The success of the strategy is critical. Failure will bring growing disillusionment with conceptions of proactive crime prevention which is central to the long term solution of disorder in South African society. And, instead, there will be a continued growth in reactive, self-help and increasingly violent solutions to crime.

Citizen Responses

The increasing failure of the criminal justice system to deter or punish offenders has been marked by a growing trend among citizens to take the law into their own hands. None of this is new, all occurring in some form or the other under apartheid rule. What is significant now is the growth of extra-state mechanisms of law and order in conjunction with declining confidence among the citizenry in the ability of the police to secure a safe environment. Forms of alternative protection vary: the wealthier components of society can afford to contract out responsibility for their safety to the private security sector, less fortunate communities are more likely to take their own initiatives.

Unlike the security business in Europe and North America, the South African private security industry has been little studied. Here the sector has, since 1980, grown rapidly; initially it expanded at about 30 per cent a year, slowing to 10–15 per cent in the last five years. (There has been an estimated annual average growth rate of 18 per cent since the late 1970s.) The exact value of the industry is difficult to quantify; a recent estimate suggested that the guarding industry alone was worth around R3.6 billion. Private security officers outnumber the public police by about 2 to 1.[11]

The South African industry, in comparison with security sectors elsewhere, shows some unique traits – a mix between a sophisticated electronic sector and the physical provision of guards. It is also distinguished by a comparatively higher growth on the reactive side. Traditionally, both in South Africa and elsewhere, security companies have played a proactive function: guards patrol defined areas to prevent crime, modelled very much on the concept of the 'bobby on the beat'. In South Africa the combination of electronic and guarding functions has led to a marked growth in the 'armed response' sector: panic buttons relay electronic signals via a control room to armed security officers patrolling in cars, who, therefore, play roles far more similar to the state's traditional law and order function.

The growth in the South African industry has not reflected broader trends in the economy. Indeed, there seems to be an inverse relationship, with the industry growing remarkably in poor economic conditions: in the pre-election months, when most business in the country stagnated, security reflected record growth. Since the election there has been some stabilization, although rises in crime are again boosting security companies. But, to some degree, parts of the market, like guarding, are increasingly showing signs of saturation.

The development of the private security sector in South Africa, however, has not been untroubled. Appeals for more powers for certain categories of security guards is likely to fall on deaf ears if the public and official perception is that private security officers are untrained and act unprofessionally. Public perceptions, whether the industry likes it or not, are shaped by individual instances of abuse; for example, the deaths of 16 people in a stampede caused by security guards armed with electric batons at Tembisa north-east of Johannesburg in July 1996 or the notorious case of security officer 'Louis' van Schoor's shooting dead of 41 alleged burglars over several years.

The danger of replicating the Tembisa incident is real. More and more, private security companies operate in the so-called private-public sphere; that is, private property which is open for public usage – for example, shopping malls or university campuses. And, there is a growing trend of using private means in purely public spheres such as policing urban neighbourhoods or central business districts. In more extreme cases, private firms engage directly in public order activities like the clearance of squatters.

Growth in the private security industry does not necessarily release pressure on the public police. In fact, quite the opposite: the industry puts in place mechanisms – guards, alarms and detection devices – to gather information which can be fed to police: rather than decreasing demands on the police, private security may overburden it in some areas. The clearest indicator of this in South Africa is the issue of 'false alarms': in KwaZulu-Natal between January and April 1996 the SAPS travelled 170,000 km in response to electronic alarm activations, accounting for 40 per cent of all complaints in the province, with only 1 percent being valid.[12]

Also, to argue – as the industry increasingly does – that private security serves as a useful component to state structures ignores their differing goals: the private company seeks to protect the interests of its client, while the police theoretically defend the rights of citizens. In the main (and barring some cases in the private investigation sector), private companies are more concerned with the prevention of loss than the detection of offenders: in particular, the exercise of discretion by such private security personnel will often be far more influenced by their perceptions of their immediate employer than any generalized concept of the public interest. Thus, offenders will only be handed over to justice if this is in the perceived interest of the client. This implies that in South Africa as elsewhere public and private policing do not fit as neatly together as first assumed.

But if the public policing activities of private security continue to grow, what are the policy alternatives? Greater regulation, beyond that offered by the Security Officers Board, a statutory body staffed and funded by the industry, is only valid if it is possible to enforce – which, is not currently the case in South Africa. One option, given that the public at large are exposed to private policing, is the establishment of an independent complaints mechanism– over and above any ordinary recourse individuals may have under the law – to provide a publicly accessible means to oversee the industry. But, with or without such a mechanism, the industry will remain contract driven, responsible in the final analysis to individual clients rather than the public at large.

While business and the wealthier sections of society seek to buy safety the less fortunate have sought to confront the problem more directly. While by no means the first of such actions, the campaign by the vigilante group People Against Gangsterism and Drugs (Pagad) in the Western Cape – who publicly murdered an alleged drug dealer and have maintained an armed presence in parts in some Cape townships – has brought the issue of citizen action to a head. But there are a real dangers to the new order should such initiatives become a permanent feature of the debate on community safety in South Africa.[13]

Indeed, South Africa is beginning to display many similar characteristics to the crime wracked states of Latin America. In Brazil, where the army have been summoned to control crime in major urban areas, vigilante policing is nothing new. The use of vigilante squads in the crowded urban complexes around Rio and São Paulo (and increasingly in small towns in the interior) are justified because of the inefficiency of Brazil's established judicial institutions. There are in this experience some profound lessons for South Africa.

Ironically, and this rings true in South Africa, vigilante action which (at least in the rhetoric of its proponents) is an attempt to strengthen state institutions often has the opposite effect: the further weakening and undermining of official criminal justice channels and the creation of alternative centres of power (and by definition coercion) outside the state security apparatus. In South Africa, as in Latin America, vigilante actions against criminals are essentially a response to state ineffectiveness, combined with a culture of violence and an inability of the state to defend its own areas of responsibility from vigilante incursions.

Perhaps more to the point, vigilante actions are encouraged by perceptions that its perpetrators themselves will not be threatened by counter-measures from the state. Indeed, that conclusion is easy for citizens to draw: if a state is ineffective in deterring the criminals who originally contributed to the potential for vigilantism, it also lacks the capacity to deter the vigilantes. This is illustrated by state responses in Latin America to vigilantism – essentially an attempt to co-opt rather than to confront. Police Commissioner George Fivaz's assertion (while of course not condoning vigilante violence) that the police wish to work in 'partnership' in the Western Cape with vigilante groups is a classic response.

It must be recognized that what is achieved by vigilante behaviour is not necessarily useful. Vigilante action is essentially reactive – it aims to suppress (violently). And, vigilante action tends to be applied in an *ad hoc* manner, even though the violation of formal legal boundaries may be supported by the majority of the community (as in São Paulo and on the Cape Flats), vigilantism is disorderly and unpredictable, *having consequences unforeseen at the time it was begun.* Often it simply solidifies the very opposition which it aimed to undercut; it is not for nothing that the gangs on the Cape Flats have resolved their differences in order to counter the common threat that now faces them.

Moreover, when law enforcement officials themselves participate, either directly or indirectly, in acts of violence, the moral validity (or the remains of it) of the formal system of laws is undercut. So one of the most serious developments around vigilante violence in the Western Cape is the widespread public perception that the police (frustrated by their own inability) stood back and allowed 'natural justice' to take its course.

Over the medium to longer term the greatest danger of vigilante action is that it will spread and become institutionalized – an accepted mechanism to police what is increasingly viewed as the unpolicable. Be assured that new complexities will develop over time. Police who are viewed to be in cahoots with criminals, for instance, could become targets for attack, upscaling and complicating the conflict.

Vigilante actions in South Africa, while their causes and aims may differ, are nothing new. The use of vigilantism to achieve political ends was a common feature of the last decade of apartheid and the transition to democracy in South Africa. The difference was of course that such forms, like the '*wit doeke*' (state-sponsored vigilantes operating in Cape Town's shack settlements during the mid-1980s. They wore white rags around their heads, hence their name.) on the Cape Flats and the impis (Zulu armed units) in KwaZulu-Natal enjoyed state support. The principle of using violent action outside the formal institutions of the state is an already well established principle.

The growth of self and private policing provides a ready base from which violent vigilante actions can grow. In Soweto, for example, groups like Youth Against Crime – a motley collection of youngsters who patrol some section of the township – can easily be upgraded into violence driven vigilante groups. Indeed, the events in the Western Cape were watched with interest by the groups in Soweto. While their organizing principles are not as strong as those of Pagad, nor are they as tightly organized, they do contain the potential for violent action.

If the dangers of vigilante action are manifest what then are the solutions? The only alternative is the most difficult one. The establishment of an effective system of criminal justice as a matter of *national priority*. The South African state, no matter what the degree of breakdown within its institutions of criminal justice, still retains the capacity for such an alternative if it is confronted in a targeted way. Seeking to co-opt vigilante leaders and placate criminals, while it will ensure peace in the short term, will over time undermine the last shreds of public confidence in the criminal justice system. The greatest danger is to do nothing – allowing vigilantism, because it has short term advantages to the state, to run its course.

Conclusion: Crime and Democracy

Just as the transition affects crime, so crime affects the transition. Not long ago, the new government's willingness to compromise politically – and the affluent minority's willingness to compromise in turn – in the interests of racial accommodation seemed the most likely determinant of democratic prospects. Ironically, however, unexpected success in this area could be nullified by the emergence of crime as a – if not the – central determinant of the attitudes towards the new democracy of local affluent minorities, and perhaps also of international investors.

High levels of crime affect all South Africans. But the effect in the new democracy appears to vary between racial groups. For affluent, suburban whites, growing evidence suggests that it is the prime threat to confidence in the new order and the factor most likely to prompt continued emigration among a sector of the society whose mobility is high and commitment to majority rule conditional. Since skills and resources are disproportionately concentrated in this group, its flight from attacks on persons and property would weaken democracy's economic foundation. There is also evidence that predominately white residents of the suburbs may react to crime by seeking to insulate themselves physically from the mainly black poor who are seen as its perpetrators. That would entrench a form of social distance which will impede attempts to create a common South African loyalty.

For much of the black majority, exit is neither a feasible nor a desired option. And, since this section of society has been living with high rates of violent crime for decades, concern at a relative increase is far outweighed by enthusiasm for a new order in which black people are full citizens: there is no visible evidence yet that crime is substantially denting black confidence in democracy. In addition recent research suggests that black citizens see crime as a symptom of social and economic inequalities rather than a product of democracy's 'weakness'. Survey evidence suggest that white and black citizens view increasing crime and state responses from diametrically opposed positions: whites see crime as a breakdown of policing standards and the weakness of the new order, blacks view increasing lawlessness as a sign that the new democracy has not consolidated and that its institutions need strengthening.[14]

This state of affairs will not last; indeed, among important constituencies in the growing black middle-classes views are beginning to converge with their white compatriots. If the personal safety of black citizens declines still further, enthusiasm for measures to 'restore order' which threaten democratic liberties could grow. The majority of black South Africans (and indeed ANC members) now support a return to capital punishment.[15]

The perception that achieving safer communities is beyond the means of the state or an apprehension that citizen's sanest response to the threat is to insulate themselves from society could ensure declining political participation. The signs of this, although only partly a response to crime, are already there; recent survey evidence suggests that the ANC has lost 10 per cent of its support, but that this has not been distributed to any of the other parties in the political system.[16] The perception that an elected government cannot perform the most fundamental function of state authority – protecting the persons of its citizens – could reduce confidence in the new democracy.

What are the prospects, then, that crime will decline significantly? The evidence does not permit a clear and confident answer. Both here and in other societies, the roots and cures of crime are far too complex to permit definitive predictions or trends. The polar conventional wisdoms of the debate – that crime will decline as soon as development takes off, or the moment the police are elevated to their 'rightful' place and adequately resourced – are at best unproven and likely to remain so for some time. And even if crime stabilizes, it appears likely that reported crime will rise. This could influence public debate by masking success, if any, in combating crime.

An underemphasized constraint on the reduction of crime, particularly its violent variety, is a grim legacy of the transition period: the ready availability of weaponry, which also erodes one of the key prerequisites of democratic transition – the state's ability to monopolize the instruments of coercion. This may be enhanced by a vicious circle in which the widespread use of illegal arms prompts continued demands for greater access to legal ones, despite the fact that widespread legal white access to weapons since the 1980s has not prevented the growth of violent crime (and in fact probably encouraged it).

These realities create ironic dilemmas for a new democratic government. On the one hand, confidence in the new order will decline if the authorities are seen to abandon any attempt to address crime in the (probably dubious) hope that citizens will adjust to an unpleasant reality. On the other, promises of a concerted 'war on crime' in a context in which the capacity to tackle the problem is clearly limited may have destructive consequences, not only for the authorities but also for the democratic system – both by creating expectations on which it may be unable to deliver, and by encouraging support for strategies which may be both inimical to civil liberties and unlikely to succeed.

The longer the dilemma remains unresolved, the more likely is it that the democratic authorities, and therefore the political process, will cease to be seen as credible guarantors of personal safety: for those unable or disinclined to emigrate, 'self-policing' and reliance on private security will be seen as more viable protections. While the impact of these choices on democracy may be difficult to determine, at the very least they suggest a declining relationship between security on the one hand, and accountability and legality on the other. As the more affluent, in particular, are forced to rely on their own responses to crime, the more likely they are to seek to insulate themselves from the rest of society, entrenching in a new form the old divisions which the transition was meant to overcome.

NOTES

1. Quoted in the *Business Day*, Johannesburg, 4 Aug. 1994.
2. For a more detailed argument on the relationship between crime and political transition, see M. Shaw, *Partners in Crime? Crime, Political Transition and Changing Forms of Policing Control* (Johannesburg: Centre for Policy Studies 1995).
3. See M. Shaw and L. Camerer, *Policing the Transformation? New issues in South Africa's crime debate* (Johannesburg: Inst. for Defence Policy 1996).
4. Unpublished crime statistics, Jan.–June 1996, Crime Information Management Centre, South African Police Service, Pretoria.
5. See M. Shaw, 'The Development of Organised Crime in South Africa', in Shaw and Camerer (note 3).
6. Lorraine Glanz, 'Crime in Gauteng', unpub. paper, Human Science Research Council 1995.
7. For an overview of problems across the criminal justice system, see *Re-engineering the Criminal Justice System*, a joint project of the Ministries of Safety and Security, Justice, Welfare and Correctional Services and Business Against Crime, June 1996.
8. The actual figure is in fact probably lower than this. See Lorraine Glanz, 'The Not so Long Arm of the Law', *Indicator SA: Crime and Conflict*, No.5, Autumn 1996.
9. See Molefi Thinane, 'End of the Line: South Africa's Overcrowded Prisons', *Indicator SA: Crime and Conflict*, No.7, Spring 1996.
10. *National Crime Prevention Strategy*, Dept. of Correctional Services, Defence, Intelligence, Justice, Safety and Security and Welfare, Pretoria, May 1996.
11. For more detailed overview of the industry, see M Shaw, 'Privatising Crime Control? South Africa's private security industry', in *Partners in Crime?* (note 2) pp.83–7.
12. *Re-engineering the Criminal Justice System* (note 7). The figures for the other provinces where statistics are available are similar.
13. M Shaw, 'Buying time? Vigilante Action, Crime Control and State Responses', *Indicator SA: Crime and Conflict*, No.7, Spring 1996.
14. D. Ehlers, I. Hirshfeld and C. Schutte, *Perceptions of Current Sociopolitical Issues in South Africa* (Centre for Sociopolitical Analysis, Human Sciences Research Council, Pretoria, June 1996). This confirms previous survey data. A confidential government poll also drew similar conclusions.
15. Ibid.
16. Ibid.

Biographical Notes

Abiodun Alao is a Nigerian and a Lecturer at the Department of War Studies, King's College, University of London. He has published many articles on African security, and he is the author of *African Conflicts: The Future Without the Cold War* (London: Brassey's for Centre for Defence Studies 1993) and *Brothers at War: Dissidence and Rebellion in Southern Africa* (London: British Academic Press 1994). He has recently received a SSRC-MacArthur award to do a major study on Mining and Conflict in West Africa.

Chris Alden is a Lecturer in International Relations with the University of the Witwatersrand. The author of *Apartheid's Last Stand: The Rise and Fall of the South African Security State* (London: Macmillan 1995), he has published on Mozambican politics, the UN and regional security issues. Dr Alden was a MacArthur Fellow at Cambridge University studying the UN and demilitarization of regional conflicts.

Jakkie Cilliers obtained a DLitt et Phil in Strategic Studies at UNISA in 1987. Since 1991 he has served as Co-Director and since 1993 as Executive-Director of the Institute for Defence Policy. He had 14 years military service in the South African Defence Force from which he resigned in 1988, having held the rank of commandant (lt-col). His service included extensive operational deployment as an artillery officer and various staff postings in Pretoria. His awards include a Bronze Medal from the South African Society for the Advancement of Science; H. Bradlow Research Bursary; Southern Cross Medal and Chief of The SA Defence Force Commendation Medal. He served as divisional manager, operations research, at Analysis, Management and Systems (Pty) Ltd (1988–91). Dr Cilliers is a well-known political analyst and commentator on local and international radio and television. He regularly lectures on defence policy issues and has published and contributed to numerous publications.

William Gutteridge is Professor Emeritus (Int. Studies) Aston University and Director of the Research Institute for the Study of Conflict and Terrorism (RISCT). He was formerly Senior Lecturer in Commonwealth History and Government at RMA Sandhurst and Head of Department at Lanchester Polytechnic (now Coventry University). He edited *South Africa's Defence and Security in the 21st Century* (Dartmouth 1996).

Judith Hudson, was educated at the University of Natal (MA in Political Science) and King's College, London (senior visiting research fellow in the Department of War Studies). A former lecturer in Political Science at the University of Natal, she is currently studying towards a doctorate at the University of the Witwatersrand. Before becoming senior researcher at the Community Agency for Social Enquiry, Braamfontein, she was a research co-ordinator at the Centre for Development and Enterprise (CDE), based in Johannesburg. There she edited *Business and Government in South Africa* and *Perspectives on business, government and civil society*, and managed a major research project on the international experience of migration.

Alexander Johnston is head of the Department of Politics at the University of Natal, Durban and (with R.W. Johnson) co-director of the KwaZulu-Natal Monitoring Project, an initiative of the Helen Suzman Foundation (Johannesburg). Among his recently published articles and chapters are, 'The Political World of KwaZulu-Natal', 'Conflict in South Africa' and (with R.W. Johnson) 'The KwaZulu-Natal Local Elections of June 1996'.

Mark Shaw is currently a senior researcher analyst at the Institute for Defence Policy (IDP) heading the Crime and Policing Project at the Institute. Studied at the University of the Witwatersrand and the London School of Economics. He completed a first-class honours degree and is completing a PhD at Wits. He has received the award for best political science student in South Africa in 1992 and the HSRC President's award for hostel research in 1993. He has written and published on a wide range of security and development issues. He worked for the Peace Secretariat on the East Rand during 1993 and was seconded to the Goldstone Institute in the pre-election period. Before joining IDP he worked as a senior research officer at the Centre for Policy Studies in Johannesburg of which he is still a research associate. A portion of his time is now spent working at Rand Merchant Bank.

Keith Somerville is Editor of the 'World Today', 'Assignment' and 'Business Programmes' in the News and Current Affairs Department of the BBC World Service. He is the author of *Angola: Politics, Economics and Society* (London: Pinter 1986); *Foreign Military Intervention in Africa* (ibid. 1990) and *Southern Africa and the Soviet Union: From Communist International to Commonwealth of Independent States* (London: Macmillan 1993). He would like to thank the International Committee of the Red Cross, Halo Trust, Norwegian People's Aid and UNAVEM for assistance they gave him in Luanda, Malanje, Kuito and Huambo during a research trip in June 1995.

J. E. Spence is Director of Studies, Royal Institute of International Affairs, London. He was formerly head of the Department of Politics and Pro-Vice Chancellor at the University of Leicester (1973–91). He was Founding Editor of the *Review of International Studies*; President of the African Studies Association of the UK (1976/77); and Chairman of the British International Studies Association (1985/87). He is an Honorary Fellow of the University of Staffordshire, University College of Wales, Swansea and Nene College, Northampton. He has published widely on Southern African themes.

Index